D1498544

HOLT FRENCH 1A

Allez, viens!

En avant!

HOLT, RINEHART AND WINSTON

A Harcourt Education Company

Orlando • **Austin** • New York • San Diego • Toronto • London

ASSOCIATE DIRECTOR
Barbara Kristof

EXECUTIVE EDITOR
Priscilla Blanton

SENIOR EDITORS
Marion Bermondy
Jaishree Venkatesan

ASSOCIATE MANAGING EDITOR
Amber P. Martin

EDITORIAL STAFF
Yamilé Dewailly
Virginia Dosher
Ruthie Ford
Serge Laîné
Géraldine Touzeau-Patrick
Mark Eells, *Editorial Coordinator*

EDITORIAL PERMISSIONS
Carrie Jones, *CCP Supervisor*
Nicole Svobodny, *Permissions Editor*
Brigida Donohue, *Interpreter-Translator*

BOOK DESIGN
Marta L. Kimball, *Design Director*
Robin Bouvette, *Senior Designer*
Ed Diaz, *Design Associate*

IMAGE ACQUISITIONS
Curtis Riker, *Director*
Tim Taylor, *Photo Research Supervisor*
Cindy Verheyden, *Senior Photo Researcher*
Elisabeth McCoy, *Photo Researcher*

Michelle Rumpf, *Art Buyer Supervisor*
Coco Weir, *Senior Art Buyer*

DESIGN NEW MEDIA
Edwin Blake, *Design Director*
Kimberly Cammerata, *Design Manager*
Czeslaw Sornat, *Design Manager*
Grant Davidson, *Senior Designer*

COVER DESIGN
Marta L. Kimball, *Design Director*
Robin Bouvette, *Senior Designer*

PRODUCTION
Bill Medellin, *Production Supervisor*

MANUFACTURING
Jevara Jackson, *Senior Manufacturing Coordinator*
Rhonda Faris, *Inventory Analyst*
Kimberly Harrison, *Media Manufacturing Coordinator*

NEW MEDIA
Liz Kline, *Senior Project Manager*
Lydia Doty, *Senior Project Manager*

VIDEO PRODUCTION
Video materials produced by Edge Productions, Inc., Aiken, S.C.

ACKNOWLEDGMENTS

PHOTOGRAPHY CREDITS

Abbreviations used: (t) top, (c) center, (b) bottom, (l) left, (r) right, (bkgd) background

Front Cover: © Cosmo Condina

Back Cover: © Earl & Nazima Kowall/CORBIS; (frame) © 2006 Image Farm, Inc.

Acknowledgements appear on page R64, which is an extension of the copyright page.

ALLEZ, VIENS! is a trademark licensed to Holt, Rinehart and Winston, registered in the United States of America and/or other jurisdictions.

Printed in the United States of America

ISBN 0-03-036971-1

3 4 5 6 7   751   08 07 06

AUTHORS

John DeMado
Washington, CT

Mr. DeMado helped form the general philosophy of the French program and wrote activities to practice basic material, functions, grammar, and vocabulary.

Emmanuel Rongiéras d'Usseau
Le Kremlin-Bicêtre, France

Mr. Rongiéras d'Usseau contributed to the development of the scope and sequence, created the basic material and listening scripts, selected realia, and wrote activities.

CONTRIBUTING WRITERS

Jayne Abrate
The University of Missouri
Rolla Campus
Rolla, MO

Sally Adamson Taylor
Publishers Weekly
San Francisco, CA

Linda Bistodeau
Saint Mary's University
Halifax, Nova Scotia

Betty Peltier
Consultant
Batz-sur-Mer, France

REVIEWERS

Dominique Bach
Rio Linda Senior High School
Rio Linda, CA

Jeannette Caviness
Mount Tabor High School
Winston-Salem, NC

Jennie Bowser Chao
Consultant
Oak Park, IL

Pierre F. Cintas
Penn State University
Abington College
Abington, PA

Donna Clementi
Appleton West High School
Appleton, WI

Cathy Cramer
Homewood High School
Birmingham, AL

Robert H. Didsbury
Consultant
Raleigh, NC

Jennifer Jones
U.S. Peace Corps volunteer
Côte d'Ivoire 1991–1993
Austin, TX

Joan H. Manley
The University of Texas at El Paso
El Paso, TX

Jill Markert
Pflugerville High School
Pflugerville, TX

Inge McCoy
Southwest Texas State University
San Marcos, TX

Gail Montgomery
Foreign Language Program
Administrator
Greenwich, CT Public Schools

Agathe Norman
Consultant
Austin, TX

Audrey O'Keefe
Jordan High School
Los Angeles, CA

Sherry Parker
Selvidge Middle School
Ballwin, MO

Sherron N. Porter
Robert E. Lee High School
Baton Rouge, LA

Marc Prévost
Austin Community College
Austin, TX

Norbert Rouquet
Consultant
La Roche-sur-Yon, France

Michèle Shockey
Gunn High School
Palo Alto, CA

Ashley Shumaker
Central High School West
Tuscaloosa, AL

Antonia Stergiades
Washington High School
Massillon, OH

Frederic L. Toner
Texas Christian University
Fort Worth, TX

Jeannine Waters
Harrisonburg High School
Harrisonburg, VA

Jo Anne S. Wilson
Consultant
Glen Arbor, MI

FIELD TEST PARTICIPANTS

Marie Allison
New Hanover High School
Wilmington, NC

Gabrielle Applequist
Capital High School
Boise, ID

Jana Brinton
Bingham High School
Riverton, UT

Nancy J. Cook
Sam Houston High School
Lake Charles, LA

Rachael Gray
Williams High School
Plano, TX

Katherine Kohler
Nathan Hale Middle School
Norwalk, CT

Nancy Mirsky
Museum Junior High School
Yonkers, NY

Myrna S. Nie
Whetstone High School
Columbus, OH

Jacqueline Reid
Union High School
Tulsa, OK

Judith Ryser
San Marcos High School
San Marcos, TX

Erin Hahn Sass
Lincoln Southeast High School
Lincoln, NE

Linda Sherwin
Sandy Creek High School
Tyrone, GA

Norma Joplin Sivers
Arlington Heights High School
Fort Worth, TX

Lorabeth Stroup
Lovejoy High School
Lovejoy, GA

Robert Vizena
W.W. Lewis Middle School
Sulphur, LA

Gladys Wade
New Hanover High School
Wilmington, NC

Kathy White
Grimsley High School
Greensboro, NC

TO THE STUDENT

Some people have the opportunity to learn a new language by living in another country.
Most of us, however, begin learning another language and getting acquainted with
a foreign culture in a classroom with the help of a teacher, classmates, and a textbook.
To use your book effectively, you need to know how it works.

Allez, viens! (*Come along!*) is organized to help you learn French and become familiar
with the cultures of people who speak French. The Preliminary Chapter presents basic
concepts in French and strategies for learning a new language. This chapter is followed
by six Location Openers and twelve chapters.

Location Opener Six four-page
photo essays called Location
Openers introduce different
French-speaking places. You can
also see these locations on video,
the *CD-ROM Tutor,* and the *DVD
Tutor.*

Chapter Opener The Chapter
Opener pages tell you the chapter
theme and goals.

Mise en train (*Getting Started*)
This illustrated story, which is also
on video, shows you French-speaking people in real-life situations,
using the language you'll learn in
the chapter.

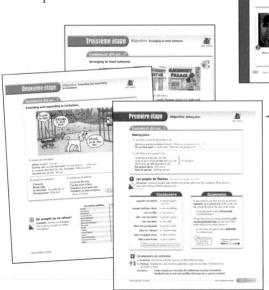

Première, Deuxième, and **Troisième étape** (*First, Second,
Third Part*) After the **Mise en train**, the chapter is divided into three sections called **étapes**. Within the **étape**,
are **Comment dit-on... ?** (*How Do You Say . . . ?*) boxes
that contain the French expressions you'll need to communicate and **Vocabulaire** and **Grammaire/Note de
grammaire** boxes that give you the French words and
grammatical structures you'll need to know. Activities in
each **étape** enable you to develop your skills in listening,
reading, speaking, and writing.

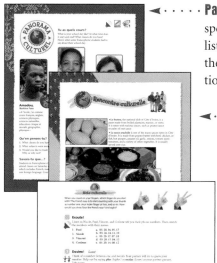

Panorama Culturel *(Cultural Panorama)* On this page are interviews with French-speaking people from around the world. You can watch these interviews on video or listen to them on audio CD. You can also watch them using the *CD-ROM Tutor* and the *DVD Tutor*, then check to see how well you understood by answering some questions about what the people say.

Rencontre culturelle *(Cultural Encounter)* This section, found in six of the chapters, gives you a firsthand encounter with some aspect of a French-speaking culture.

Note culturelle *(Culture Note)* In each chapter, there are notes with more information about the cultures of French-speaking people.

Lisons! *(Let's Read!)* The reading section follows the three **étapes**. The selections are related to the chapter themes and help you develop your reading skills in French.

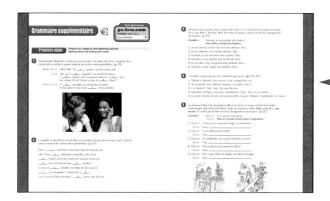

Grammaire supplémentaire *(Additional Grammar Practice)* This section begins the chapter review. You will find four pages of activities that provide additional practice on the grammar concepts you learned in the chapter.

Mise en pratique *(Review)* The activities on these pages practice what you've learned in the chapter and help you improve your listening, reading, and communication skills. You'll also review what you've learned about culture. A section called **Ecrivons!** *(Let's Write!)* in Chapters 3–12 will help develop your writing skills.

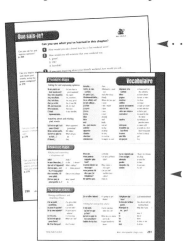

Que sais-je? *(Let's See if I Can . . .)* This page at the end of each chapter contains a series of questions and short activities to help you see if you've achieved the chapter goals.

Vocabulaire *(Vocabulary)* On the French-English vocabulary list on the last page of the chapter, the words are grouped by **étape**. These words and expressions will be on the quizzes and tests.

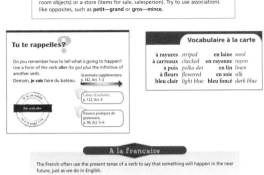

Tu te rappelles?

Do you remember how to tell what is going to happen? Use a form of the verb **aller** (to go) plus the infinitive of another verb.
Demain, **je vais** faire du bateau.

Grammaire supplémentaire, p. 342, Act. 1–2

Cahier d'activités, p. 122, Act. 4

Travaux pratiques de grammaire, p. 90, Act. 5–6

Vocabulaire à la carte

à rayures	striped	en laine	wool
à carreaux	checked	en rayonne	rayon
à pois	polka dot	en lin	linen
à fleurs	flowered	en soie	silk
bleu clair	light blue	bleu foncé	dark blue

A la française

The French often use the present tense of a verb to say that something will happen in the near future, just as we do in English.
Samedi matin, je vais jouer au tennis. *Saturday morning, I'm going to play tennis.*
Samedi matin, je joue au tennis. *Saturday morning, I'm playing tennis.*

You'll also find special features in each chapter that provide extra tips and reminders.

De bons conseils (*Helpful advice*) offers study hints to help you succeed in a foreign language class.

Tu te rappelles? (*Do you remember?*) and **Si tu as oublié** (*If you forgot*) remind you of expressions, grammar, and vocabulary you may have forgotten.

A la française (*The French way*) gives you additional expressions to add more color to your speech.

Vocabulaire à la carte (*Additional Vocabulary*) lists extra words you might find helpful. These words will not appear on the quizzes and tests unless your teacher chooses to include them.

You'll also find French-English and English-French vocabulary lists at the end of the book. The words you'll need to know for the quizzes and tests are in boldface type.

At the end of your book, you'll find more helpful material, such as:
- a summary of the expressions you'll learn in the **Comment dit-on... ?** boxes
- additional vocabulary words you might want to use
- a summary of the grammar you'll study
- a grammar index to help you find where structures are presented

Allez, viens! Come along on an exciting trip to new cultures and a new language!

Bon voyage!

Explanation of Icons in *Allez, viens!*

Throughout Allez, viens!, you'll see these symbols, or icons, next to activities and presentations. The following key will help you understand them.

 Video/DVD Whenever this icon appears, you'll know there is a related segment in the *Allez, viens! Video* and *DVD* Programs.

 Listening Activities

 Pair Work/Group Work Activities

 Writing Activities

 Interactive Games and Activities Whenever this icon appears, you'll know there is a related activity on the *Allez, viens! Interactive CD-ROM Tutor* and on the *DVD Tutor*.

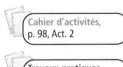

Cahier d'activités, p. 98, Act. 2

Travaux pratiques de grammaire, p. 75, Act. 9–10

Practice Activities These icons tell you which activities from the *Cahier d'activités* and the *Travaux pratiques de grammaire* practice the material presented.

 Grammaire supplémentaire, p. 286, Act. 15–16

Grammaire supplémentaire This reference tells you where you can find additional grammar practice in the review section of the chapter.

 Internet Activities This icon provides the keyword you'll need to access related online activities at **go.hrw.com**.

En avant! Contents

Come along—to a world of new experiences!

En avant! offers you the opportunity to learn the language spoken by millions of people in countries in Europe, Africa, Asia, and around the world. Let's find out what those countries are.

ALLEZ, VIENS

à Poitiers!

CHAPITRE 1

Faisons connaissance! 16

CHAPITRE 2
Vive l'école! 46

CHAPITRE 3
Tout pour la rentrée.....74

CHAPITRE 4
Sports et passe-temps 106

ALLEZ, VIENS
à Paris!

LOCATION • CHAPITRES 5, 6, 7 136

CHAPITRE 5
On va au café? 140

CHAPITRE 6
Amusons-nous! 168

CULTURAL REFERENCES

LA FRANCE

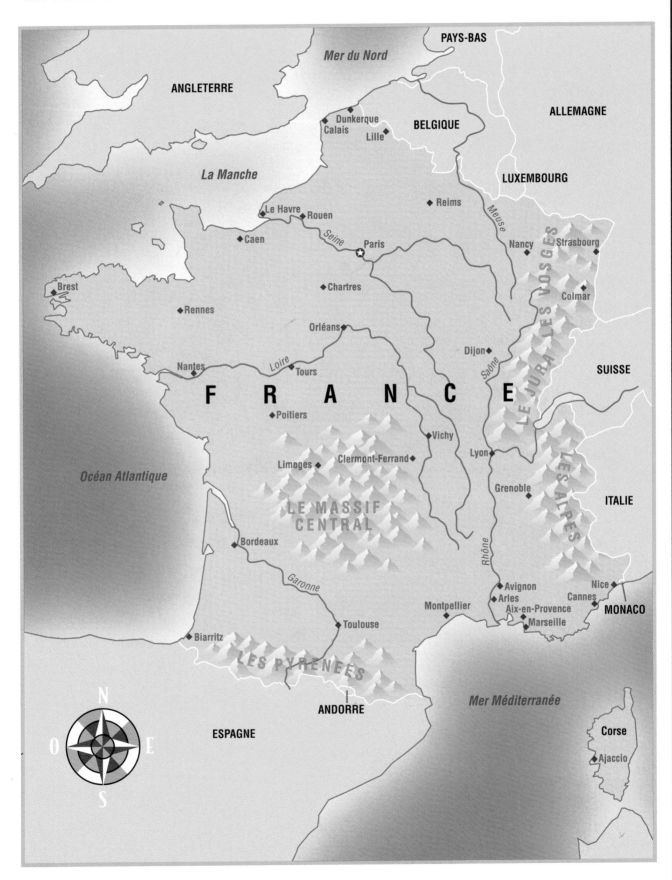

L'AFRIQUE FRANCOPHONE

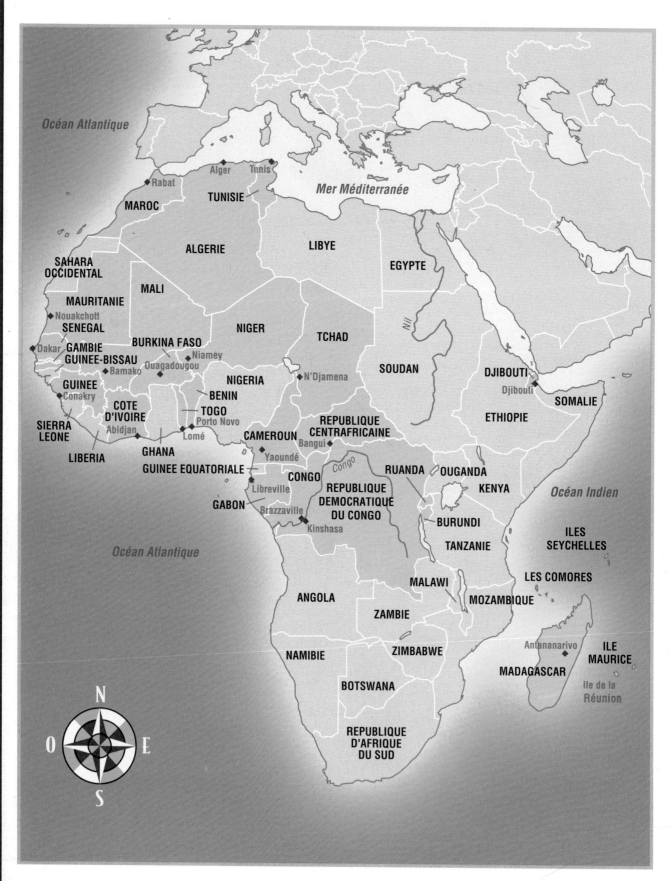

Océan Atlantique

Mer Méditerranée

Alger   Tunis

Rabat

MAROC   TUNISIE

ALGERIE   LIBYE

EGYPTE

SAHARA OCCIDENTAL

Nil

MAURITANIE   MALI

Nouakchott   SENEGAL   NIGER   TCHAD

Dakar   GAMBIE   BURKINA FASO   SOUDAN   DJIBOUTI
GUINEE-BISSAU   Niamey   Djibouti

Bamako   Ouagadougou   N'Djamena   SOMALIE

GUINEE   NIGERIA
Conakry   BENIN   ETHIOPIE

COTE   TOGO
SIERRA   D'IVOIRE   Porto Novo   REPUBLIQUE
LEONE   Abidjan   Lomé   CAMEROUN   CENTRAFRICAINE

LIBERIA   GHANA   Bangui

GUINEE EQUATORIALE   Yaoundé   RUANDA   OUGANDA

CONGO   Congo   KENYA   Océan Indien

Libreville   REPUBLIQUE
DEMOCRATIQUE
GABON   Brazzaville   DU CONGO   BURUNDI

Kinshasa   ILES
TANZANIE   SEYCHELLES

LES COMORES

MALAWI

Océan Atlantique   ANGOLA   MOZAMBIQUE

ZAMBIE

Antananarivo   ILE
ZIMBABWE   MAURICE

NAMIBIE   MADAGASCAR
Ile de la
Réunion

BOTSWANA

REPUBLIQUE
D'AFRIQUE
DU SUD

O   N   E   S

L'AMÉRIQUE FRANCOPHONE

Québec

CANADA

Saint-Pierre-
et-Miquelon

Québec ◆
Montréal ◆

Nouvelle-
Angleterre

ÉTATS-UNIS

Océan Atlantique

Louisiane
La Nouvelle-Orléans ◆

Golfe du Mexique

CUBA

REP.
DOMINICAINE

HAITI
JAMAIQUE
Port-au-Prince

Porto Rico

MEXIQUE

BELIZE

Mer des Caraïbes

GUATEMALA   HONDURAS

NICARAGUA

SALVADOR

COSTA RICA

PANAMA

Océan Pacifique

VENEZUELA

COLOMBIE

GUYANA

Cayenne ◆

SURINAM   Guyane
française

BRESIL

Guadeloupe

Pointe-à-Pitre

Marie-
Galante

DOMINIQUE

Martinique

Fort-de-France

Guadeloupe

Martinique

Allez, viens!

Bienvenue dans le monde francophone!

Welcome to the French-speaking world!

You know, of course, that French is spoken in France, but did you know that French is spoken by many people in North America? About one-third of Canadians speak French, mostly in Quebec province. In the United States, about 375,000 people in New England, whose ancestors immigrated from Canada, speak or understand French. French is also an official language in the state of Louisiana.

French is the official language of France's overseas possessions. These include the islands of Martinique and Guadeloupe in the Caribbean Sea, French Guiana in South America, the island of Réunion in the Indian Ocean, and several islands in the Pacific Ocean. French is also spoken in Haiti.

French is also widely used in over twenty African countries where it is an official language. Many people in West and Central African countries, such as Senegal, the Republic of Côte d'Ivoire, Mali, Niger, and Chad, speak French. In North Africa, French has played an important role in Algeria, Tunisia, and Morocco. Although Arabic is the official language of these North African countries, French is used in many schools across North Africa.

Take a minute to find France on the map. Several of the countries bordering France use French as an official language. It's the first or second language of many people in Belgium, Switzerland, Luxembourg, and Andorra, as well as in the principality of Monaco.

As you look at the map, what other places can you find where French is spoken? Can you imagine how French came to be spoken in these places?

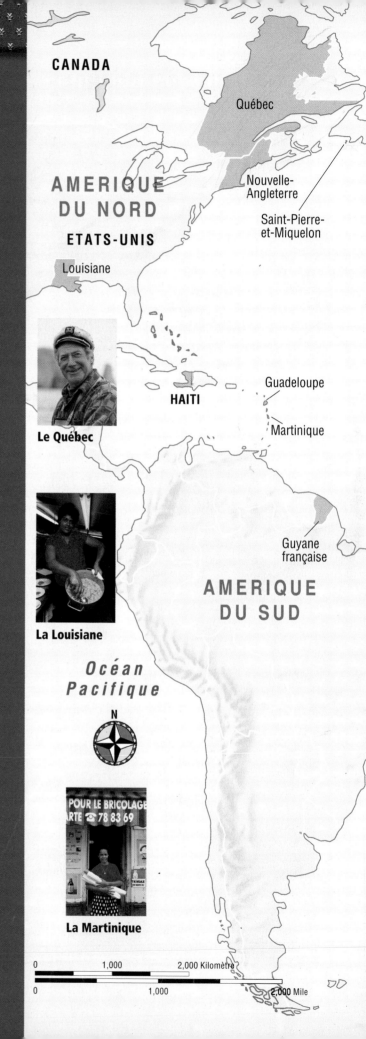

CANADA

Québec

AMERIQUE DU NORD

ETATS-UNIS

Louisiane

Nouvelle-Angleterre

Saint-Pierre-et-Miquelon

HAITI

Guadeloupe

Martinique

Le Québec

La Louisiane

Guyane française

AMERIQUE DU SUD

Océan Pacifique

N

POUR LE BRICOLAGE
ARTE ☎ 78 83 69

La Martinique

0   1,000   2,000 Kilomètre

0   1,000   2,000 Mile

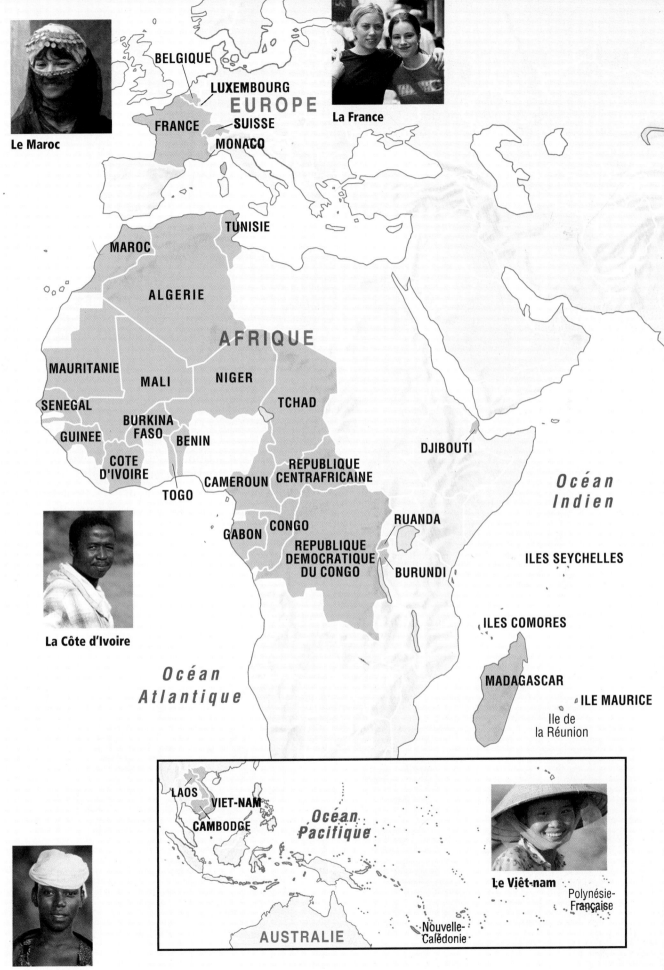

Le Maroc

La France

BELGIQUE
LUXEMBOURG
EUROPE
FRANCE
SUISSE
MONACO

TUNISIE

MAROC

ALGERIE

AFRIQUE

MAURITANIE
MALI
NIGER

SENEGAL
TCHAD

BURKINA
FASO
GUINEE
BENIN

DJIBOUTI

COTE
D'IVOIRE

REPUBLIQUE
CENTRAFRICAINE

Océan
Indien

CAMEROUN

TOGO

La Côte d'Ivoire

GABON
CONGO
RUANDA

REPUBLIQUE
DEMOCRATIQUE
DU CONGO

ILES SEYCHELLES

BURUNDI

ILES COMORES

Océan
Atlantique

MADAGASCAR

ILE MAURICE

Ile de
la Réunion

LAOS
VIET-NAM
Océan
Pacifique

CAMBODGE

Le Viêt-nam

Polynésie-
Française

Le Sénégal

AUSTRALIE

Nouvelle-
Calédonie

Tu les connais? · *Do you know them?*

In science, politics, technology, and the arts, French-speaking people have made important contributions. How many of these people can you match with their descriptions?

❶ Isabelle Adjani (b. 1955) A talented actress and producer, Isabelle Yasmine Adjani is well known for her award-winning roles in French films. In the 1980s, Adjani publicly acknowledged her Algerian heritage and began a personal campaign to raise consciousness about racism in France.

❷ Jacques Cousteau (1910-1997) Jacques-Yves Cousteau first gained worldwide attention for his undersea expeditions as the commander of the Calypso and for inventing the aqualung. In order to record his explorations, he invented a process for filming underwater.

❸ Léopold Senghor (1906-2001) A key advocate of Négritude, which asserts the values and the spirit of black African civilization, Senghor was a man of many talents. He was the first black African high school teacher in France. He was President of Senegal from 1960 to 1980. He was also the first black member of the **Académie Française.**

❹ Marie Curie (1867-1934) Along with her husband Pierre, Marie Curie won a Nobel prize in physics for her study of radioactivity. Several years later, she also won an individual Nobel prize for chemistry. Marie Curie was the first woman to teach at the Sorbonne in Paris.

5 **Victor Hugo** (1802-1885) Novelist, poet, and political activist, Hugo led the Romantic Movement in French literature. In his most famous works, *Notre-Dame de Paris (The Hunchback of Notre Dame)* and *Les Misérables,* he sympathizes with the victims of poverty and condemns a corrupt political system.

6 **Zinedine Zidane** (b. 1972) Zinedine Zidane, one of the most well-known soccer players in France and Europe, has received numerous awards and recognition for his accomplishments in soccer. In 1998, he helped lead the National French Team to victory by scoring two important goals to win the World Soccer Championship. He also received the Golden Ball award and was elected Best Player of the World.

7 **Céline Dion** (b. 1968) A native of Quebec, Dion is an award-winning singer whose work includes hit songs in both English and French. In 1996, her album *Falling Into You* was awarded the Grammy® for Album of the Year and Best Pop Album. Dion also performed in the opening ceremonies of the 1996 Olympic Games in Atlanta, Georgia.

8 **Gérard Depardieu** (b. 1948) Gérard Depardieu is a popular actor, director, and producer, who has appeared in over 70 films. His performance in the 1990 movie *Green Card,* which won him a Golden Globe award, marked his American film debut.

1C 2D 3G 4A 5B 6H 7E 8F

Pourquoi apprendre le français?

Why learn French?

To expand your horizons

When you study a language, you learn much more than vocabulary and grammar. You learn about the people who speak the language and the influence they've had on our lives. Francophone (French-speaking) cultures continue to make notable contributions to many fields, including art, literature, movies, fashion, cuisine, science, and technology.

For travel

Someday you may live, travel, or be an exchange student in one of the more than 30 countries all over the world where French is spoken. You can imagine how much more meaningful your experience will be if you can talk to people in their own language.

For career opportunities

Being able to communicate in another language can be an advantage when you're looking for employment in almost any field. As a journalist, sportscaster, hotel receptionist, tour guide, travel agent, buyer for a large company, lawyer, engineer, economist, financial expert, flight attendant, diplomat, translator, teacher, writer, interpreter, publisher, or librarian, you may have the opportunity to use French in your work. Did you know that nearly 4,000 American companies have offices in France?

For fun!

Perhaps the best reason for studying French is for the fun of it. Studying another language is a challenge to your mind, and you'll get a great feeling of accomplishment the first time you have a conversation in French.

Qui suis-je? • *Who am I?*

Here's how to introduce yourself to young people who speak French.

To ask someone's name:
Tu t'appelles comment?
To give your name:
Je m'appelle...

Note culturelle

French-speaking people use **tu** *(you)* when they talk to a friend, a family member, or a person their own age or younger. In Chapter 1, you'll learn how to address an adult using the more formal **vous.**

Here's a list of some popular French names for girls and boys. Can you find your name, or a name similar to yours?

Noms de filles		*Noms de garçons*	
	Dominique	Vincent	
	Corinne	Bernard	
	Stéphanie	Stéphane	
	Julie	Eric	
	Audrey	Jean	
	Emilie	Daniel	
	Sabrina	Philippe	Mathieu
Delphine	Séverine	Frédéric	Christian
Nathalie	Virginie	Cédric	David
Laurence	Valérie	Nicolas	Laurent
Céline	Lætitia	Michel	Marc
Elodie	Karine	Olivier	Gilles
Sandrine	Aurélie	Jérôme	Etienne
Claudine	Christelle	Christophe	Pierre

1 **Présente-toi!**   *Introduce yourself!*

If you like, choose a French name for yourself. Introduce yourself to two or three students in the class, using your own name or your new French name. Ask them their names, too.

L'alphabet ▪ *The alphabet*

The French alphabet looks the same as the English alphabet. The difference is in pronunciation. Look at the letters and words below as your teacher pronounces them or as you listen to the audio recording. Which letters sound similar in English and French? Which ones have a different sound?

A astronaute	**B** banane	**C** croissant	**D** dessert	**E** Europe
F fille	**G** girafe	**H** hélicoptère	**I** igloo	**J** judo
K kangourou	**L** lion	**M** microscope	**N** Noël	**O** orange
P parachute	**Q** quiche	**R** rose	**S** serpent	**T** trompette
U uniforme	**V** voyage	**W** western	**X** xylophone	**Y** yo-yo
		Z zèbre		

Have you noticed that many French words look like English words? Words in different languages that look alike are called cognates. Although they're pronounced differently, cognates have the same meaning in French and English. You may not realize it, but you already know hundreds of French words.

Can you figure out what these words mean?

chocolat

musique

carotte

adresse

examen

2 Le dictionnaire

Scan the French-English vocabulary list in the back of your book to see if you can find ten cognates.

3 Les animaux

Ecoutons Write down the words as you hear them spelled. Then, match the words you've written with the pictures. Be careful! One of the words isn't a cognate.

a.

b.

c.

d.

e.

f.

4 Tu t'appelles comment?

Can you spell your name, pronouncing the letters in French?

Les accents · *Accent marks*

Have you noticed the marks over some of the letters in French words? These marks are called accents. They're very important to the spelling, the pronunciation, and even the meaning of French words.

The **accent aigu** (´) tells you to pronounce an *e* similar to the *a* in the English word *date*:	éléphant Sénégal
The **accent grave** (`) tells you to pronounce an *e* like the *e* in the English word *jet*:	zèbre chèque
However, an **accent grave** over an *a* or *u* doesn't change the sound of these letters:	à où
The **accent circonflexe** (ˆ) can appear over any vowel, and it doesn't change the sound of the letter:	pâté forêt île hôtel flûte
The **cédille** (¸) under a *c* tells you to pronounce the *c* like an *s*:	français ça
When two vowels appear next to each other, a **tréma** (¨) over the second one tells you to pronounce each vowel separately:	Noël Haïti
You usually will not see accents on capital letters.	île Ile état Etats-Unis

When you spell a word aloud, be sure to say the accents, as well as the letters.

5 **Quelle est l'orthographe?**   *What is the spelling?*

Ecoutons Write down the words as you hear them spelled.

Les chiffres de 0 à 20 ▪ *Numbers from 0 to 20*

How many times a day do you use numbers? Giving someone a phone number, checking grades, and getting change at the store all involve numbers. Here are the French numbers from 0 to 20.

 Note culturelle

When you count on your fingers, which finger do you start with? The French way is to start counting with your thumb as number one, your index finger as two, and so on. How would you show four the French way? And eight?

 6 **Mon numéro de téléphone**

Ecoutons Listen as Nicole, Paul, Vincent, and Corinne tell you their phone numbers. Then, match the numbers with their names.

1. Paul
2. Nicole
3. Vincent
4. Corinne

a. 03. 20. 16. 05. 17
b. 03. 20. 18. 11. 19
c. 03. 20. 17. 07. 18
d. 03. 20. 15. 04. 13
e. 03. 20. 14. 08. 12

 7 **Devine!** *Guess!*

Think of a number between one and twenty. Your partner will try to guess your number. Help out by saying **plus** *(higher)* or **moins** *(lower)* as your partner guesses. Take turns.

 8 **Plaques d'immatriculation** *License plates*

Look at the license plates pictured below. Take turns with a partner reading aloud the numbers and letters you see.

1. 90 ZD 972
2. 275 PS 13
3. 1 872 LD 94
4. Québec WFW 547 Je me souviens
5. 2463 RP 13
6. 1869 AR01

A l'école · *At school*

You should familiarize yourself with these common French instructions. You'll hear your teacher using them in class.

Ecoutez!	Listen!
Répétez!	Repeat!
Levez-vous!	Stand up!
Levez la main!	Raise your hand!
Asseyez-vous!	Sit down!
Ouvrez vos livres à la page... !	Open your books to page . . . !
Fermez la porte!	Close the door!
Sortez une feuille de papier!	Take out a sheet of paper!
Allez au tableau!	Go to the blackboard!
Regardez la carte!	Look at the map!

9 Les instructions

Ecoutons Listen to the teacher in this French class tell his students what to do. Then, decide which student is following each instruction.

Conseils pour apprendre le français

Tips for studying French

Listen

It's important to listen carefully to what is going on in class. Ask questions if you don't understand, even if you think your question is silly. Other people are probably wondering the same thing! You won't be able to understand everything you hear, but you will quickly realize that you don't need to! Don't get frustrated. You're actually absorbing the language even when you don't realize it.

Speak

Practice speaking French every day. Talking with your teachers and classmates is an easy and fun way to learn. Don't be afraid to take risks with the language. Your mistakes will help you identify problems and will show you important differences in the way English and French work.

Practice

Learning a new language is like learning to play a sport or an instrument. You can't spend one night practicing and then expect to play perfectly the next morning. You didn't learn English that way either! Short, daily study sessions are more effective than once-a-week cramming sessions. Also, try to practice with a friend or a classmate, since language is all about communication.

Expand

Increase your contact with French outside of class in every way you can. You might find French-language programs on TV, on the radio, or at the video store, or even someone living near you who speaks French. Magazines, French newspapers, and the Internet are other great sources for French-language material. Don't be afraid to read, watch, or listen! You don't need to understand every word. You can get a lot out of a story or an article by concentrating on the words you recognize and doing a little intelligent guesswork.

Organize

As you learn French, your memory is going to get a workout, so it's important to be organized and efficient. Throughout the textbook you'll see tips (**De bons conseils**) that will help you study smart. For starters, try looking for cognates when you read. Cognates are words that look similar and have the same meaning in French and English, such as **chocolat** and *chocolate*, **musique** and *music*. Once you recognize which words are cognates, you can then spend more of your time studying the words that are completely unfamiliar.

Connect

Some English and French words have common roots in Latin, so your knowledge of English can give you clues about the meaning of many French words. Look for an English connection when you need to guess unfamiliar words. You may also find that learning French will help you in English class!

Have fun!

Above all, remember to have fun!
The more you try, the more you'll learn.
Bonne chance! *(Good luck!)*

Allez, viens à Poitiers!

Capital of Poitou-Charentes

Population : more than 120,000

Points of interest : the Futuroscope theme park, the Saint-Pierre Cathedral, the Palais de Justice

Museums : Sainte-Croix, Hypogée des Dunes

Industries : agriculture, fishing, electrical and mechanical manufacturing, forestry, furniture production

Famous people : saint Hilaire, Diane de Poitiers, Aliénor d'Aquitaine

Regional specialties : goat cheese, nougat, snails, cream-cheese pastries, chocolates

go.hrw.com
WA3 POITIERS

VIDEO

CD-ROM 1
DVD 1

Poitiers, ville d'art et d'histoire ▶

Poitiers

Poitiers is famous for its art and history. It was here in 732 A.D. that Charles Martel defeated the Saracens in the Battle of Poitiers. Home to an important university and attractions such as a futuristic park devoted to cinematic technology, Poitiers is also a very modern city.

Visit Holt Online

go.hrw.com

KEYWORD: WA3 POITIERS

Activités Internet

1 Le Futuroscope
People of all ages enjoy this popular futuristic theme park filled with cinematic exhibits. Of particular interest are the 360-degree theater and the **Kinémax** with its 600-square-meter screen.

2 L' Hôtel de ville
In most French cities you will find the **Hôtel de ville,** which houses the government administration offices.

3 La Pierre Levée

This kind of prehistoric monument, called a dolmen, is constructed of upright stones supporting a horizontal stone. Found especially in Britain and France, dolmens are believed to be tombs. This one dates from about 3000 B.C.

4 La cathédrale Saint-Pierre

Construction of this Gothic cathedral of incredible height was begun at the end of the twelfth century. Its elaborate façade has three gabled portals like this one and a rose window.

In chapters 1, 2, and 3,

you will meet some students who live in Poitiers. Once among the biggest cities in France (in the sixteenth century), Poitiers is now a mid-size city, a university town full of young people. It is known for its pleasant atmosphere and Romanesque churches.

5 Le centre-ville

The heart of French cities and towns is called **le centre-ville**. In Poitiers, it is the bustling center of town where people gather in cafés and frequent the many shops.

6 Les marchés

At least once a week, French towns usually have an outdoor market such as this **marché aux fleurs.**

1
Faisons connaissance!

Objectives

In this chapter you will learn to

Première étape

- greet people and say goodbye
- ask how people are and tell how you are
- ask someone's name and age and give yours

Deuxième étape

- express likes, dislikes, and preferences about things

Troisième étape

- express likes, dislikes, and preferences about activities

Visit Holt Online

go.hrw.com

KEYWORD: WA3 POITIERS-1

Online Edition ⬍

◀ **Salut! Ça va?**

MISE EN TRAIN ▪ *Salut, les copains!*

Stratégie **pour comprendre**
What can you tell about these teenagers just by looking at their photos? Look for hints about where they live, how old they are, and what they like to do.

1

Claire
Bonjour! Ça va? Je m'appelle Claire. J'ai 15 ans. Je suis française, de Poitiers. J'adore le cinéma. Mais j'aime aussi danser, lire, voyager et écouter de la musique.

2

Djeneba
Salut! Je m'appelle Djeneba. J'ai 16 ans. Je suis ivoirienne. J'aime étudier, mais j'aime mieux faire du sport. C'est super cool!

3

Ahmed
Salut! Je m'appelle Ahmed. Je suis marocain. J'aime tous les sports, surtout le football. J'aime aussi faire du vélo.

4

Thuy
Salut! Ça va? Je m'appelle Thuy. J'ai 14 ans. Je suis vietnamienne. J'aime faire les magasins. En général, je n'aime pas la télévision. J'aime mieux aller au cinéma.

Didier
Salut! Je m'appelle Didier. J'ai 13 ans. Je suis belge.
J'aime écouter de la musique. J'aime aussi les
vacances. J'aime surtout voyager!

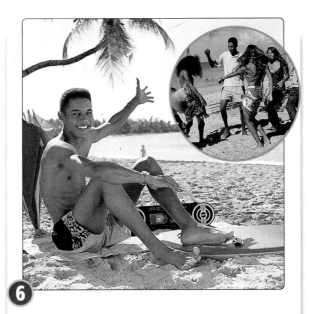

Stéphane
Bonjour! Je m'appelle Stéphane. J'ai 15 ans et je suis
martiniquais. J'aime la plage, la mer, le soleil, la
musique et j'aime aussi nager. J'aime surtout danser.

André
Tiens, bonjour! Comment ça va? Je m'appelle André.
J'ai 17 ans et je suis suisse. Je parle français et
allemand. J'aime beaucoup la télévision. J'aime aussi
parler au téléphone avec mes copains.

Emilie
Bonjour! Je m'appelle Emilie. J'ai 16 ans. Je suis
québécoise. J'adore faire du sport, surtout du ski et
du patin. J'aime bien aussi faire de l'équitation.

Cahier d'activités, p. 3, Act. 1–2

1 Tu as compris? *Did you understand?*

Answer the following questions about the teenagers you've just met. Look back at *Salut, les copains!* if you have to. Don't be afraid to guess.

1. What are these teenagers talking about?
2. What information do they give you in the first few lines of their introductions?
3. What are some of the things they like?
4. Which of them have interests in common?

2 Vrai ou faux? *True or false?*

According to *Salut, les copains!,* are the following statements true (**vrai**) or false (**faux**)?

1. André aime parler au téléphone.
2. Ahmed n'aime pas le sport.
3. Stéphane aime écouter de la musique.
4. Claire aime voyager et danser.
5. Didier n'aime pas voyager.
6. Emilie aime faire de l'équitation.
7. Thuy aime la télévision.
8. Djeneba n'aime pas faire du sport.

3 Cherche les expressions *Look for the expressions*

Look back at *Salut, les copains!* How do the teenagers . . .

1. say hello?
2. give their name?
3. give their age?
4. say they like something?

J'ai... ans. J'aime... Je suis...

Bonjour. Salut. Je m'appelle...

4 Qui est-ce? *Who is it?*

Can you identify the teenagers in *Salut, les copains!* from these descriptions?

1. Elle est québécoise.
2. Il parle allemand.
3. Il a quinze ans.
4. Il aime voyager.
5. Elle adore le ski.
6. Elle n'aime pas la télévision.
7. Il adore le football.
8. Elle aime étudier.

5 Et maintenant, à toi *And now, it's your turn*

Which of the students in *Salut, les copains!* would you most like to meet? Why? Jot down your thoughts and share them with a classmate.

CHAPITRE 1 Faisons connaissance!

Rencontre culturelle

Look at what the people in these photos are doing.

—Salut, Mireille!
—Salut, Lucien!

—Bonjour, Maman!
—Bonjour, mon chou!

—Salut, Lucien!
—Salut, Jean-Philippe!

—Salut, Agnès!
—Tchao, Mireille!

—Bonjour, Monsieur Balland.
—Bonjour, Marc.

—Au revoir, Monsieur Legrand.
—Au revoir, Isabelle.

Qu'en penses-tu?   *What do you think?*

1. How do these teenagers greet adults? Other teenagers? What gestures do they use?
2. How do they say goodbye? What gestures do they use?
3. Is this similar to the way you greet people and say goodbye in the United States?

Savais-tu que...?   *Did you know . . . ?*

In France, girls kiss both girls and boys on the cheek when they meet or say goodbye. The number of kisses varies from two to four depending on the region. Boys shake hands with one another. Teenagers may kiss adults who are family members or friends of the family, but they shake hands when they greet other adults.

To address adults who aren't family members, teenagers generally use the titles **madame, mademoiselle,** or **monsieur. Mme, Mlle,** and **M.** are the written abbreviations of these titles.

Première étape

Objectives Greeting people and saying goodbye; asking how people are and telling how you are; asking someone's name and age and giving yours

WA3 POITIERS-1

Comment dit-on...?

Greeting people and saying goodbye

To anyone:

Bonjour. *Hello.*

Au revoir. *Goodbye.*
A tout à l'heure. *See you later.*
A bientôt. *See you soon.*
A demain. *See you tomorrow.*

To someone your own age or younger:

Salut. *Hi.*

Salut. *Bye.*
Tchao. *Bye.*

Cahier d'activités, p. 4, Act. 3

6 Bonjour ou Au revoir?

Ecoutons Imagine you overhear the following short conversations on the street in Poitiers. Listen carefully and decide whether the speakers are saying hello or goodbye.

7 Comment le dire? *How should you say it?*

Parlons How would you say hello to these people in French?

Mme Leblanc

M. Diab

Nadia

Eric

Mme Desrochers

8 Comment répondre? *How should you answer?*

Parlons How would you respond to the greeting from each of the following people?

1.

2.

3.

4.

Comment dit-on...?

Asking how people are and telling how you are

To ask how your friend is:

Comment ça va? or **Ça va?**

To tell how you are:

Super! *Great!*
Très bien. *Very well.*

Ça va. *Fine.*
Comme ci comme ça. *So-so.*
Pas mal. *Not bad.*
Bof! *(expression of indifference)*

Pas terrible. *Not so great.*

To keep a conversation going:

Et toi? *And you?*

Cahier d'activités, p. 4, Act. 4

Travaux pratiques de grammaire, p. 1, Act. 1

A la française

To ask an adult how he or she is, you can say:

Comment allez-vous?

To keep a conversation with an adult going, you can say:

Et vous?

You'll learn more about using **vous** later in this chapter.

---

9 **Comment ça va?**

Ecoutons You're going to hear a student ask Valérie, Jean-Michel, Anne, Marie, and Karim how they're feeling. Are they feeling good, fair, or bad?

Note culturelle

Gestures are an important part of communication. They often speak louder than words. Can you match the gestures with these expressions?

a. Super!

b. Comme ci comme ça.

c. Pas terrible!

When you say **super,** use a thumbs-up gesture. When you say **comme ci comme ça,** hold your hand in front of you, palm down, and rock it from side to side. When you say **pas terrible,** shrug your shoulders and frown.

1.

2.

3.

PREMIERE ETAPE

vingt-trois **23**

10 Méli-mélo! *Mishmash!*

Ecrivons/Parlons Work with a classmate to rewrite the conversation in the correct order, using your own names. Then, act it out with your partner. Remember to use the appropriate gestures.

> Très bien.　Super! Et toi?
> Tchao.　Salut,... ! Ça va?
> Bon. Alors, à tout à l'heure!　Bonjour,... !

11 Et ton voisin (ta voisine)? *And your neighbor?*

Parlons Create a conversation with a partner. Be sure to greet your partner, ask how he or she is feeling, respond to any questions your partner asks you, and say goodbye. Don't forget to include the gestures you learned in the **Note culturelle** on page 23.

Comment dit-on...?

Asking someone's name and giving yours

—**Tu t'appelles comment?**
—**Je m'appelle Magali.**

To ask someone his or her name:

Tu t'appelles comment?

To give your name:

Je m'appelle...

> Travaux pratiques de grammaire, p. 2, Act. 5

To ask someone else's name:

Il/Elle s'appelle comment? *What is his/her name?*

To give someone else's name:

Il/Elle s'appelle... *His/Her name is . . .*

12 Il ou elle?

Ecoutons Listen as some French teenagers tell you about their friends. Are they talking about a boy (**un garçon**) or a girl (**une fille**)?

13 **Il s'appelle comment?**

Ecoutons You're going to hear a song called *S'appeler rap.* Which of the following names are mentioned in the song?

Emilie   Jean   Thomas

Laurence   Pierre

Robert   Julie

Linda   Laurent

 14 **Je te présente...** *Let me introduce . . .*

Parlons Select a French name for yourself from the list of names on page 5, or ask your teacher to suggest others. Then, say hello to a classmate, introduce yourself, and ask his or her name. Now, introduce your partner to the rest of the class, using **il s'appelle** or **elle s'appelle.**

Comment dit-on...?

Asking someone's age and giving yours

To find out someone's age:

Tu as quel âge?

To give your age:

J'ai douze **ans.**
treize
quatorze
quinze
seize
dix-sept
dix-huit

CD-ROM **1**
DVD **1**

Grammaire supplémentaire, p. 38, Act. 1–2

Travaux pratiques de grammaire, pp. 1–2, Act. 2–4, 6

 15 **Je me présente...**

Ecoutons Listen as Bruno, Véronique, Laurent, and Céline introduce themselves to you. Write down each student's age.

 16 **Faisons connaissance!** *Let's get to know one another!*

Parlons Create a conversation with two other classmates. Introduce yourself, ask your partners' names and ages, and ask how they are.

 17 **Mon journal** *My journal*

Ecrivons A good way to learn French is to use it to express your own thoughts and feelings. From time to time, you'll be asked to write about yourself in French in a journal. As your first journal entry, identify yourself, giving your name, your age, and anything else important to you that you've learned how to say in French.

Comment dit-on...?

Expressing likes, dislikes, and preferences about things

To ask if someone likes something:

> **Tu aimes** les hamburgers?
> **Tu aimes** le vélo **ou** le ski? *Do you like . . . or . . . ?*

To say that you dislike something:

> **Je n'aime pas** les hamburgers.

To say that you like something:

> **J'adore** le chocolat.
> **J'aime bien** le sport.
> **J'aime** les hamburgers.

To say that you prefer something:

> J'aime les frites, **mais j'aime mieux** le chocolat. *I like . . . , but I prefer . . .*
> **Je préfère** le français.

Note de grammaire

J'aime la pizza.

Je n'aime pas la pizza.

Look at the sentences in the illustrations to the left. Can you figure out when to use **ne (n')... pas**?

You put **ne (n')... pas** around the verb **aime** to make the sentence negative. Notice the contraction **n'** before the vowel.

> J'aime le sport.
> Je **n'**aime **pas** le sport.

Travaux pratiques de grammaire, p. 3, Act. 7–8

Grammaire supplémentaire, p. 39, Act. 3

18 Grammaire en contexte

a. **Ecoutons** Listen to Paul and Sophie Dubois discuss names for their baby girl. Which of the names does Paul prefer? And Sophie?

b. **Parlons** Do you agree with Paul and Sophie's choices? With a partner, discuss whether you like or dislike the names Paul and Sophie mention. What's your favorite French girl's name? And your favorite French boy's name? You might refer to the list of names on page 5.

> EXEMPLE — Tu aimes...?
>
> — Oui, mais je n'aime pas...

> Claude   Sandrine   Claudette
>
> Lætitia   Claudine

19 Quel film? *Which movie?*

Parlons With two of your classmates, decide on a movie you all like.

> EXEMPLE — J'aime *The Truman Show!* Et toi?
>
> — Moi, je n'aime pas *The Truman Show.* Tu aimes *Chicken Run*®?
>
> — Oui, j'aime *Chicken Run,* mais j'aime mieux *Wallace and Gromit!*

CASABLANCA RE

1942. 1h40. Film d'aventures américain en noir et blanc de Michael Curtiz avec Humphrey Bogart, Ingrid Bergman, Paul Henreid, Conrad Veidt, Claude Rains. Casablanca à l'heure de Vichy. Un réfugié américain retrouve une femme follement aimée et fuit la persécution nazie. Une distribution étincelante et une mise en scène efficace.

• V.O. Saint Lambert 96

CD-ROM **1**
DVD **1**

les amis (m.)

le cinéma

le ski

le football

le magasin

la plage

le vélo

la glace

l'école (f.)

le français

les frites (f.)

le chocolat

l'anglais (m.)

les examens (m.)

les vacances (f.)

les escargots (m.)

You can probably guess what these words mean:

les concerts (m.)   les hamburgers (m.)   les maths (f.)   la pizza   le sport

Cahier d'activités,
p. 8, Act. 12

Travaux pratiques de
grammaire, p. 4, Act. 9–11

20 **Moi, j'aime...**

Ecoutons Listen as several French teenagers call in to a radio talk-show poll of their likes and dislikes. Match their names with the pictures that illustrate the activities they like or dislike.

Paul   Pierre   Robert

Monique   Suzanne   Emilie

a.

b.

c.

d.

e.

f.

Grammaire

The definite articles *le, la, l',* and *les*

There are four ways to say *the* in French: **le, la, l',** and **les.** These words are called *definite articles.* Look at the articles and nouns below. Can you tell when to use **les?** When to use **l'?**

| le français | la glace | l'école | les escargots |
| le football | la pizza | l'anglais | les magasins |

• As you may have guessed, you always use **les** before plural nouns.

• Before a singular noun, you use **l'** if the noun begins with a vowel sound, **le** if the noun is masculine, or **la** if the noun is feminine. How do you know which nouns are masculine and which are feminine? While it is usually true that nouns that refer to males are masculine (**le garçon** *the boy*) and those that refer to females are feminine (**la fille** *the girl*), there are no hard-and-fast rules for other nouns. You'll just have to learn the definite article that goes with each one.

Grammaire supplémentaire, p. 39, Act. 4–5

Travaux pratiques de grammaire, p. 5, Act. 12–14

21 Grammaire en contexte

Lisons/Parlons Lucie and Gilbert are talking about the things they like. With a partner, complete their conversation according to the pictures.

LUCIE   Moi, j'aime bien . Et toi?

GILBERT   Moi, j'aime mieux J'aime bien aussi sortir avec  .

J'adore le sport aussi. Et toi, tu aimes le sport?

LUCIE   Oui, j'adore et j'aime bien aussi.

22 Grammaire en contexte

Ecrivons/Parlons Choose six things from the vocabulary on page 27. Next, write down which of those things you like and which you dislike. Then, with a partner, try to guess each other's likes and dislikes by asking **Tu aimes... ?**

A la française

Two common words you can use to connect your ideas are **et** *(and)* and **mais** *(but)*. Here's how you can use them to combine sentences.

J'aime les hamburgers. J'aime le chocolat.
J'aime les hamburgers **et** le chocolat.

J'aime le français. Je n'aime pas les maths.
J'aime le français **mais** je n'aime pas les maths.

DE BONS CONSEILS

How can you remember if a noun is masculine or feminine? Here are a few hints. Choose the one that works best for you.

- Practice saying each noun aloud with **le** or **la** in front of it. (NOTE: This won't help with nouns that begin with vowels!)
- Write the feminine nouns in one column and the masculine nouns in another. You might even write the feminine nouns in one color and the masculine nouns in a second color.
- Make flash cards of the nouns, writing the feminine and masculine nouns in different colors.

23 Mon journal

Ecrivons In your journal, write down some of your likes and dislikes. Use **et** and **mais** to connect your sentences. You might want to illustrate your journal entry.

DEUXIEME ETAPE   *vingt-neuf*   **29**

Qu'est-ce que tu aimes faire après l'école?

What do you like to do when you have free time? Do you think teenagers in French-speaking countries like to do the same things? Here's what some students had to say about their favorite leisure-time activities.

Gabrielle,
Québec

«J'aime lire. J'aime écouter de la musique. J'aime parler... discuter avec mes amis.»

Fabienne,
Martinique

«Alors, quand j'ai du temps libre, j'aime aller au cinéma, aller à la plage, lire et puis voilà, c'est tout.»

Caroline,
France

«Après l'école, j'aime regarder la télévision, aller à la piscine ou lire des livres.»

Qu'en penses-tu?

1. What do all three of these people have in common?
2. What interests do you and your friends share with these people?
3. What do these people do that you don't like to do?
4. Which of these people would you most like to meet? Why?

Savais-tu que...?

In general, French-speaking teenagers enjoy the same kinds of activities you do. However, some activities do tend to be especially popular in certain areas, such as badminton and hockey in Canada, dancing and soccer in West Africa, and soccer and cycling in France. In many francophone countries, students have a great deal of homework, so they do not have very much leisure time after school. Of course, people are individuals, so their tastes vary. In French, you might say **Chacun ses goûts!** *(To each his own!).*

Vocabulaire

CD-ROM 1
DVD 1

Stéphanie adore **regarder la télé.**

Etienne aime **sortir avec les copains.**

Nicolas aime **parler au téléphone.**

Olivier aime **dormir.**

Danielle aime **étudier.**

Sylvie aime bien **faire du sport.**

Michèle aime **faire les magasins.**

Hervé aime **faire le ménage.**

Raymond aime **faire de l'équitation.**

Serge aime **voyager.**

Eric aime **écouter de la musique.**

Laurence aime bien **nager.**

Solange adore **danser.**

Annie aime **lire.**

Cahier d'activités, p. 10, Act. 18–19

Travaux pratiques de grammaire, pp. 6–7, Act. 15–17

24 **Mon activité préférée**

Ecoutons You're going to hear six students tell you what they like to do. For each statement you hear, decide which of the students pictured on page 31 is speaking.

Comment dit-on...?

Expressing likes, dislikes, and preferences about activities

To ask if someone likes an activity:

Tu aimes voyager?

To tell what you like to do:

J'aime voyager.
J'adore danser.
J'aime bien dormir.

To tell what you don't like to do:

Je n'aime pas aller aux concerts.

To tell what you prefer to do:

J'aime mieux regarder la télévision.
Je préfère lire.

Cahier d'activités,
p. 9, Act. 16

25 **Sondage** *Poll*

a. Lisons Complete the following poll.

1. J'aime...
   a. faire de l'équitation.
   b. sortir avec les copains.
   c. parler français.
   d. dormir.
   e. écouter le professeur.
   f. faire du sport.

2. Chez moi, j'aime...
   a. regarder la télévision.
   b. écouter de la musique.
   c. dormir.
   d. parler au téléphone.

3. Avec mes copains, j'aime mieux...
   a. faire du sport.
   b. manger au restaurant.
   c. faire les magasins.
   d. danser.
   e. nager.
   f. aller au cinéma.

4. J'aime surtout...
   a. le chocolat.
   b. les hamburgers.
   c. la salade.
   d. les frites.
   e. la pizza.

5. J'aime aussi...
   a. le ski.
   b. le vélo.
   c. le volley.
   d. le basket-ball.

6. Je n'aime pas...
   a. les escargots.
   b. la pollution.
   c. l'école.
   d. la violence.
   e. les dentistes.
   f. les examens.

 b. Parlons Compare your responses to the poll with those of a classmate. Which interests do you have in common?

Subject pronouns and *-er* verbs

The verb **aimer** has different forms. In French, the verb forms change according to the subjects just as they do in English: *I like, you like,* but *he* or *she likes*.

Most **-er** verbs, that is, verbs whose infinitive ends in **-er,** follow the pattern below:

aimer *(to like)*

J' aim**e**	Nous aim**ons**
Tu aim**es**	Vous aim**ez**
Il/Elle aim**e**	Ils/Elles aim**ent**

- The forms **aime, aimes,** and **aiment** sound the same.
- The subject pronouns in French are **je/j'** *(I),* **tu** *(you),* **il** *(he or it),* **elle** *(she or it),* **nous** *(we),* **vous** *(you),* **ils** *(they),* and **elles** *(they).*
- Notice that there are two pronouns for *they.* Use **elles** to refer to a group of females. Use **ils** to refer to a group of males or a group of males and females.
- **Tu** and **vous** both mean *you.* Use **vous** when you talk to more than one person or to an adult who is not a family member. Use **tu** when you talk to a friend, family member, or someone your own age.
- Noun subjects take the same verb forms as their pronouns.

Philippe aime la salade.　　　　**Sophie et Julie aiment** faire du sport.

Il aime la salade.　　　　**Elles aiment** faire du sport.

Cahier d'activités,
pp. 9–10, Act. 14, 17

Travaux pratiques de grammaire,
pp. 7–9, Act. 18–23

Grammaire supplémentaire,
pp. 40–41, Act. 6–10

26　**Grammaire en contexte**

    a. Parlons Would you use **tu** or **vous** to greet the following people? How would you ask them if they like a certain thing or activity?

Mes amis

Mlle Normand

Flore et Loïc

Lucie

    b. Parlons Now complete the following phrases to tell what these people like, according to the illustrations above.

      1. Mes amis...　　　　　　3. Flore et moi, nous...

      2. Mlle Normand...　　　　4. Moi, je m'appelle Lucie. J'...

27 Grammaire en contexte

Parlons Your French pen pal wants to know what your friends like to do. Use the following photographs as cues.

Julio

Robert

Mark, David et Thomas

Agnès

Marie

Eric

Karen

Pamela

Emily et Raymond

28 Les vedettes! *Celebrities!*

 a. Ecrivons Make a list of three public figures (movie stars, musicians, athletes, and so on) you admire. Write down one or two things you think each person might like to do.

> **EXEMPLE** **Shaquille O'Neal aime faire du sport, surtout** *(especially)* **du basket-ball!**

 b. Parlons Now, get together with a classmate. Tell your partner what one of the celebrities you've chosen likes to do. Use **il** or **elle** instead of the person's name. Your partner will try to identify the celebrity. Take turns.

29

Parlons During your summer vacation you're working as a reporter for a French news-paper. Your new assignment for the paper is to do a survey about what is popular with young people right now. Interview your classmates, making sure to ask them a variety of questions in French about what foods they like, how they feel about school, and what activities they like and dislike.

30 **Mon journal**

Ecrivons Expand your previous journal entry by adding the activities you like and dislike. Tell which activities you and your friends like to do together. Find or draw pictures to illustrate the activities.

PRONONCIATION

Intonation

As you speak, your voice rises and falls. This is called *intonation.*

A. A prononcer

In French, your voice rises at the end of each group of words within a statement and falls at the end of a statement. Repeat each of the following phrases:

J'aime les frites, les hamburgers et la pizza.

Il aime le football mais il n'aime pas le vélo.

If you want to change a statement into a question, raise your voice at the end of the sentence. Repeat these questions.

Tu aimes l'anglais?

Tu t'appelles Julie?

B. A écouter

Decide whether each of the following is a statement or a question.

C. A écrire

You're going to hear two short dialogues. Write down what the people say.

Petites Annonces

A. Look at the pictures and titles of this article from a French magazine. What do you think the article is about?

B. Do you remember what you've learned about cognates? Can you find at least five cognates in this article?

C. What do you think **Petites Annonces** means?

D. Which of the pen pals would you choose if you were searching for the following?

Quelqu'un qui (*someone who*)…

aime faire les boutiques

aime les animaux

parle français et espagnol

aime la musique et le cinéma

aime le rap et la techno

Petites Annonces

Christiane Saulnier
Marseille

Si vous aimez la télévision, les animaux et les vacances, qu'est-ce que vous attendez pour m'écrire et m'envoyer votre photo! Je voudrais correspondre avec des filles ou des garçons de 13 à 16 ans. J'attends votre réponse avec impatience!

Karim Marzouk
Tunis, Tunisie

J'adorerais recevoir des lettres de personnes habitant le monde entier; j'adore voyager, écouter de la musique, aller au concert et lire sur la plage. J'aime bien les langues et je parle aussi l'arabe et l'espagnol. A bientôt.

Mireille Lacombe
Nantes

J'ai 15 ans et je voudrais bien correspondre avec des filles et des garçons de 13 à 17 ans. J'aime le rap et surtout la techno. Je fais aussi de l'équitation. Ecrivez-moi vite et je promets de vous répondre (photos S.V.P.)!

Didier Kouassi
Abidjan, Côte d'Ivoire

La techno me fait délirer et je suis aussi très sportif. Je cherche des correspondants filles ou garçons entre 15 et 17 ans. N'hésitez pas à m'écrire!

★ COPAINS ★ COPINES ★

Laurence Simon
Le Marin, Martinique

J'ai 16 ans, je suis dingue de sport, j'aime les soirs de fête entre copains. Le week-end, j'aime faire les magasins. Alors, si vous me ressemblez, dépêchez-vous de m'écrire. Réponse assurée à 100%!

Etienne Hubert
Poitiers

Je suis blond aux yeux bleus, assez grand, timide mais très sympa. J'aime sortir et j'aime lire la science-fiction. Je cherche des amis entre 14 et 16 ans. Répondez vite!

Hugues Vallet
La Rochelle

Je voudrais correspondre avec des filles et des garçons de 16 à 18 ans. J'aime sortir, délirer et faire les boutiques. Je suis fan de Vanessa Paradis et de Julia Roberts. Alors, j'attends vos lettres!

Amélie Perrin
Périgord

Je voudrais correspondre avec des jeunes de 14 à 17 ans qui aiment faire la fête, écouter de la musique et aller au cinéma. Moi, j'étudie la danse et la photographie. Ecrivez-moi et je me ferai une joie de vous répondre.

Vous voulez correspondre avec des gens sympas? Écrivez votre petite annonce en précisant vos nom, prénom, âge et adresse, et en y joignant une photo d'identité.

E. Several of your friends are looking for pen pals. Based on their wishes, find a good match for each of them in **Petites Annonces.**

   1. My pen pal should like sports.

   2. I'd like to hear from someone who likes going out.

   3. I'm looking for a pen pal who likes to go to the movies.

   4. It would be great to have a pen pal who enjoys shopping.

   5. I'd like to hear from someone from Africa.

   6. I'd like a pen pal who likes to travel.

F. If you want to place an ad for a pen pal, what should you do?

G. One of your classmates is looking for a pen pal. Make a short list of questions that will help you identify which pen pal has the most in common with your classmate. Then, interview your classmate, compare his or her answers with the ads included in **Petites Annonces,** and decide which pen pal would be the best match. Find out if your classmate agrees with your decision.

H. Jot down a few things you might like to include in your own letter requesting a pen pal. Using your notes, write your own request for a pen pal like the ones you read in **Petites Annonces.**

Cahier d'activités, p. 11, Act. 20–21

trente-sept **37**

Grammaire supplémentaire

CD-ROM 1
DVD 1

Visit Holt Online

go.hrw.com

KEYWORD: WA3 POITIERS-1

Jeux interactifs

Première étape   **Objectives** Greeting people and saying goodbye; asking how people are and telling how you are; asking someone's name and age and giving yours

1   Can you find the pattern in these phone numbers? Figure out which number completes each pattern. Then, write out the number in French. (**pp. 9, 25**)

> **EXEMPLE**   02. **11**. 20. 29. 38; <u>onze</u>

1. 05. 12. _____ . 26. 33; _____

2. 03. 10. _____ . 24. 31; _____

3. 01. _____ . 25. 37. 49; _____

4. 05. _____ . 35. 50. 65; _____

5. 04. 10. _____ . 22. 28; _____

6. 02. _____ . 22. 32. 42; _____

2   These French speakers are telling you their name and age. The age of each speaker corresponds to the number of letters in his or her place of origin. Make two statements for each speaker by following the example below. (**pp. 9, 24, 25**)

> **EXEMPLE**   Pierre/France
> **Je m'appelle Pierre. J'ai six ans.**

1. Bernard/Martinique

2. Aurélie/Belgique

3. Ousmane/Sénégal

4. Cédric/Guyane française

5. Lætitia/Mali

6. Lisette/Burkina Faso

3 Complete the following sentences, using the correct form of **aimer** and **ne (n')... pas** when appropriate. (**p. 26**)

EXEMPLE   — Tu adores la plage, mais tu **n'aimes pas** la piscine.

1. Moi, j'aime bien la musique classique, mais je/j' _____ le rock.
2. Tu n'aimes pas le sport, mais tu _____ le vélo.
3. J'adore la glace, mais je/j' _____ le chocolat.
4. J'aime bien l'école, mais je/j' _____ les examens.
5. Tu aimes les concerts, mais tu _____ le cinéma.
6. Tu n'aimes pas les hamburgers, mais tu _____ les frites.
7. J'aime la télé, mais je/j' _____ le cinéma.
8. Tu n'aimes pas l'anglais, mais tu _____ le français.

4 Complete Gabrielle's journal entry with the appropriate definite articles **le, la, l',** or **les**. (**p. 28**)

J'aime ___1___ école. J'aime bien ___2___ anglais et ___3___ français, mais je n'aime pas ___4___ examens. J'adore ___5___ sport et ___6___ plage. J'aime ___7___ football et ___8___ vélo aussi.

5 Use the following cues to create four questions and four answers. Remember to add the appropriate definite articles: **le, la, l',** or **les**. (**p. 28**)

EXEMPLE   salade/Eric/tu/aimes?   aime/j'/hamburgers/aussi *(also)*
            Eric, tu aimes la salade?   **Oui, et j'aime aussi les hamburgers.**

1. tu/aimes/frites/Marianne?   3. aimes/escargots/Nathalie/tu?
   aime/j'/pizza/aussi   j'/aussi/aime/chocolat
   —Oui, et...   —Oui, et...

2. tu/ne/pas/maths/aimes/Isabelle?   4. tu/aimes/ne/pas/magasins?
   français/aussi/aime/j'   plage/j'/aussi/aime
   —Si *(yes),* et...   —Si, et...

Grammaire supplémentaire

WA3 POITIERS-1

Troisième étape **Objective** Expressing likes, dislikes, and preferences about activities

6 Séverine is looking for a pen pal. Complete her ad with the appropriate forms of the verbs in parentheses. (**p. 33**)

J'ai 16 ans. Je/J' ___1___ (adorer) faire du sport. Je/J' ___2___ (aimer) aussi sortir avec les copains. Nous ___3___ (aimer) bien aller au cinéma, mais nous ___4___ (préférer) aller danser. Parfois, nous ___5___ (écouter) de la musique. Nous ___6___ (adorer) le rap, surtout MC Solaar; il ___7___ (danser) très bien. Nous ___8___ (aimer) aussi les fast-foods. Si vous ___9___ (aimer) le sport, écrivez-moi! A bientôt!

7 Etienne and Solange don't have much in common. Complete their conversation with the appropriate forms of the verbs in parentheses. (**p. 33**)

ETIENNE Dis, Solange, tu ___1___ (aimer) faire du vélo?

SOLANGE Non, je n' ___2___ (aimer) pas le sport, mais j' ___3___ (adorer) danser.

ETIENNE Moi, je ne ___4___ (danser) pas, mais j' ___5___ (écouter) souvent la radio.

SOLANGE Ah oui? Tu ___6___ (écouter) quel type de musique?

ETIENNE Moi, j' ___7___ (adorer) le rap. Mes copains ___8___ (aimer) aller à des concerts de rap, mais moi, j' ___9___ (aimer) mieux regarder des vidéo-clips à la télé. Et toi, tu ___10___ (regarder) la télé?

SOLANGE Moi, non. J' ___11___ (aimer) mieux aller au cinéma.

8 There are many things these students like to do, but what do they prefer to do? Complete these conversations with the appropriate subject pronouns. (**p. 33**)

EXEMPLE —Pierre aime les frites. —Oui, mais **il** aime mieux les escargots.

1. —Lucie et Marie aiment regarder la télé.
   —Oui, mais _____ préfèrent aller au cinéma.

2. —Hugo et toi, vous aimez parler au téléphone?
   —Oui, mais _____ préférons sortir avec les copains.

3. —Olivier et Lise aiment faire les magasins.
   —Oui, mais _____ aiment mieux faire du sport.

4. —Aurélie aime lire.
   —Oui, mais _____ aime mieux dormir.

5. —Christelle et moi, nous aimons le volley.
   —Oui, mais _____ préférez le basket-ball, non?

9 Given their likes and dislikes, what do the following students probably do on weekends? Complete each sentence, using a personal pronoun and the correct form of the appropriate verb. (**p. 33**)

EXEMPLE   Hervé et moi, nous aimons danser.
Le week-end, <u>nous dansons</u>.

1. Mary aime bien parler français avec sa copine.

Le week-end, ...

2. Jules et Loïc aiment regarder des matches de football.

Le week-end, ...

3. Moi, j'adore écouter de la musique.

Le week-end, ...

4. Sylvie et Marianne aiment bien nager.

Le week-end, ...

5. Stéphane et toi, vous aimez parler au téléphone.

Le week-end, ...

6. Toi, tu adores danser.

Le week-end, ...

10 Complete the following sentences, using the correct form of **aimer** and **ne (n')... pas** when appropriate. (**pp. 26, 33**)

EXEMPLE   —Jean adore la plage, mais il **n'aime pas** la piscine.
—Julio n'aime pas voyager, mais il **aime** lire.

1. Jean aime bien les frites, mais il _____ les escargots.

2. Stéphanie n'aime pas les discothèques, mais elle _____ danser.

3. Victor adore écouter la radio, mais il _____ regarder la télé.

4. Yvette aime bien parler au téléphone, mais elle _____ étudier.

5. José aime sortir avec ses copains, mais il _____ le cinéma.

6. Agnès n'aime pas faire le ménage, mais elle _____ faire les magasins.

Mise en pratique

CD-ROM 1
DVD 1

Visit Holt Online
go.hrw.com
KEYWORD: WA3 POITIERS-1
Self-Test

1 Do the following photos represent French culture, American culture, or both?

1.

2.

3.

4.

5.

2 **L'Organisation internationale de correspondants (l'O.I.C.),** a pen-pal organization you wrote to, has left a phone message on your answering machine. Listen carefully to the message and write down your pen pal's name, age, phone number, likes, and dislikes.

Nom :

Age :

Numéro :

Aime :

N'aime pas :

3 Tell a classmate, in French, about your new pen pal.

4 You've received your first letter from Robert Perrault. Read it twice—the first time for general understanding, the second time for details. Then, answer the questions below in English.

Robert Perrault
25, Boulevard Saint-Germain
92700 TANNAY
FRANCE

Bonjour,

Je suis bien content d'être ton correspondant. J'ai quinze ans. J'aime bien sortir avec les copains et écouter de la musique aussi, mais je n'aime pas danser. J'adore la pizza et la glace au chocolat. Et toi? Le week-end, j'adore faire du sport. J'aime bien le vélo, mais pendant les vacances, j'aime mieux nager; c'est super! Toi aussi, tu aimes nager? Écris-moi.

À bientôt,

Robert

1. How old is Robert?

2. What sports does he like?

3. What foods does he like?

4. What doesn't he like to do?

5 Now, answer Robert's letter. Begin your reply with **Cher Robert.** Be sure to . . .

- introduce yourself.
- ask how he's doing.
- tell about your likes and dislikes.
- ask him about other likes and dislikes he might have.
- answer his questions to you.
- say goodbye.

6 **Jeu de rôle**

A French exchange student has just arrived at your school. How would you find out his or her name? Age? Likes and dislikes? Act out the scene with a partner. Take turns playing the role of the French student.

Que sais-je?

Can you use what you've learned in this chapter?

Can you greet people and say goodbye?
p. 22

1 How would you say hello and goodbye to the following people? What gestures would you use?
  1. a classmate
  2. your French teacher

Can you ask how people are and tell how you are?
p. 23

2 Can you ask how someone is?

3 If someone asks you how you are, what do you say if . . .
  1. you feel great?
  2. you feel OK?
  3. you don't feel well?

Can you ask someone's name and age and give yours?
pp. 24–25

4 How would you . . .
  1. ask someone's name?
  2. tell someone your name?

5 How would you . . .
  1. find out someone's age?
  2. tell someone how old you are?

Can you express likes, dislikes, and preferences about things?
p. 26

6 Can you tell whether you like or dislike the following?
  1. horseback riding
  2. soccer
  3. going out with friends
  4. shopping
  5. the movies

Can you express likes, dislikes, and preferences about activities?
p. 32

7 Can you ask a friend in French if he or she likes . . .

a.

b.

c.

d.

e.

8 Can you tell in French what these people like, dislike, or prefer?
  1. Robert never studies.
  2. Emilie thinks reading is the greatest.
  3. Hervé prefers pizza.
  4. Nathalie never goes to the beach.
  5. Nicole is always biking or playing soccer.

CHAPITRE 1   Faisons connaissance!

Greeting people and saying goodbye

Bonjour!	Hello!
Salut!	Hi! or Goodbye!
Au revoir!	Goodbye!
A tout à l'heure!	See you later!
A bientôt.	See you soon.
A demain.	See you tomorrow.
Tchao!	Bye!
madame (Mme)	ma'am; Mrs.
mademoiselle (Mlle)	miss; Miss
monsieur (M.)	sir; Mr.

Asking how people are and telling how you are

(Comment) ça va?	How's it going?
Ça va.	Fine.
Super!	Great!
Très bien.	Very well.
Comme ci comme ça.	So-so.
Bof!	(expression of indifference)
Pas mal.	Not bad.
Pas terrible.	Not so great.
Et toi?	And you?

Asking someone's name and giving yours

Tu t'appelles comment?	What's your name?
Je m'appelle...	My name is . . .
Il/Elle s'appelle comment?	What's his/her name?
Il/Elle s'appelle...	His/Her name is . . .

Asking someone's age and giving yours

Tu as quel âge?	How old are you?
J'ai... ans.	I am . . . years old.
douze	twelve
treize	thirteen
quatorze	fourteen
quinze	fifteen
seize	sixteen
dix-sept	seventeen
dix-huit	eighteen

Deuxième étape

Expressing likes, dislikes, and preferences about things

j'aime (bien)...	I (really) like . . .
Je n'aime pas...	I don't like . . .
J'aime mieux...	I prefer . . .
Je préfère...	I prefer . . .
J'adore...	I adore . . .
Tu aimes... ?	Do you like . . . ?
les amis (m.)	friends
l'anglais (m.)	English
le chocolat	chocolate
le cinéma	the movies
les concerts (m.)	concerts
l'école (f.)	school
les escargots (m.)	snails
les examens (m.)	tests
le football	soccer
le français	French
les frites (f.)	French fries
la glace	ice cream
les hamburgers (m.)	hamburgers
les magasins (m.)	stores
les maths (f.)	math
la pizza	pizza
la plage	beach
le ski	skiing
le sport	sports
les vacances (f.)	vacation
le vélo	biking

Other useful expressions

et	and
mais	but
non	no
oui	yes
ou	or

Troisième étape

Expressing likes, dislikes, and preferences about activities

aimer	to like
danser	to dance
dormir	to sleep
écouter de la musique	to listen to music
étudier	to study
faire de l'équitation	to go horseback riding
faire les magasins	to go shopping
faire le ménage	to do housework
faire du sport	to play sports
lire	to read
nager	to swim
parler au téléphone	to talk on the phone
regarder la télé	to watch TV
sortir avec les copains	to go out with friends
voyager	to travel

Other useful expressions

aussi	also
surtout	especially

For subject pronouns, see page 33.

2

Vive l'école!

Objectives

In this chapter you will learn to

Première étape

- agree and disagree

Deuxième étape

- ask for and give information
- tell when you have class

Troisième étape

- ask for and express opinions

Visit Holt Online

go.hrw.com

KEYWORD: WA3 POITIERS-2

Online Edition

◀ **Tu as quels cours ce matin?**

MISE EN TRAIN · *La rentrée*

Stratégie pour comprendre

Make a list of the cognates you hear or see from **La rentrée**. Do these words have a common theme? Based on your list of cognates, what do you think these teenagers are talking about? Can you guess where they are?

Les jeunes de Poitiers :

Claire   **Delphine**

et du Texas :

Ann

Jérôme   **Marc**

C'est la première semaine de cours...

1

Claire :	Tu as quel cours maintenant?
Delphine :	Allemand. J'adore. Et toi, tu as quoi?
Claire :	Sciences nat.

2

Delphine :	Ecoutez, Je ne veux pas être en retard. Bon courage!
Ann :	Pourquoi?
Delphine :	C'est difficile, les sciences nat.
Claire :	Mais non, c'est passionnant. Et le prof est sympa.

3

Claire :	Alors, les garçons, ça boume?
Jérôme :	Super.
Marc :	Bof. Pas terrible.

4

Claire :	Qu'est-ce qu'il y a?
Marc :	Oh rien. J'ai maths.
Ann :	Tu n'aimes pas les maths?
Marc :	Non, c'est nul.

5

Ann : Moi, j'adore. C'est super intéressant.

Marc : J'aime mieux le sport. C'est plus cool.

6

Claire : Et après, tu as quoi?

Marc : Après les maths, j'ai géographie.

7

Ann : Et toi, Jérôme, tu as quoi maintenant?

Jérôme : Euh, je ne sais pas très bien.

Claire : Tu n'as pas allemand?

Jérôme : Si, tu as raison.

8

Ann : Tu aimes l'allemand, toi?

Jérôme : Oui, mais j'aime encore mieux l'espagnol. C'est plus facile pour moi.

Ann : Tu étudies aussi l'espagnol?

Jérôme : Oui. Et l'anglais aussi.

9

Claire : Dis, tu as sport cet aprèm?

Marc : Oui, à quatorze heures.

Ann : Génial! Nous aussi!

Jérôme : Alors, on a tous sport cet aprèm.

10

Ann : Il est quelle heure?

Claire : Huit heures! Vite. Allons-y! On est en retard!

Marc : Eh bien, Jérôme? Qu'est-ce qu'il y a?

Jérôme : Je n'ai pas mes baskets.

Cahier d'activités, p. 13, Act. 1

1 Tu as compris?

Réponds aux questions suivantes sur *La rentrée.*

1. What are the students discussing?
2. What do you think the title *La rentrée* means?
3. What class do they all have together?
4. Why are they in a hurry at the end of the conversation?
5. What is Jérôme worried about?

2 Vrai ou faux?

1. Ann est américaine.
2. Jérôme n'aime pas l'espagnol.
3. Ann et Marc n'aiment pas les maths.
4. Jérôme a allemand.
5. Marc n'a pas sport cet aprèm.

3 Cherche les expressions

In *La rentrée,* what do the students say to . . .

1. ask what class someone has?
2. tell why they like a class?
3. tell why they don't like a class?
4. tell which class they prefer?
5. ask what time it is?

> C'est difficile.   C'est nul.   Il est quelle heure?
>
> C'est super intéressant.   J'aime encore mieux...
>
> C'est plus cool.
>
> Tu as quel cours?   Tu as quoi?
>
> Le prof est sympa.   J'aime mieux...
>
> C'est passionnant.

4 Ils aiment ou pas?

Do these students like or dislike the subjects or teachers they're talking about?

1. «Les sciences nat, c'est passionnant.»
2. «Les maths, c'est nul.»
3. «C'est super intéressant, les maths.»
4. «Le prof est sympa.»

5 Qu'est-ce qui manque?

Choose the correct words from the box to complete these sentences based on *La rentrée.*

1. Après maths, Marc a _____.
2. Jérôme a _____.
3. Jérôme aime mieux _____ que l'allemand.
4. On a tous sport à _____ heures.
5. On est en retard! Il est _____ heures.

> géographie   allemand   quatorze
>
> huit   l'espagnol

6 Et maintenant, à toi

Which students in *La rentrée* share your own likes or dislikes about school subjects?

Vocabulaire

CD-ROM 1
DVD 1

LYCEE VOLTAIRE

LES SCIENCES NATURELLES — 322

L'INFORMATIQUE — 323

LES TRAVAUX PRATIQUES DE CHIMIE — 222

L'HISTOIRE — 1944 — 223

LA GEOGRAPHIE — 122

L'ALLEMAND — Wie geht's? — 123

L'EDUCATION PHYSIQUE ET SPORTIVE

L'ESPAGNOL — ¡Gracias! — 022

LES ARTS PLASTIQUES — 023

l'algèbre (f.) *algebra*
la biologie *biology*
la chimie *chemistry*
la géométrie *geometry*
la physique *physics*
la chorale *choir*
le cours de développement personnel et social (DPS) *health*

la danse *dance*
le latin *Latin*
la musique *music*
le cours *course, school subject*
les devoirs (m.) *homework*
l'élève (m./f.) *student*
le professeur *teacher*

Cahier d'activités,
pp. 14–16, Act. 2–5, 7

Travaux pratiques de grammaire,
pp. 10–11, Act. 1–4

*You can abbreviate **Education Physique et Sportive** as **EPS.** In conversation, students often say **le sport** instead of **EPS.**

7 C'est où?

Ecoutons On the first day of school, Céline and Aurélie are looking for their French class. As you listen to their conversation, look at the drawing of the school on page 51 and write the numbers of the classrooms they're looking into.

8 Ils aiment quels cours?

Parlons Name three subjects Nicole and Gérard probably like, according to their interests.

Nicole   **Gérard**

9 C'est qui?

Parlons Tell your partner what subject one of these students likes, without naming the person. Your partner will try to guess the person's name. Take turns until you've identified all of the students.

EXEMPLE   — Il aime le français.
             — C'est Michel.

Michel

Julien   **Nathalie**   **Virginie**

Guillaume   **Franck**   **Karine**

DE BONS CONSEILS

Study at regular intervals. It's best to learn language in small chunks and to review frequently. Cramming will not usually work for French. Study at least a little bit every day, whether you have an assignment or not. The more often you review words and structures, the easier it will be for you to understand and participate in class.

Note culturelle

In France and other countries that follow the French educational system, the grade levels are numbered in descending order. When students begin junior high (**le collège**) at about 10 or 11 years of age, they enter the grade called **sixième**. Then they go into **cinquième, quatrième,** and **troisième.** The grade levels at the high school (**le lycée**) are called **seconde, première,** and **terminale.**

Le baccalauréat, or **le bac,** is a national exam taken at the end of study at a **lycée.** Not all students take the **bac,** but those who plan to go on to a university must pass it. It's an extremely difficult oral and written test that covers all major subjects. Students spend the final year of the **lycée, la terminale,** preparing for this exam. There are three major categories of **baccalauréat** exams: **le bac général, le bac technologique,** and **le bac professionnel.** Each category is divided into a more specialized series of exams, depending upon a student's chosen field of study. For example, a student specializing in literature would take the **bac général littéraire,** or simply **le bac L.**

Cahier d'activités, p. 24, Act. 25

Baccalauréat : Les hauts et les bas

Taux de réussite par série (en %).

Examen et série	Total
Bac Général	
Littéraire (L)	76,5
Economique et social (ES)	76
Sciences (S)	76,3
Bac Technologique	
Sciences et technologies industrielles (STI)	73,4
Sciences et technologies de laboratoire (STL)	79,7
Sciences médico-sociales (SMS)	81
Sciences et technologies tertiaires (STT)	80,6
Bac Professionnel	
Industriel	74,3
Tertiaire	81
Hôtellerie	79,5

10 Mon journal

Ecrivons Make a list of your favorite school subjects in your journal. If you were taking these subjects in France, which **bac** do you think you would take?

EXEMPLE **Je passerais le bac...**

Agreeing and disagreeing

To agree:

Oui, beaucoup. *Yes, very much.*
Moi aussi. *Me too.*
Moi non plus. *Neither do I.*

To disagree:

Moi, non. *I don't.*
Non, pas trop. *No, not too much.*
Moi, si. *I do.*
Pas moi. *Not me.*

Cahier d'activités, p. 15, Act. 6

Note de grammaire

Use **si** instead of **oui** to contradict a negative statement or question.

— Tu **n'**aimes **pas** la biologie?
— Mais **si!** J'adore la bio!

Grammaire supplémentaire, p. 66, Act. 1–2

Cahier d'activités, p. 16, Act. 8

Travaux pratiques de grammaire, p. 11, Act. 5

---

11 ### Grammaire en contexte

Ecoutons Listen as Hélène and Gérard talk about the subjects they like and dislike. Which one do they agree on? Which one do they disagree on?

12 ### Grammaire en contexte

Parlons Ask your partner's opinion about several subjects and then agree or disagree. Take turns.

EXEMPLE — Tu aimes les arts plastiques?
— Non, pas trop.
— Moi, si.

---

13 ### Ça te plaît?

Parlons Get together with two classmates. Find at least two things or activities that you all like. Then, tell the rest of the class what you agree on.

EXEMPLE   ELEVE 1 — J'aime les hamburgers. Et toi?
ELEVE 2 — Oui, beaucoup.
ELEVE 3 — Moi aussi.
ELEVE 1 — Nous aimons tous les hamburgers.

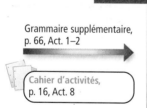

le cinéma   le foot   les concerts
la pizza   faire du sport
écouter de la musique
la glace   faire les magasins   le ski

Comment dit-on...?

Asking for and giving information

To ask about someone's classes:

> **Tu as quels cours** aujourd'hui?
> *What classes do you have . . . ?*
> **Tu as quoi** le matin?
> *What do you have . . . ?*
> **Vous avez** espagnol l'après-midi?
> *Do you have . . . ?*

To tell what classes you have:

> **J'ai** arts plastiques et physique.
> *I have . . .*
> **J'ai** algèbre, DPS et sport.
>
> Oui, et **nous avons** aussi géo.
> *. . . we have . . .*

Vocabulaire

le matin	*in the morning*
l'après-midi (m.)	*in the afternoon*
aujourd'hui	*today*
demain	*tomorrow*
maintenant	*now*

Travaux pratiques de grammaire, p. 12, Act. 6

14 **On a quoi?**

a. **Parlons** Find out what subjects your partner has in the morning and in the afternoon.

> EXEMPLE
> — Tu as quoi le matin (l'après-midi)?
> — Bio, algèbre et chorale. Et toi?
> — Moi, j'ai algèbre, chimie, chorale et DPS.

b. **Parlons** Now, tell the rest of the class which subjects you and your partner have in common.

> EXEMPLE
> Marc et moi, nous avons algèbre et chorale.

Grammaire

The verb *avoir*

Avoir is an irregular verb. That means it doesn't follow the pattern of the **-er** verbs you learned in Chapter 1.

avoir *(to have)*

J'	**ai**	Nous	**avons**
Tu	**as**	Vous	**avez**
Il/Elle/On	**a**	Ils/Elles	**ont**

As you saw in Chapter 1, you often use an article (**le, la, l',** or **les**) before a noun. When you're telling which school subjects you have, however, you don't use an article.

> **Elle a chimie** maintenant.
> **Vous avez** quoi le matin?

Grammaire supplémentaire, p. 66, Act. 3

Cahier d'activités, p. 17, Act. 12

Travaux pratiques de grammaire, pp. 12–13, Act. 7–9

15 **Grammaire en contexte**

Parlons Some students are day-dreaming about the future. What classes are they taking to prepare for these careers?

EXEMPLE   **Ils ont géométrie, physique et géographie.**

1.

2.

3.

4.

Voilà l'emploi du temps de Stéphanie Lambert.

CD-ROM **1**
DVD **1**

EMPLOI DU TEMPS

NOM: Stéphanie Lambert   **CLASSE:** 3ᵉ

		LUNDI	MARDI	MERCREDI	JEUDI	VENDREDI	SAMEDI	DIMANCHE
MATIN	8h00	Allemand	Arts plastiques	Mathématiques	Mathématiques	Français		L I B R E
	9h00	Français	Arts plastiques	Anglais	Sciences nat	Français	Anglais	
	10h00	**Récréation**	**Récréation**	**Récréation**	**Récréation**	**Récréation**	TP physique	
	10h15	EPS	Allemand	Français	EPS	Sciences nat	TP physique	
	11h15	Sciences nat	**Etude**	Histoire/Géo	**Etude**	Arts plastiques	**[Sortie]**	
	12h15	**Déjeuner**	**Déjeuner**	**[Sortie]**	**Déjeuner**	**Déjeuner**	**APRES-MIDI**	
APRES-MIDI	14h00	Histoire/Géo	Mathématiques	**APRES-MIDI**	Histoire/Géo	Allemand	**LIBRE**	
	15h00	Anglais	Physique/Chimie	**LIBRE**	Physique/Chimie	Mathématiques		
	16h00	**Récréation**	**[Sortie]**		**Récréation**	**[Sortie]**		
	16h15	Mathématiques			Arts plastiques			
	17h15	**[Sortie]**			**[Sortie]**			

Cahier d'activités, pp. 18–19, Act. 14–15

Travaux pratiques de grammaire, pp. 13–14, Act. 10–12

Grammaire supplémentaire, p. 67, Act. 4

16 Tu comprends?

Lisons/Parlons Answer the following questions about Stéphanie Lambert's schedule on page 56.

1. Can you find and copy the words in the schedule that refer to days of the week?
2. **Déjeuner** and **Récréation** don't refer to school subjects. What do you think they mean?
3. What do you think **14h00** means?
4. If **étudier** means *to study,* what do you think **Etude** means?
5. You know that **sortir** means *to go out.* What do you think **Sortie** means?
6. Can you list two differences between Stéphanie's schedule and yours?

17 L'emploi du temps de Stéphanie

Lisons/Ecrivons Stéphanie is telling a friend about her schedule. Complete her statements according to her schedule on page 56.

Le ___1___ matin, j'ai allemand, français, EPS et sciences nat. Je n'aime pas trop les sciences. J'ai histoire-géo le ___2___, le ___3___ et le ___4___. J'adore l'histoire! Et le mercredi ___5___, je n'ai pas cours. Normalement, j'ai ___6___ à 10h00, mais le ___7___, j'ai travaux pratiques de physique à 10h00. Je n'ai pas cours le ___8___.

18 Elles ont quels cours?

Ecoutons Look at Stéphanie's schedule as you listen to three of her friends call her on the phone. They're going to tell her what subjects they have on a certain day of the week. Do they have the same subjects as Stéphanie on that day?

Vocabulaire

You've already learned the numbers 0–20. Here are the numbers 21–59 in French.

21	22	23	24	25
vingt et un(e)	vingt-deux	vingt-trois	vingt-quatre	vingt-cinq

26	27	28	29	30
vingt-six	vingt-sept	vingt-huit	vingt-neuf	trente

31	32	40	41	42
trente et un(e)	trente-deux	quarante	quarante et un(e)	quarante-deux

50	51	52	59	
cinquante	cinquante et un(e)	cinquante-deux	cinquante-neuf	

Cahier d'activités, p. 17, Act. 11   Travaux pratiques de grammaire, pp. 14–15, Act. 13–14

19 **Tu connais les nombres?**

1. **Parlons** Say these numbers in French.

   a. 25   **b.** 37   **c.** 46   **d.** 53

2. **Ecrivons** Write the numerals for these numbers.

   a. vingt-huit   **b.** trente-quatre   **c.** quarante et un   **d.** cinquante-cinq

Comment dit-on...?

Telling when you have class

To find out at what time someone has a certain class:

   Tu as maths **à quelle heure?**

To tell at what time you have a certain class:

   J'ai maths **à neuf heures.**

| **huit heures** | **dix heures quinze** | **sept heures vingt** | **quinze heures trente** | **seize heures quarante-cinq** |

 Cahier d'activités, p. 18, Act. 13

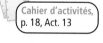  Travaux pratiques de grammaire, p. 15, Act. 15–17

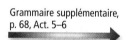 Grammaire supplémentaire, p. 68, Act. 5–6

20 **A quelle heure?**

Ecoutons Listen as Jérôme answers Anne's questions about his schedule. At what time does he have these classes: **anglais, espagnol, histoire,** and **maths?**

À la française

In casual conversation, you might try using the abbreviated forms of words just as French teenagers do. For example, **la récréation** can be abbreviated to **la récré.** Do you recall the abbreviated forms of the words listed to the right? If not, look for them in *La rentrée* or in Stéphanie's schedule.

> les sciences naturelles
> la géographie
> l'éducation physique et sportive
> l'après - midi
> les mathématiques
> le professeur

21 Une journée chargée

Parlons Claudine is busy today. What does she have at each of the times listed?

EXEMPLE   **A huit heures, elle a géographie.**

8h00

1. 9h35

2. 11h50

3. 14h05

4. 16h20

22 Nos emplois du temps

a. Ecrivons/Parlons   You and your partner prepare blank schedules showing only the times classes meet at your school. Take turns asking at what time you each have the classes listed here. Fill in each other's schedule, writing the subjects next to the appropriate times.

> **EXEMPLE**   — **Tu as histoire à quelle heure?**
>   — **A onze heures trente.**

b. Parlons/Ecrivons   Now complete the schedules by asking what subjects you each have at the remaining times.

> **EXEMPLE**   — **Tu as quoi à treize heures?**

français	histoire	sport
maths	sciences	anglais

23 Mon journal

Ecrivons Make a list of your classes in your journal. Include the days and times they meet and the names of your teachers.

Tu as quels cours?

What is your school day like? At what time does it start and end? What classes do you have? Here's what some francophone students had to say about their school day.

Yannick,
Martinique

«Comme je suis en première S, j'ai de l'économie. Je fais de l'anglais, du portugais, du français, de l'éducation physique, de l'histoire, de la géographie et des maths.»

Tu peux décrire ton emploi du temps?

«Je commence à huit heures. Je termine à midi. J'ai l'interclasse de midi à deux heures et [j'ai cours] de deux heures à dix-sept heures.»

Amadou,
Burkina Faso

«A l'école, j'ai comme cours français, anglais, sciences physiques, sciences naturelles, éducation civique et morale, les épreuves physiques.»

Patrice,
Québec

«Comme cours, j'ai le français, l'anglais, les maths. J'ai aussi éducation physique. J'ai l'art plastique, l'informatique... beaucoup de matières comme ça.»

Qu'en penses-tu?

1. What classes do you have in common with these students?
2. What subjects were mentioned that aren't taught at your school?
3. Would you like to trade schedules with any of these students? Why or why not?

Savais-tu que...?

Students in francophone countries commonly have Wednesday afternoons free and attend classes on Saturday mornings. In general, they follow the same core curriculum, which includes French, math, science, history, geography, physical education, and at least one foreign language. Courses like industrial arts and band are not often taught.

Comment dit-on...?

Asking for and expressing opinions

To ask someone's opinion:

Comment tu trouves ça?
Comment tu trouves le cours de biologie?

To express a favorable opinion:

C'est... *It's . . .*
  facile. *easy.*
  génial. *great.*
  super. *super.*
  cool. *cool.*
  intéressant.
    interesting.
  passionnant.
    fascinating.

To express indifference:

C'est pas mal.
  It's not bad.
Ça va.
  It's OK.

To express an unfavorable opinion:

C'est... *It's . . .*
  difficile. *hard.*
  pas terrible. *not*
    so great.
  pas super. *not*
    so hot.
  zéro. *a waste of*
    time.
  nul. *useless.*
  barbant. *boring.*

Cahier d'activités,
pp. 20–21, Act. 17–19

Travaux pratiques de grammaire,
p. 16, Act. 18–20

Grammaire supplémentaire,
p. 69, Act. 8–9

A la française

In informal conversation, French speakers will often leave out the **ne** in a negative sentence.
    J'aime pas les hamburgers, moi.
    C'est pas super, la géo.
In writing, you should include the **ne** in negative sentences.

Grammaire supplémentaire,
p. 69, Act. 7

24   **Quel cours aiment-ils?**

Ecoutons Listen as Aurélie and Eric talk about their subjects. Which ones does Eric like? Which doesn't he like? And Aurélie?

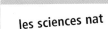

les sciences nat
l'anglais
l'histoire
les maths
la géo
l'allemand
l'espagnol

Note culturelle

The French system of grading is based on a scale of 0–20. A score of less than 10 isn't a passing grade. Students are usually pleased with a score of 10 or higher. They must work very hard to receive a 17 or an 18, and it's very rare to earn a 19 or a 20.

25 Qu'est-ce qu'on dit?

Parlons What do you think these students are saying?

1. L'histoire, c'est...

2. La géométrie, c'est...

3. L'algèbre, c'est...

4. La biologie, c'est...

5. L'espagnol, c'est...

6. Les arts plastiques, c'est...

26 La vie scolaire

Lisons/Ecrivons Read this letter that your new pen pal Laurent wrote to you after his first day of class. Then, write your reply.

27 Comment tu trouves?

Parlons With your partner, discuss how you feel about your classes.

EXEMPLE
— Tu as maths?
— Oui, à neuf heures.
— Comment tu trouves ça?
— C'est super!

Salut!

Ça va au lycée? Tu aimes tes cours? Moi, mes cours sont pas mal. J'adore les maths, c'est facile. Mais la physique, c'est barbant. Et la bio, c'est difficile. Et toi? Tu aimes les sciences? Pas moi. J'aime mieux les langues. C'est génial, et c'est plus intéressant. J'ai sport l'après-midi. J'aime bien; c'est cool. Et toi? Tu as sport aussi? Ça te plaît?

A bientôt,
Laurent

28  **De l'école au travail**

Parlons/Ecrivons You work part-time as an office aide for the school board. You've been asked to interview some French exchange students to get their opinion on the American school system. Create a conversation in which you interview the exchange student, your partner, about his or her classes. Ask questions about his or her class schedule and level of difficulty of each class. Then, switch roles. Be sure to take notes during the interview to provide to the school board.

EXEMPLE   — Tu as quels cours le matin?

                 — ...

                 — Comment tu trouves ça?

PRONONCIATION

Liaison

In French you don't usually pronounce consonants at the end of a word, such as the **s** in **les** and the **t** in **c'est.** But you do pronounce some final consonants if the following word begins with a vowel sound. This linking of the final consonant of one word with the beginning vowel of the next word is called **liaison.**

les examens	**C'est intéressant.**	**vous avez**	**deux élèves**
∨	∨	∨	∨
z	t	z	z

A. A prononcer

Repeat the following phrases and sentences.

les maths / les escargots
nous n'aimons pas / nous aimons
C'est super. / C'est intéressant.
les profs / les élèves

B. A lire

Take turns with a partner reading the following sentences aloud. Make all necessary liaisons.

1. Ils ont maths.
2. Elles ont histoire.
3. Elles aiment l'espagnol.
4. Elle a deux examens lundi.
5. Vous avez cours le samedi?
6. Nous aimons les arts plastiques.

C. A écrire

You're going to hear two short dialogues. Write down what you hear.

SONDAGE
Les lycéens ont-ils le moral?

Stratégie pour lire
You'll find photos, drawings, charts, and other visual clues when you read newspapers, magazines, and even your textbooks! These illustrations will usually give you an idea of what you're going to read before you begin.

A. First, look at the illustrations. Based on what you see, do you think you're going to read . . .
1. price lists?
2. math exercises?
3. results from a survey?
4. ads from a sales catalogue?

B. Now, scan the titles and texts. Based on the titles and the drawings, do you think these articles are about . . .
1. teenagers' favorite pastimes?
2. grades given to students on exams?
3. students' attitudes toward school?
4. prices at several stores?

C. Here are some cognates from the graph entitled **Profs.** What do you think these words mean in English?

distants   respectueux
    compétents   absents

SONDAGE

Les lycéens ont-ils le moral?

PROFS
Dans l'ensemble, jugez-vous que la majorité de vos professeurs sont…

assidus	trop souvent absents
86 %	8
compétents	incompétents
80 %	13 %
intéressants	pas intéressants
68 %	25 %
respectueux	méprisants
64 %	21 %
amicaux	distants
48 %	43%

ENTHOUSIASME
Le matin, quand vous allez au lycée, êtes-vous habituellement...

...très content
6 %

...assez content
52 %

58 %

Et pourquoi êtes-vous content ?

• Parce que vous retrouvez vos copains ——— **69 %**
• Parce que vos études vous intéressent ——— **45 %**
• Parce que l'ambiance du lycée vous plaît ——— **28 %**
• Parce que c'est toujours mieux qu'à la maison —**12 %**
• Parce que vous y retrouvez votre petit(e) copain(ine) **9 %**
• Parce que vos professeurs sont sympas ——— **9 %**

Ne se prononcent pas — **1 %**

Sur 100 lycéens contents d'aller au lycée, soit 58 % de l'échantillon. Total supérieur à 100, les interviewés ayant pu donner 2 réponses.

...peu content
29 %

...pas content du tout
11 %

40 %

Et pourquoi êtes-vous mécontent ?

• Parce que vos professeurs vous énervent ——— **36 %**
• Parce que l'ambiance est déplorable ——— **34 %**
• Parce que votre travail scolaire vous prend trop de temps et vous empêche un peu de vivre ——— **33 %**
• Parce qu'après tout on est mieux à la maison ——— **22 %**
• Parce que vos études vous ennuient——— **22 %**
• Parce que vous ne supportez pas d'être traité comme un gosse——— **13 %**

Ne se prononcent pas — **2 %**

Sur 100 lycéens mécontents d'aller au lycée, soit 40 % de l'échantillon. Total supérieur à 100, les interviewés ayant pu donner 2 réponses.

D. Knowing that the words at each end of the bar on the graph are opposites, what do you think the following words mean?
1. **assidus**
2. **incompétents**
3. **pas intéressants**
4. **méprisants**
5. **amicaux**

E. According to the graph, . . .
1. do French students generally have a positive or negative image of their teachers?
2. how do most of the students feel about their teachers?
3. what do the students criticize the most?

F. Look at the drawings for **Enthousiasme.** What do you think the following categories mean in English? Which category is the best? Which is the worst?

peu content	**très content**
pas content du tout	**assez content**

G. According to the percentages, do most of the students have a positive or a negative attitude when they go to the **lycée?**

H. Conduct the same surveys in your class and compile the results. How do the attitudes of your classmates compare with those of the French **lycéens?**

Cahier d'activités, p. 23, Act. 23–24

Visit Holt Online

go.hrw.com

KEYWORD: WA3 POITIERS-2

Jeux interactifs

Première étape   Objective Agreeing and disagreeing

1 Would you answer **si** or **oui** to each of the following questions? (**p. 54**)

1. Hervé n'aime pas faire le ménage?
2. Vous aimez le cours de physique?
3. Tu aimes écouter de la musique?
4. Annick et Ahmed n'aiment pas le prof de français?
5. Jean-Paul aime la chorale?
6. Olivia n'aime pas faire du sport?

2 Complete the following conversations, using **si, oui,** or **non,** as appropriate. (**p. 54**)

1. —Tu aimes les sciences naturelles?
   — _____, j'adore!
2. —Marc n'aime pas parler au téléphone?
   — _____, il aime bien parler avec ses copains.
3. —Ils aiment la physique?
   — _____, ils n'aiment pas les cours de science.
4. —Tu n'aimes pas le ski?
   — _____, j'aime bien le sport en général.
5. —Tu aimes faire de l'équitation?
   — _____, mais je préfère lire et regarder la télévision.
6. —Nicole aime les concerts?
   — _____, elle adore la musique.

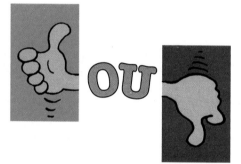

Deuxième étape   Objectives Asking for and giving information; telling when you have class

3 Complete the conversation below with the correct forms of the verb **avoir.** (**p. 55**)

—Céline, tu __1__ quels cours aujourd'hui?

—Le matin, j' __2__ sciences nat et français. L'après-midi, j' __3__ histoire et géométrie.

—Et Vincent, il __4__ quels cours?

—Il __5__ chimie et espagnol le matin, et l'après-midi, il __6__ informatique.

—Le mardi et le jeudi matin, nous __7__ travaux pratiques de chimie.

4 Using the information from Marc's and Ingrid's schedules, answer the questions that follow. (**pp. 55, 56**)

EXEMPLE —Marc a français le mardi?
—Non, il n'a pas français le mardi.

EMPLOI DU TEMPS   NOM: Marc Champlain

		LUNDI	MARDI	MERCREDI	JEUDI	VENDREDI	SAMEDI	DIMANCHE
MATIN	8h00	Arts plastiques	Allemand	Français	Sciences nat	Mathématiques		
	9h00	Sciences nat	Histoire/Géo	EPS	Allemand	Physique	Mathématiques	
	10h00	Récréation	Récréation	Récréation	Récréation	Récréation	TP Physique	
	10h15	Allemand	Physique	Anglais	Mathématiques	Français	TP Physique	
	11h15	Mathématiques	Etude	Histoire/Géo	Etude	Français	[Sortie]	
	12h15	**Déjeuner**	**Déjeuner**	**[Sortie]**	**Déjeuner**	**Déjeuner**	**APRES-MIDI**	
APRES-MIDI	14h00	Anglais	Mathématiques	**APRES-MIDI**	Arts plastiques	Arts plastiques	**LIBRE**	
	15h00	EPS	Chimie	**LIBRE**	Arts plastiques	Anglais		
	16h00	Récréation	[Sortie]		Récréation	[Sortie]		
	16h15	Histoire/Géo			Chimie			
	17h15	[Sortie]			[Sortie]			

DIMANCHE: L I B R E

EMPLOI DU TEMPS   NOM: Ingrid Valmont

		LUNDI	MARDI	MERCREDI	JEUDI	VENDREDI	SAMEDI	DIMANCHE
MATIN	8h00	Arts plastiques	Français	Anglais	Français	Géométrie		
	9h00	DPS	Géométrie	EPS	Français	Géométrie	Anglais	
	10h00	Récréation	Récréation	Récréation	Récréation	Récréation	TP Biologie	
	10h15	Espagnol	Sciences nat	Espagnol	Biologie	Sciences nat	TP Biologie	
	11h15	Géométrie	Etude	Histoire/Géo	Etude	Espagnol	[Sortie]	
	12h15	**Déjeuner**	**Déjeuner**	**[Sortie]**	**Déjeuner**	**Déjeuner**	**APRES-MIDI**	
APRES-MIDI	14h00	Anglais	Biologie	**APRES-MIDI**	Arts plastiques	Arts plastiques	**LIBRE**	
	15h00	Biologie	EPS	**LIBRE**	Arts plastiques	Français		
	16h00	Récréation	[Sortie]		Récréation	[Sortie]		
	16h15	Histoire/Géo			Géométrie			
	17h15	[Sortie]			[Sortie]			

DIMANCHE: L I B R E

1. Ingrid n'a pas biologie le lundi?
2. Marc a anglais le mercredi?
3. Ingrid a espagnol le jeudi?
4. Ingrid et Marc n'ont pas arts plastiques le lundi?
5. Marc et Ingrid ont EPS le lundi?
6. Ingrid a histoire le mercredi?
7. Marc a allemand le samedi?
8. Marc et Ingrid ont français le samedi?
9. Ingrid et Marc ont l'après-midi libre le samedi?
10. Marc n'a pas mathématiques le vendredi?

5 Mathieu and some of his friends are discussing their school schedules. Complete each of the following sentences with the correct form of the verb **avoir.** Then, write out the time given in parentheses. (**pp. 55, 58**)

EXEMPLE   Sylvie _____ latin à (9h30). Sylvie **a** latin à **neuf heures trente**.

1. J' _____ sciences nat à (8h45).
2. Anne et moi, nous _____ EPS à (13h50).
3. Mathieu et Jeanne, vous _____ latin à (11h20), non?
4. Séverine, tu _____ quoi à (15h30)?
5. Chad et Mireille _____ maths à (16h15).
6. André et Hélène _____ français à (9h45).
7. Jean, Alain et moi, nous _____ récréation à (14h25).

6 Unscramble each of these sentences, using the correct form of **avoir.** Then, match each clock with the sentence that mentions the corresponding time. (**pp. 55, 58**)

a.

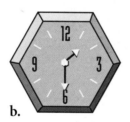
b.

c.

d.

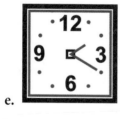
e.

f.

g.

1. avoir / huit / mathématiques / heures / à / j'
2. DPS / quinze / à / heures / avoir / neuf / nous
3. quarante / chimie / avoir / à / heures / dix / Audrey
4. treize / Florent / à / Bernard / quarante-cinq / géographie / et / avoir / heures
5. avoir / et / quatorze / Sophie / à / moi, / nous / heures / français / vingt
6. plastiques / heures / à / trente / arts / avoir / treize / tu
7. heures / à / vous / seize / EPS / avoir / vingt-cinq

7 Rewrite these informal remarks and questions in formal French. (**pp. 26, 61**)

1. «C'est pas super, l'algèbre.»
2. «Elle aime pas la chimie?»
3. «Ils aiment pas les devoirs.»
4. «Mais non! L'anglais, c'est pas difficile!»
5. «Tu aimes pas la géographie?»

8 David and Olivia are discussing their schedules and their classes. Complete their conversation with either the correct form of the verb in parentheses or the word or phrase that expresses their opinion. (**pp. 33, 55, 61**)

—Olivia, tu __1__ (avoir) quels cours le lundi matin?

—J' __2__ (avoir) histoire, maths et français. Et toi, tu __3__ (avoir) quels cours?

—Florent et moi, nous __4__ (avoir) chimie, allemand et anglais.

—Vous __5__ (aimer) la chimie?

—Florent n' __6__ (aimer) pas ça. Mais moi, j' __7__ (adorer) la chimie. C'est __8__ (passionnant/pas super)!

—Ah bon! Florent __9__ (avoir) biologie le mardi. Il __10__ (adorer) ça. Et toi, tu __11__ (aimer) ça, la biologie?

—Moi, non. C'est __12__ (pas mal/nul).

9 Some friends are talking about their courses and school schedules. Complete each sentence with the correct verb form. Then, select the word from the box that most logically tells how each person feels about his or her course. (**pp. 33, 55, 61**)

—J' __1__ (avoir) maths à huit heures. Je __2__ (ne pas aimer). Je __3__ (préférer) dormir. Les maths, c'est __4__.

—J' __5__ (adorer) nager. J' __6__ (avoir) natation à quatre heures de l'après-midi. C'est __7__.

—J' __8__ (aimer) lire. J' __9__ (avoir) français à neuf heures vingt. C'est __10__.

—J' __11__ (avoir) chimie à dix heures cinquante. J' __12__ (ne pas aimer) étudier, et je __13__ (ne pas aimer) la chimie. C'est __14__.

—J' __15__ (avoir) anglais à deux heures vingt-cinq. J' __16__ (aimer bien) la littérature. C'est __17__!

cool

facile

nul

génial

difficile

GRAMMAIRE SUPPLEMENTAIRE

CD-ROM **1**
DVD **1**

1
Listen as André, a French exchange student, tells you how he feels about his American schedule. What is his reaction to his schedule in general? At what times does he have the following subjects: **chimie, sport, latin, informatique?**

2
Answer these questions according to Eliane's schedule.

1. Eliane a quoi le lundi matin?

2. Elle a quels cours le jeudi après-midi?

3. Quels jours et à quelle heure est-ce qu'elle a histoire? Anglais? Maths?

EMPLOI DU TEMPS

NOM: Eliane Soulard   **CLASSE:** 3ᵉ

		LUNDI	MARDI	MERCREDI	JEUDI	VENDREDI	SAMEDI	DIMANCHE
MATIN	8h00	Anglais	Arts plastiques	Histoire/Géo	Mathématiques	Musique		L
	9h00	Français	Musique	Anglais	Sciences nat	Arts plastiques	Anglais	I
	10h00	Récréation	Récréation	Récréation	Récréation	Récréation	TP physique	
	10h15	EPS	Mathématiques	Sciences nat	EPS	Sciences nat	TP physique	B
	11h15	Sciences nat	Etude	Arts plastiques	Etude	Français	[Sortie]	
	12h15	**Déjeuner**	**Déjeuner**	**[Sortie]**	**Déjeuner**	**Déjeuner**	**APRES-MIDI**	R
APRES-MIDI	14h00	Arts plastiques	Mathématiques	**APRES-MIDI**	Histoire/Géo	Physique	**LIBRE**	
	15h00	Musique	Physique	**LIBRE**	Physique	Anglais		E
	16h00	Récréation	[Sortie]		Récréation	[Sortie]		
	16h15	Mathématiques			Français			
	17h15	[Sortie]			[Sortie]			

3
Tell three classmates whether or not you like Eliane's schedule and why. Then, ask them if they like it.

EXEMPLE   **J'aime l'emploi du temps d'Eliane. Elle a étude et arts plastiques. C'est cool! Et vous?**

4
How does an American class schedule compare with Eliane's? With a partner, make a list of similarities and differences.

SIMILARITES

DIFFERENCES

Eliane n'a pas cours le mercredi après-midi.

5 Answer these questions according to Eliane's report card.

1. What are Eliane's best subjects?

2. What would she probably say about French class? Music class? Science class?

BULLETIN TRIMESTRIEL

Année scolaire : 20**02**- 20**03**

NOM et Prénom: *Soulard Eliane*   Classe de: **3ᵉ**

MATIERES D'ENSEIGNEMENT	Moyenne de l'élève	OBSERVATIONS
Français	5	Montre peu d'enthousiasme
Anglais	8	Assez mauvais travail!
Mathématiques	18	Très bonne élève!
Histoire-Géographie	11	Travail moyen
Sciences naturelles	17	Elève sérieuse
Education physique	12	Un peu paresseuse
Physique-Chimie	18	Très douée pour la physique
Arts plastiques	14	Bon travail.
Musique	15	Fait des efforts.

Ce bulletin doit être conservé précieusement par les parents.
Il n'en sera pas délivré de duplicata.

6 Create your ideal schedule showing subjects, days, and times. Write it down in the form of a French **emploi du temps.**

7 **J e u   d e   r ô l e**

Create a conversation with two classmates. Talk about . . .

a. the subjects you like best and your opinion of them.

b. the subjects you don't like and your opinion of them.

c. whether or not you agree with your classmates' likes and dislikes.

Que sais-je?

Can you use what you've learned in this chapter?

Can you agree and disagree?
p. 54

1 How would you agree if your friend said the following? How would you disagree with your friend?
1. J'adore l'histoire!
2. J'aime les sciences nat. Et toi?
3. Je n'aime pas le français.

Can you ask for and give information?
p. 55

2 How would you ask . . .
1. what subjects your friend has in the morning?
2. what subjects your friend has in the afternoon?
3. what subjects your friend has on Tuesdays?
4. if your friend has music class?
5. if your friend has English today?

3 How would you say in French that the following students have these classes, using the verb **avoir**?
1. you / French and choir   3. we / gym
2. Paul / physics   4. Francine and Séverine / Spanish

Can you tell when you have class?
p. 58

4 How would you ask your friend at what time he or she has these classes?

1.   2.   3.

5 How would you tell your friend that you have the following classes at the times given?

1. 9h15   2. 11h45   3. 15h50

Can you ask for and express opinions?
p. 61

6 How would you tell your friend that your geography class is . . .
1. fascinating?   2. not so great?   3. boring?

Première étape

School subjects

l'algèbre (f.)	algebra
l'allemand (m.)	German
les arts (m.) plastiques	art class
la biologie	biology
la chimie	chemistry
la chorale	choir
le cours de développement personnel et social (DPS)	health
la danse	dance
l'éducation (f.) physique et sportive (EPS)	physical education

l'espagnol (m.)	Spanish
la géographie	geography
la géométrie	geometry
l'histoire (f.)	history
l'informatique (f.)	computer science
le latin	Latin
la musique	music
la physique	physics
les sciences (f.) naturelles	natural science
le sport	gym
les travaux (m.) pratiques	lab

School-related words

le cours	course

les devoirs (m.)	homework
l'élève (m./f.)	student
le professeur (le prof)	teacher

Agreeing and disagreeing

Oui, beaucoup.	Yes, very much.
Moi aussi.	Me too.
Moi, non.	I don't.
Non, pas trop.	No, not too much.
Moi non plus.	Neither do I.
Moi, si.	I do.
Pas moi.	Not me.

Deuxième étape

Asking for and giving information

Tu as quels cours... ?	What classes do you have . . . ?
Tu as quoi... ?	What do you have . . . ?
J'ai...	I have . . .
Vous avez... ?	Do you have . . . ?
Nous avons...	We have . . .
avoir	to have

Telling when you have class

Tu as... à quelle heure?	At what time do you have . . . ?

à... heures	at . . . o'clock
à... heures quinze	at . . . fifteen
à... heures trente	at . . . thirty
à... heures quarante-cinq	at . . . forty-five
aujourd'hui	today
demain	tomorrow
maintenant	now
le matin	in the morning
l'après-midi (m.)	in the afternoon
le lundi	on Mondays
le mardi	on Tuesdays
le mercredi	on Wednesdays
le jeudi	on Thursdays

le vendredi	on Fridays
le samedi	on Saturdays
le dimanche	on Sundays

Parts of the school day

la récréation	break
l'étude (f.)	study hall
le déjeuner	lunch
la sortie	dismissal
l'après-midi libre	afternoon off

Numbers

See page 57 for the numbers 21 through 59

Troisième étape

Asking for and expressing opinions

Comment tu trouves ça?	What do you think of that/it?
Comment tu trouves... ?	What do you think of . . . ?
Ça va.	It's OK.

C'est...	It's . . .
super.	super.
cool.	cool.
facile.	easy.
génial.	great.
intéressant.	interesting.
passionnant.	fascinating.

pas mal.	not bad.
barbant.	boring
difficile.	difficult.
nul.	useless.
pas super.	not so hot.
pas terrible.	not so great.
zéro.	a waste of time.

3
Tout pour la rentrée

Objectives

In this chapter you will learn to

Première étape

- make and respond to requests
- ask others what they need and tell what you need

Deuxième étape

- tell what you'd like and what you'd like to do

Troisième étape

- get someone's attention
- ask for information
- express and respond to thanks

Visit Holt Online

go.hrw.com

KEYWORD: WA3 POITIERS-3

Online Edition

◀ C'est combien, cette calculatrice?

MISE EN TRAIN · *Pas question!*

Stratégie pour comprendre
Where are Julie and Mme Pelletier? What could they be shopping for? Use the context of the setting to guess the meanings of the words you don't know.

Madame Pelletier

Julie

La vendeuse

1

Mme Pelletier :	Alors, qu'est-ce qu'il te faut?
Julie :	Eh bien, des crayons, des stylos, une gomme, une calculatrice, un pot de colle...

2

Mme Pelletier :	Pardon, mademoiselle, vous avez des trousses, s'il vous plaît?
La vendeuse :	Oui, bien sûr. Là, à côté des cahiers.

3

Julie :	Et voilà une boîte de crayons de couleur.
Mme Pelletier :	C'est combien?
Julie :	Trois cinquante.

4

Julie :	Regarde, Maman, une calculatrice-traductrice. C'est chouette!
Mme Pelletier :	Oui. C'est pour les maths ou pour l'anglais?
Julie :	Euh, il me faut une calculatrice pour les maths. Mais une calculatrice-traductrice, c'est pratique pour l'anglais.

⑤

Mme Pelletier : C'est combien, mademoiselle?
La vendeuse : 80 euros.

⑥

Mme Pelletier : 80 euros! Oh là là! C'est pas possible!

⑦

Mme Pelletier : Et cette calculatrice-là?
La vendeuse : 20 euros.
Mme Pelletier : Bien. Alors, cette calculatrice.

⑧

Julie : Eh, Maman, regarde ce sac vert. Il est super!
Mme Pelletier : Oui. Pas mal. Mais cher. 33 euros!

⑨

Mme Pelletier : Moi, j'aime mieux ce sac-là, à 12 euros.
Julie : Non! Il est horrible!
Mme Pelletier : Pourquoi?
Julie : Je n'aime pas ce rouge.

⑩

Mme Pelletier : Moi, je n'achète pas un sac à 33 euros.
Julie : Alors, j'aime mieux aller à l'école sans sac!

Cahier d'activités, p. 25, Act. 1

1 Tu as compris?

Réponds aux questions suivantes d'après l'épisode de *Pas question!*

1. What is the relationship between Julie and Mme Pelletier? How do you know?
2. Where are they?
3. What are they doing there?
4. Why does Julie need a calculator?
5. What is Mme Pelletier's main concern?
6. What do you think of Julie's decision at the end of *Pas question!*?

2 Julie ou sa mère?

Dans les phrases suivantes, on parle de Julie ou de Mme Pelletier?

1. Elle aime la calculatrice à 80 €.
2. Elle voudrait une calculatrice-traductrice.
3. Elle aime mieux le sac à 12 €.
4. Elle aime mieux le sac vert.
5. Elle va aller à l'école sans sac.
6. Elle n'achète pas un sac à 33 €.

3 Cherche les expressions

Can you find an expression in *Pas question!* to . . .

1. ask what someone needs?
2. tell what you need?
3. get a salesperson's attention?
4. ask the price of something?
5. say you like or prefer something?
6. say you don't like something?

> Il est horrible!   C'est combien?
> Il me faut...   J'aime mieux...
> Il est super!   Pardon, mademoiselle...
> Qu'est-ce qu'il te faut?

4 Mets en ordre

Mets les phrases suivantes dans un ordre chronologique, d'après l'épisode de *Pas question!*

1. Mme Pelletier asks the price of a calculator.
2. Mme Pelletier asks a salesperson if she has any pencil cases.
3. Julie says she will go to school without a bag.
4. Mme Pelletier asks Julie what she needs for school.
5. Mme Pelletier asks the price of a box of colored pencils.
6. Julie points out a bag she likes.

5 Et maintenant, à toi

What do you think will happen next in the story? Discuss your ideas with a partner.

Objectives Making and responding to requests; asking others what they need and telling what you need

WA3 POITIERS-3

Vocabulaire

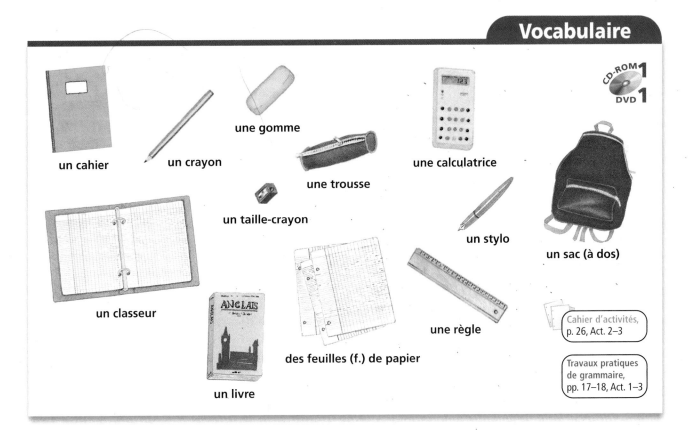

un cahier

un crayon

une gomme

une trousse

un taille-crayon

une calculatrice

un stylo

un sac (à dos)

un classeur

des feuilles (f.) de papier

une règle

un livre

CD-ROM 1
DVD 1

Cahier d'activités, p. 26, Act. 2–3

Travaux pratiques de grammaire, pp. 17–18, Act. 1–3

DE BONS CONSEILS

Make flashcards to learn new words. On one side of a card, write the French word you want to learn. If the word is a noun, include an article **(le, la, les)** to help you remember the gender. On the other side, paste or draw a picture to illustrate the meaning of the word. Then, ask a classmate to show you the picture while you try to name the object, or use the cards to test yourself.

6 **Qu'est-ce qu'il y a dans mon sac?**

Ecoutons Listen as Hafaïdh and Karine check the contents of their bookbags. Then, look at the pictures and decide which bag belongs to each of them.

a.

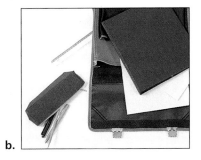

b.

c.

7 Objets trouvés

Lisons/Ecrivons When Paulette gets home from the store, she realizes that she forgot to put some of her school supplies into her bag. Look at the receipt showing what she bought and make a list, in French, of the missing items.

EXEMPLE   Elle n'a pas le...

Note culturelle

In large stores in France, customers are expected to place their items on the conveyer belt and then remove and bag them as well. Most stores provide small plastic sacks, but many shoppers bring their own basket **(un panier)** or net bag **(un filet)**. Since space is limited in small stores and boutiques, browsing inside these stores is not as common. In some cases, items and their prices are placed in window displays. Most people window-shop until they are ready to make a purchase. A sign that reads **Entrée libre** indicates that browsers are welcome.

```
VEN 13-05-03              3004
  047CA  BELLIOT  Stéphanie

GOMME CAOUTCH.          0,50
CRAYONS GRAH.           0,79
REGLE GRADUEE           3,85
CAH. BROUILLON          1,53
COPIES DBLES PF GC      1,38
CLASSEUR 17X22          4,64
TROUSSE                 7,23
SOUS/TOTAL             19,92

TOTAL                  19,92

REÇU                   50,00
RENDU                  30,08

00617      7 ARTC      16:36TM
```

8 Devine!

Parlons/Ecrivons Write down the name of one of the objects from the **Vocabulaire** on page 79. Don't let the other members of your group know what you've chosen. They will then take turns guessing which object you chose.

EXEMPLE   —C'est un taille-crayon?
            —Oui, c'est ça. *or* Non, ce n'est pas ça.

Comment dit-on...?

Making and responding to requests

To ask someone for something:

Tu as un stylo?
Vous avez un crayon?

To respond:

Oui. **Voilà.** *Here.*
Non. **Je regrette. Je n'ai pas de** crayons.
   Sorry. I don't have any . . .

Cahier d'activités, p. 27, Act. 4b

—Tu as une calculatrice, Paul?

—J'ai un stylo, un crayon, une règle et des feuilles de papier, mais je n'ai pas de calculatrice!

Grammaire

The indefinite articles *un, une,* and *des*

The articles **un** and **une** both mean *a* or *an*. Use **un** with masculine nouns and **une** with feminine nouns. Use **des** *(some)* with plural nouns. Notice that **un, une,** and **des** change to **de** after **ne... pas.**

J'ai **un** crayon, mais je n'ai pas **de** papier.

Nous avons **des** règles, mais nous n'avons pas **de** stylo.

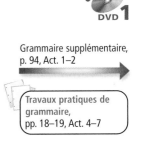

Grammaire supplémentaire, p. 94, Act. 1–2

Travaux pratiques de grammaire, pp. 18–19, Act. 4–7

9 **Grammaire en contexte**

Ecoutons Listen as Nadine asks her friends for some school supplies. Match her friends' responses to the appropriate pictures.

a.

b.

c.

d.

e.

10 **Grammaire en contexte**

Parlons With a partner, take turns pointing out the differences you notice between Christophe's desk and Annick's.

EXEMPLE **Regarde! Christophe a une gomme, mais Annick n'a pas de gomme.**

Comment dit-on...?

Asking others what they need and telling what you need

To ask what someone needs:

Qu'est-ce qu'il te faut pour les maths?
What do you need for . . . ?
(informal)
Qu'est-ce qu'il vous faut pour la géo?
What do you need for . . . ? (formal)

To tell what you need:

Il me faut un stylo et un classeur.

Cahier d'activités,
p. 28, Act. 5–6

Grammaire supplémentaire,
p. 94, Act. 3

Alors, qu'est-ce qu'il te faut pour l'anglais?

Euh, il me faut un classeur et un sac aussi.

Vocabulaire à la carte

Here are some additional words you can use to talk about your school supplies.

un compas	*a compass*
des crayons (m.) **de couleur**	*some colored pencils*
un feutre	*a marker*
du liquide (m.) **correcteur**	*some correction fluid*
du ruban (m.) **adhésif**	*some transparent tape*
une tenue de gymnastique	*a gym uniform*

11 Qu'est-ce qu'il te faut?

Ecrivons/Parlons Make a list of your school subjects. Exchange lists with a partner. Then, take turns asking each other what you need for various classes.

EXEMPLE — **Qu'est-ce qu'il te faut pour les maths?**

— **Il me faut une calculatrice et un crayon.**

12 Aide-mémoire

Ecrivons Write a note to remind yourself of the school supplies you need to buy for two or three of your classes.

13 Un petit service

Parlons You're late for class, and you've forgotten your supplies. Ask a friend if he or she has what you need. Your friend should respond appropriately. Then, change roles.

EXEMPLE — **Oh là là! J'ai histoire! Il me faut un stylo et un cahier. Tu as un stylo?**

— **Non, je regrette.**

— **Zut!**

Pour le français il me faut...

Qu'est-ce qu'il te faut comme fournitures scolaires?

We asked some francophone students what supplies they bought for the opening of school, **la rentrée.** Here's what they had to say.

Séverine,
Martinique

«Alors, donc pour l'école j'ai acheté un nouveau sac à dos, des livres pour étudier, des vêtements, entre autres des jeans, des chaussures, bien sûr et puis bon, des tee-shirts, des jupes, des robes.»

Onélia,
France

«Il faut des classeurs, des cahiers, des crayons, des règles, des instruments de géométrie, [une] calculatrice pour les mathématiques, des feuilles... C'est tout.»

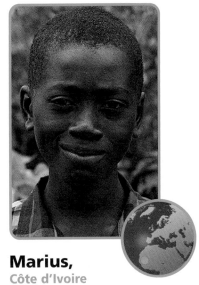

Marius,
Côte d'Ivoire

«Pour l'école, il faut des règles, des bics, des stylos, des cahiers, des livres et la tenue.»

Qu'en penses-tu?

1. What school supplies did you have to purchase for the school year?
2. What other items do you usually buy at the beginning of a school year?
3. What did these students buy that is usually provided by schools in the United States?
4. What are the advantages and disadvantages of each system?

Savais-tu que...?

In French-speaking countries, students usually buy their own textbooks and even maintain their own grade book, **un livret scolaire.** Some schools require students to purchase school uniforms. A store that specializes in school supplies, textbooks, and paper products is called **une librairie-papeterie.**

Vocabulaire

Qu'est-ce qu'on va acheter?

Hervé regarde **un short.**

Odile regarde **des baskets.**

Denis regarde **un roman.**

Stéphane regarde **un disque compact/un CD.**

Dorothée regarde **un jean.**

Mme Roussel regarde **un ordinateur.**

M. Beauvois regarde **une montre.**

M. Prévost regarde **un portefeuille.**

You can probably figure out what these words mean:

un bracelet	**un magazine**	**une radio**	**une télévision**
une cassette	**un poster**	**un sweat-shirt**	**une vidéocassette**
un dictionnaire	**un pull-over**	**un tee-shirt**	

Travaux pratiques de grammaire, p. 20, Act. 8–9

Grammaire supplémentaire, p. 95, Act. 4

 14 ### Le shopping

 Ecoutons Several shoppers in the **Vocabulaire** are going to tell you what they would like to buy. As you listen to each speaker, look at the illustrations above and identify the person. Write down his or her name.

Telling what you'd like and what you'd like to do

Je voudrais un sac. *I'd like . . .*
Je voudrais acheter un tee-shirt. *I'd like to buy . . .*

---

15 Les achats

Ecoutons Georges has just won a gift certificate from his favorite department store. Listen as he tells you what he would like to buy and make a list of his choices.

16 Vive le week-end!

Parlons What would you like to do this weekend? Find three classmates who want to do the same thing.

EXEMPLE —**Je voudrais sortir avec des copains. Et toi?**

—**Moi aussi.** *or* **Moi, je voudrais faire du sport.**

> faire les magasins
> danser   dormir   faire le ménage
> écouter de la musique
> parler au téléphone   faire du sport
> regarder la télévision
> nager   sortir avec des copains   étudier

17 Un cadeau

Ecrivons Make a list of what you would like to buy for . . .

1. a friend who likes horror movies and books.
2. a friend who loves sports.
3. someone who's always late for class.
4. a friend who loves music.
5. someone who loves French.
6. your best friend.

18 Mon journal

Ecrivons You earned 100 dollars this summer. Write down three or four items you'd like to buy for yourself.

Grammaire

The demonstrative adjectives *ce, cet, cette,* and *ces*

Ce, cet, and **cette** mean *this* or *that.* **Ces** means *these* or *those.*

	Singular	*Plural*
Masculine before a consonant sound	**ce** stylo	**ces** stylos
Masculine before a vowel sound	**cet** examen	**ces** examens
Feminine	**cette** école	**ces** écoles

Grammaire supplémentaire, pp. 95–96, Act. 5–6

Cahier d'activités, p. 29, Act. 7–8

Travaux pratiques de grammaire, p. 21, Act. 10–11

When you want to specify *that* as opposed to *this,* add **-là** *(there)* to the end of the noun.

—J'aime **ce sac.**

—Moi, j'aime mieux **ce sac-là.**

19 **Grammaire en contexte**

Lisons Claire is shopping for a gift for her mother. The salesperson is making suggestions. Choose the correct articles to complete their conversation.

Le Vendeur Vous aimez (ce/cette) montre, mademoiselle?

Claire Oui, mais ma mère a déjà (un/une) montre.

Le Vendeur Et (ces/ce) roman?

Claire Non, elle n'aime pas lire.

Le Vendeur Elle aime (la /l') musique?

Claire Oui. Elle adore le jazz.

Le Vendeur (Cet/Cette) cassette de Wynton Marsalis, peut-être?

Claire C'est une bonne idée.

20 **Grammaire en contexte**

Parlons Take turns with a partner asking and answering questions about the items below.

Moi aussi.   Non.   Non, je n'aime pas ça.

Oui, mais j'aime mieux...   Oui, j'adore!

J'aime bien.   Moi non plus.

EXEMPLE — Tu aimes ce sac?
— Non. J'aime mieux ce sac-là.

1.

2.

3.

4.

Vocabulaire

De quelle couleur est...

le sac?	la trousse?		le sac?	la trousse?
ROUGE	ROUGE		ROSE	ROSE
ORANGE	ORANGE		BLANC	BLANCHE
JAUNE	JAUNE		GRIS	GRISE
VERT	VERTE		NOIR	NOIRE
BLEU	BLEUE		MARRON	MARRON
VIOLET	VIOLETTE			

Cahier d'activités, pp. 29–30, Act. 9–10

Travaux pratiques de grammaire, p. 22, Act. 12

21 **Vrai ou faux?**

Parlons Regarde l'image et dis si les phrases
suivantes sont vraies ou fausses.

1. Claire a un sac jaune.
2. Claire et Thierry ont des tee-shirts bleus.
3. Claire a un short marron.
4. Thierry a des baskets bleues.
5. Thierry a un classeur rouge.
6. Claire et Thierry ont des shorts noirs.

Grammaire

Adjective agreement and placement

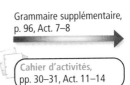

Did you notice in the **Vocabulaire** on page 86 that the spelling of some colors changes
according to the nouns they describe?

	Singular	*Plural*
Masculine	le classeur vert	les classeurs verts
Feminine	la gomme verte	les gommes vertes

- Usually, you add an **e** to make an adjective feminine; however, when an
  adjective ends in an unaccented **e,** you don't have to add another **e:**
  le classeur rouge, la gomme rouge.
- Some adjectives don't follow this pattern: **blanc, blanche; violet, violette.**
- Usually, you add an **s** to make an adjective plural; however, when an
  adjective ends in an **s,** you don't have to add another **s: les crayons gris.**
- Some adjectives don't change form. Two examples are **orange** and **marron.**
- Colors and many other adjectives are placed after the nouns they describe.

Grammaire supplémentaire,
p. 96, Act. 7–8

Cahier d'activités,
pp. 30–31, Act. 11–14

Travaux pratiques
de grammaire,
pp. 22–23, Act. 13–15

22 **Grammaire en contexte**

Ecrivons/Parlons Create a list of six objects. Ask your classmates if they have the items
on your list. When you find someone who does, find out what color each item is and
write the person's name next to the appropriate item.

un tee-shirt   une montre   un short

des baskets   une trousse   un stylo   un portefeuille   un pull-over

Vocabulaire

60	70	71	72	80	81
soixante	soixante-dix	soixante et onze	soixante-douze	quatre-vingts	quatre-vingt-un

90	91	100	101	200	201
quatre-vingt-dix	quatre-vingt-onze	cent	cent un	deux cents	deux cent un

CD-ROM 1
DVD 1

Cahier d'activités, pp. 32–33, Act. 15–17

Travaux pratiques de grammaire, p. 24, Act. 16–18

Grammaire supplémentaire, p. 97, Act. 9

23 Le top des radios

Ecoutons Listen to four French disc jockeys announce the dial frequencies of their radio stations. Then, match the frequencies to the station logos.

**RCV
99 MHZ (LILLE)**

a.

100.3 MHZ

b.

**C'ROCK
89.5 MHZ (VIENNE)**

c.

**OUÏ FM
102.3 MHZ (PARIS)**

d.

**CANAL B

RADIO ROCK
94 MHz**

e.

Note culturelle

After a transition of three years, France changed its currency in 2002. It phased out its own French **franc** to replace it with the currency shared by most of the countries of Western Europe, the **euro.** That means that if you are traveling in Europe, you could use the same money in Spain, France, and Germany without having to convert to local currencies. Euro bills come in denominations of 5, 10, 20, 50, 100, 200, and 500 euros. Euro coins, called **cents** come in denominations of 1, 2, 5, 10, 20, and 50. There are one hundred cents in each euro. Belgium and Luxembourg are among the European countries that have adopted the euro.

24 Ça fait combien?

Parlons/Écrivons How much money is shown in each illustration? Give the totals in French.

1.

2.

25 C'est combien?

Lisons Look at the drawing of the store display below. How much money does each of these customers spend in **Papier Plume**?

1. Alain achète deux stylos et une trousse.
2. Geneviève achète un classeur, un dictionnaire et un cahier.
3. Paul achète six crayons et un taille-crayon.
4. Marcel achète une règle, une gomme et un stylo.
5. Sarah achète deux cahiers et un dictionnaire.
6. Cécile achète une règle et une calculatrice.

26 Mon journal

Ecrivons Do you budget your money? Make a list of the items you've bought in the last month and the approximate price of each in euros. To convert American prices to euros, look up the current exchange rate in the newspaper or on the Web.

Comment dit-on...?

Getting someone's attention; asking for information; expressing and responding to thanks

To get someone's attention:

Pardon, monsieur/madame/ mademoiselle.

Excusez-moi, monsieur/madame/ mademoiselle.

To ask how much something costs:

C'est combien, s'il vous plaît?
How much is it, please?

To express and respond to thanks:

Merci. *Thanks*
A votre service. *You're welcome.*

Grammaire supplémentaire, p. 97, Act. 10–11

Cahier d'activités, p. 34, Act. 18–19

27 C'est combien?

Ecoutons/Ecrivons In a department store in France, you overhear shoppers asking salespeople for the prices of various items. As you listen to the conversations, write down the items mentioned and their prices.

Note culturelle

Prices expressed in euros can be said in two ways in French: either **quarante-cinq euros cinquante** or **quarante-cinq cinquante (45,50)**. Notice that prices are written in French with a comma where a decimal point would be used in American prices.

28 Jeu de rôle

Parlons You're buying school supplies in a French **librairie-papeterie.** For each item you want, get the salesperson's attention and ask how much the item costs. The salesperson will give you the price. Act out this scene with a partner. Then, change roles.

EXEMPLE — Excusez-moi, madame. C'est combien, cette trousse bleue?
— C'est six euros.
— Merci.

29 De l'école au travail

Parlons You have a job with an international distributor of magazines selling subscriptions over the telephone to French-speaking customers. With a partner, take turns playing the roles of customer and salesperson, using the advertisement to discuss the prices of subscriptions in French.

Abonnez-vous à :

FEMME A LA MODE	(12 numéros) France 35 €
DECOUVERTE SCIENTIFIQUE	(22 numéros) France 75 €
L'AFRIQUE DE NOS JOURS	(12 numéros) France 40 €, Europe 40 €, Dom-Tom 40 €, Afrique 45 €
TELE-TUBE	(52 numéros) France et Dom-Tom 90 €, USA $140, Canada $180, Autres pays 130 €
LA VOIX DU MONDE	(52 numéros) France 110 €
LES GRANDS MOUVEMENTS DE L'ECONOMIE	(12 numéros) France 25 €
LA VIE SPORTIVE	(12 numéros) France 20 €

PRONONCIATION

The r sound

The French **r** is quite different from the American *r*. To pronounce the French **r**, keep the tip of your tongue pressed against your lower front teeth. Arch the back of your tongue upward, almost totally blocking the passage of air in the back of your throat.

A. A prononcer

Repeat the following words.

1. Raoul   rouge   roman   règle
2. crayon   trente   calculatrice barbe
3. terrible   intéressant Europe   quarante
4. poster   rare   vert   montre

B. A lire

Take turns with a partner reading the following sentences aloud.

1. Fermez la porte.
2. Regardez le livre de français.
3. Prenez un crayon.
4. Ouvrez la fenêtre.
5. Je voudrais une montre.
6. Je regrette. Je n'ai pas de règle.

C. A écrire

You're going to hear a short dialogue. Write down what you hear.

TROISIEME ETAPE

quatre-vingt-onze

UNIVERS : TOUT POUR LA RENTRÉE

Stratégie pour lire

When you read material like this, you are generally looking for specific information—prices, colors, or sizes, for example. When that is your purpose, you don't have to read or understand every word. You can simply scan the material until you find what you are looking for.

A. At what time of year would you expect to see an advertisement like this?

B. When you buy school supplies, what is most important to you? Color? Price? Brand name?

C. Working with a partner, scan the ad for information about price, size, and quantity. Make a list of the words you find in the text that fit each of these categories.

D. What do you think **les 3** means?

E. The word **écolier** is used to describe the notebook. Do you recognize a word you've learned before in this word? What do you think **écolier** means?

F. What is the most expensive item? The least expensive?

UNIVERS
TOUT POUR LA RENTRÉE
VENEZ VOIR NOS PRIX REMARQUABLES!

ENSEMBLE D'ARDOISE: ardoise naturelle, éponge, crayon.

6,37€

0,68€

SURLIGNEUR FLUORESCENT divers coloris

4,18€

STYLO PLUME

0,95€

REGLE Graduation millimétrique, 30cm.

2,15€

COMPAS POINTE FIXE

BOITE DE GOUACHE 12 pastilles de 30 mm et un pinceau.

4,92€

5,76€

CALCULATRICE
8 chiffres, 4 opérations,
fonctions : mémoire, %,
√. Garantie 1 an.

0,63€

POT DE COLLE

2,55€

CLASSEUR ECOLIER
dim. 24 x 32

LES 3

0,44€

RUBAN ADHESIF
TRANSPARENT
19 mm X 33 m.

3,83€

SACHET DE
FEUTRES A DESSIN

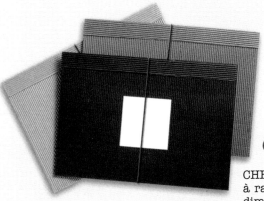

2,18€

CHEMISE
à rabat et élastique,
dim. 24 X 32 cm,
différents coloris.

ROULEAU PROTEGE-LIVRES
en polypropylène, différents coloris
et transparent, dim. 0,50 X 2 m.

0,80€

0,50 x 2m

G. What item(s) in this ad might each of these people ask for?
 1. a secretary
 2. an architect
 3. an artist

H. Do you think these prices? How can you tell?

I. What do you think these cognates mean?

adhésif	coloris
éponge	transparent

J. There are probably some items in this advertisement that you don't normally buy for school. Match the French words for these items with the English definitions. Look at the text and the pictures if you need help.

 1. rouleau protège-livres
 2. ardoise
 3. gouache
 4. colle
 5. stylo plume

 a. a writing slate
 b. glue
 c. fountain pen
 d. a roll of plastic material used to protect books
 e. paint

K. If you had 10 € to spend on school supplies, which items in the ad would you buy? Remember, you need supplies for all of your classes.

Cahier d'activités, p. 35, Act. 20

quatre-vingt-treize **93**

Grammaire supplémentaire

Première étape — **Objectives** Making and responding to requests; asking others what they need and telling what you need

1 Fill in the missing letters in the following words to find out what Amadou has on his desk. Then, write each word with the correct indefinite article. (p. 81)

EXEMPLE C __ __ I __ R -> **un cahier**

1. L __ __ R __ S
2. T __ O __ __ S __
3. S T __ __ O __
4. C __ A __ __ N
5. C __ __ C __ L __ T __ __ C __
6. F __ __ I L __ __ S

2 Create sentences, using the words that are jumbled below. To complete your sentences, you'll need to add **un, une, des, de (d')**. Remember to use the correct form of **avoir**. (p. 81)

EXEMPLE Anne/tu/avoir/montre? —**Anne, tu as une montre?**

1. Hélène/tu/sac à dos/avoir?
2. Non/ne/avoir/je/pas/sac à dos
3. Raphaël et Philippe/feuilles de papier/avoir/vous?
4. Karine/taille-crayon/tu/avoir?
5. Valérie et Mireille/vous/calculatrices/avoir?
6. Moi/pas/trousse/je/avoir/ne

3 Mamadou is asking you what you need to bring to school. Answer his questions, using the appropriate words from the box. Use each noun only once and remember to add **un, une,** or **des**. (pp. 81, 82)

EXEMPLE —Qu'est-ce qu'il te faut pour le sport?
—**Il me faut un tee-shirt.**

feuilles de papier	calculatrice	règle
	livre	
gomme	cahier	crayon

1. Qu'est-ce qu'il te faut pour la géométrie?
2. Qu'est-ce qu'il te faut pour l'anglais?
3. Qu'est-ce qu'il te faut pour l'algèbre?
4. Qu'est-ce qu'il te faut pour les arts plastiques?
5. Qu'est-ce qu'il te faut pour l'histoire?
6. Qu'est-ce qu'il te faut pour la chimie?

4 Choose the correct words (**me, te,** or **vous**) to complete the following conversations. Then, indicate whether each conversation is **logique** (logical) or **illogique** (illogical). Underline your choices. (**pp. 82, 84**)

1. —Serge, qu'est-ce qu'il (me/te) faut pour l'école?
   —Il (vous/me) faut un ordinateur, un poster et une pizza.
   Logique ou illogique?

2. —Géraldine et Nathalie, qu'est-ce qu'il (te/vous) faut pour les maths?
   —Des crayons, des gommes, deux calculatrices et des feuilles de papier.
   Logique ou illogique?

3. —Hervé, qu'est-ce qu'il (te/vous) faut pour le cours d'anglais?
   —Il (vous/me) faut un dictionnaire, des frites et un roman.
   Logique ou illogique?

4. —Alors, les garçons, qu'est-ce qu'il (vous/me) faut pour l'EPS?
   —Des baskets... c'est tout.
   Logique ou illogique?

5 You overheard these conversations at a school supplies store. Complete them with **ce, cet, cette,** or **ces.** (**p. 85**)

1. —Tu aimes _____ montre?
   —Oui, mais je préfère _____ bracelet.

2. —Vous aimez _____ jean?
   —Oui, mais il me faut _____ tee-shirt pour l'EPS.

3. —Je voudrais acheter _____ ordinateur.
   —Moi aussi, mais il te faut _____ calculatrice pour les maths.

4. —Comment tu trouves _____ baskets?
   —Super! J'aime _____ short aussi.

5. —Je voudrais acheter _____ cassette.
   —Moi, je préfère acheter _____ disque compact.

6. —Il me faut _____ feuilles de papier.
   —Moi aussi. Il me faut _____ règle aussi.

6 Match a verb from column A with a noun from column B, using each word only once. Then, write six logical sentences telling what you would like to do, using **je voudrais,** and **ce, cet, cette,** or **ces.** (**p. 85**)

EXEMPLE étudier roman **Je voudrais étudier ce roman.**

A	B
1. sortir avec	a. magazines
2. regarder	b. amis
3. lire	c. cours (m. pl.)
4. avoir	d. calculatrice
5. acheter	e. disque compact
6. écouter	f. vidéocassette

7 Unscramble the colors. Then, use them to describe the items you would like to have. Remember to add the appropriate endings to the colors if necessary. (**p. 87**)

EXEMPLE LEBU/des tee-shirts **Je voudrais des tee-shirts bleus.**

1. RARONM/des trousses
2. NLCAB/des calculatrices
3. ORUEG/des stylos
4. ETVR/une règle
5. RNIO/un sac
6. RIGS/des cahiers
7. OLEVIT/une gomme

8 You're telling the salesperson what school supplies you need to buy. Rewrite each sentence to include the given adjective in its correct form and position. (**p. 87**)

1. Il me faut une calculatrice. (gris)
2. Il me faut des baskets. (noir)
3. Il me faut des feuilles. (blanc)
4. Il me faut deux règles. (jaune)
5. Il me faut une trousse. (marron)

9 Murielle needs to buy a calculator, two tee-shirts, three pencils, a dictionary, and a pair of sneakers for school. First, write out the total amount she will spend for each of these items. Remember that she is buying more than one of some of the items. Then, write out the total amount of all her purchases. (**p. 88**)

1. Une calculatrice—25,98 €: _____

2. Un tee-shirt—13,86 €: _____

3. Un crayon—1,80 €: _____

4. Un dictionnaire—35,76 €: _____

5. Des baskets—58,63 €: _____

   Total : _____

10 Complete this conversation with the appropriate form of the words in parentheses. (**pp. 81, 85, 87, 90**)

JULIE   Excusez-moi, madame. C'est combien, ___**1**___ (ce/cet/cette) montre ___**2**___ (gris)?

LA VENDEUSE   Vingt euros, mademoiselle. Elle vous plaît?

JULIE   Oui, beaucoup. J'aime aussi ___**3**___ (ce/cet/cette) télévision ___**4**___ (blanc). Et vous avez ___**5**___ (des/de/d') calculatrices ___**6**___ (violet)?

LA VENDEUSE   Non. Je regrette, mademoiselle. Je n'ai pas ___**7**___ (des/de/d') calculatrices.

11 Ask how much the following items cost, using **ce, cet, cette,** or **ces,** and the appropriate form of the adjectives. (**pp. 85, 87, 90**)

EXEMPLE   trousse/bleu   **C'est combien, cette trousse bleue?**

1. crayons/noir
2. montre/violet
3. télévision/gris
4. classeurs/orange
5. bracelet/rose

MINIPRIX
Tout pour la rentrée

- une calculatrice ✓
- un dictionnaire ✓
- des gommes ✓
- des cahiers ✓
- une règle ✓
- des crayons ✓
- une montre ✗

Mise en pratique

1 You want to buy your friend a birthday gift. Listen as she gives you some ideas and then make a list of the things she would like.

2 You and a friend are browsing through a magazine. Point out several items you like and several you dislike.

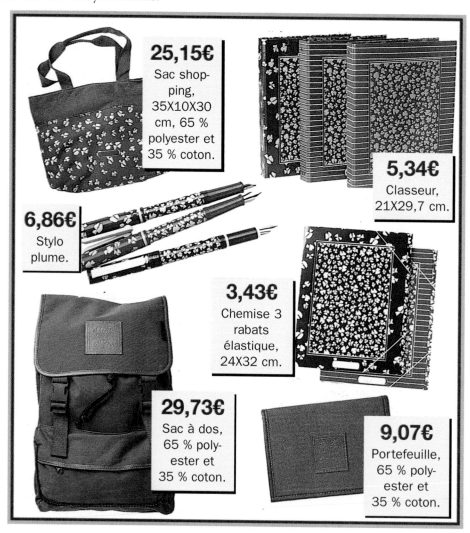

25,15€
Sac shop-ping, 35X10X30 cm, 65 % polyester et 35 % coton.

5,34€
Classeur, 21X29,7 cm.

6,86€
Stylo plume.

3,43€
Chemise 3 rabats élastique, 24X32 cm.

29,73€
Sac à dos, 65 % poly-ester et 35 % coton.

9,07€
Portefeuille, 65 % poly-ester et 35 % coton.

3 Make a list in French of two or three of the items pictured above that you'd like to buy. Include the colors and prices of the items you choose.

4 Tell your partner about the items you've chosen in Activity 3. Give as much detail as you can, including the color and price.

5 Your friend has been passing notes to you during study hall. Write a response to each one.

Il me faut un stylo!

Qu'est-ce qu'il faut pour l'algèbre ?

Qu'est-ce qu'il faut pour la chimie ?

6 If you were in France, what differences would you notice in these areas?

1. money   **2.** school supplies   **3.** stores

7 Ecrivons!

You're creating your own department store. First, make a list of possible names for your store. Then, create a list of items you would like to sell in your store, and begin thinking about how these items might be grouped together. Before you start, organize your ideas in a cluster diagram.

Stratégie pour écrire

Cluster diagrams are a helpful way to organize the ideas you develop in your brainstorming. Start by drawing a circle and label it with the name you chose for your store. Then draw two or three other circles, each connected to the first circle. In each of the new circles you draw, write the name of an item you plan to sell. Add more circles as you need them. Connect your circles with lines to group similar items together as they might be organized in a department store.

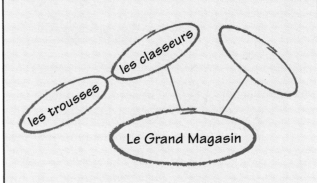

les trousses — les classeurs

Le Grand Magasin

8 Jeu de rôle

Visit the "store" your partner created and decide on something you'd like to buy. Your partner will play the role of the salesperson. Get the salesperson's attention, tell what you want, ask the price(s), pay for your purchase(s), thank the salesperson, and say goodbye. Your partner should respond appropriately. Then, change roles, using the store you created. Remember to use **madame, monsieur,** or **mademoiselle,** and **vous.**

MISE EN PRATIQUE

Que sais-je?

Can you use what you've learned in this chapter?

Can you make and respond to requests?
p. 80

1 How would you ask for the following items, using the verb **avoir?** How would you respond to someone's request for one of these items?

1.

2.

3.

Can you ask others what they need?
p. 82

2 How would you ask your friend what he or she needs for each of these school subjects?

1.

2.

3.

Can you tell what you need?
p. 82

3 How would you tell a friend that you need . . .
1. a calculator and an eraser for math?
2. a binder and some sheets of paper for Spanish class?
3. some pens and a notebook for English?
4. a pencil and a ruler for geometry?
5. a backpack and a book for history?

Can you tell what you'd like and what you'd like to do?
p. 85

4 How would you tell your friend that you'd like . . .
1. those white sneakers?
2. this blue bag?
3. that purple and black pencil case?
4. to listen to music and talk on the phone?
5. to go shopping?

Can you get someone's attention, ask for information, and express and respond to thanks?
p. 90

5 What would you say in a store to . . .
1. get a salesperson's attention?
2. politely ask the price of something?
3. thank a clerk for helping you?

Making and responding to requests

Tu as... ?	Do you have . . . ?
Vous avez... ?	Do you have . . . ?
Voilà.	Here.
Je regrette.	Sorry.
Je n'ai pas de...	I don't have a/any . . .

Asking others what they need and telling what you need

Qu'est-ce qu'il vous faut pour... ?	What do you need for . . . ? (formal)

Qu'est-ce qu'il te faut pour... ?	What do you need for . . . ? (informal)
Il me faut...	I need . . .
un	a; an
une	a; an
des	some

School supplies

un cahier	notebook
une calculatrice	calculator
un classeur	loose-leaf binder
un crayon	pencil

des feuilles (f.) de papier	sheets of paper
une gomme	eraser
un livre	book
une règle	ruler
un sac (à dos)	bag; backpack
un stylo	pen
un taille-crayon	pencil sharpener
une trousse	pencil case

Other useful expressions

Zut!	Darn!

Deuxième étape

Telling what you'd like and what you'd like to do

Je voudrais...	I'd like . . .
Je voudrais acheter...	I'd like to buy . . .

For school and fun

des baskets (f.)	sneakers
un bracelet	bracelet
une cassette	cassette tape
un dictionnaire	dictionary
un disque compact/un CD	compact disc/CD
un jean	(a pair of) jeans
un magazine	magazine

une montre	watch
un ordinateur	computer
un portefeuille	wallet
un poster	poster
un pull-over	pullover
une radio	radio
un roman	novel
un short	(a pair of) shorts
un sweat-shirt	sweatshirt
un tee-shirt	T-shirt
une télévision	television
une vidéocassette	videotape
ce, cet, cette	this; that
ces	these; those
-là	there (noun suffix)

Colors

De quelle couleur est... ?	What color is . . . ?
blanc(he)	white
bleu(e)	blue
gris(e)	grey
jaune	yellow
marron	brown
noir(e)	black
orange	orange
rose	pink
rouge	red
vert(e)	green
violet(te)	purple

Troisième étape

Getting someone's attention; asking for information; expressing and responding to thanks

Pardon.	Pardon me.
Excusez-moi.	Excuse me.
C'est combien?	How much is it?
Merci.	Thank you.
A votre service.	At your service; You're welcome.
s'il vous/te plaît	please

un euro	(the European monetary unit)
soixante	sixty
soixante et un	sixty-one
soixante-dix	seventy
soixante et onze	seventy-one
soixante-douze	seventy-two
quatre-vingts	eighty
quatre-vingt-un	eighty-one
quatre-vingt-dix	ninety

quatre-vingt-onze	ninety-one
cent	one hundred
cent un	one hundred and one
deux cents	two hundred

Other useful expressions

Bien sûr.	Of course.

Allez, viens à Québec!

Capitale de la province du Québec

Population : plus de 600.000

Points d'intérêt : le château Frontenac, l'université Laval, la terrasse Dufferin, le musée du Québec, les fortifications de Québec, les chutes Montmorency, le mont Sainte-Anne, Québec Expérience

Québécois célèbres : Samuel de Champlain, François de Montmorency-Laval, le marquis de Montcalm

Ressources et industries : dérivés du bois, du cuir et de l'érable; tourisme

Spécialités : ragoût de boulettes, tourtière, cretons, soupe aux pois, tarte au sucre, tarte à la ferlouche

WA3 QUEBEC CITY

Le château Frontenac ▶

Québec

Quebec City, one of the oldest cities in North America, is the capital of La Nouvelle-France, as the French-speaking province of Quebec used to be called. The Québécois people are fiercely proud of their heritage and traditions, and they work hard to maintain their language and culture. The narrow streets and quaint cafés of Vieux-Québec have an old-world feeling, but Quebec is also a dynamic, modern city — as exciting as any you'll find in North America!

Visit Holt Online

go.hrw.com

KEYWORD: WA3 QUEBEC CITY

Activités Internet

1 **Le Vieux-Québec**
These are typical houses in the historical part of the city.

2 **Les chutes Montmorency**
Spectacular waterfalls are found just outside of the city.

3 **La Grande Allée**
A boulevard lined with businesses and cafés, it is the longest road in Quebec.

4 **La terrasse Dufferin**
This bustling boardwalk overlooks the St. Lawrence River.

5 La rue du Trésor
This street in the heart of the old section of town is very popular among tourists. Local artists sell their work here.

6 Les plaines d'Abraham
This 250-acre park was the site of the battle in which the English defeated the French on September 13, 1759.

In chapter 4, you will meet Leticia and her Canadian pen pal, Emilie. Emilie and her friends will take you on a video tour of Quebec City. You will also find out what activities they do at different times of the year.

7 Le quartier Petit-Champlain
This picturesque shopping district is filled with boutiques and cafés.

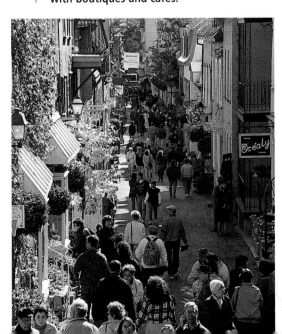

8 Le Vieux-Québec
Musicians, jugglers, and other entertainers frequently perform in the streets.

C H A P I T R E

4
Sports et passe-temps

Objectives

In this chapter you will learn to

Première étape

- tell how much you like or dislike something

Deuxième étape

- exchange information

Troisième étape

- make, accept, and turn down suggestions

Visit Holt Online

go.hrw.com

KEYWORD: WA3 QUEBEC CITY-4

Online Edition ⬍

◀ **On aime faire du théâtre!**

cent sept **107**

MISE EN TRAIN · *Nouvelles de Québec*

Stratégie pour comprendre

Emilie is eager to get to know her American pen pal Leticia. What kind of information do you think Emilie might include in a letter to her new pen pal? Look at the photos she included, and see if you can guess what Emilie is telling Leticia. What sort of questions might Emilie ask Leticia?

Emilie Tremblay
185, rue des Grisons
Québec, Québec
G-1R 4M9
Canada

Leticia Garza
10286 Balboa Ave.
San Diego, CA 92123
U.S.A.

Par avion

Salut, Leticia!

Comment ça va? Juste une petite lettre pour accompagner ces photos, une brochure sur le mont Sainte-Anne, une montagne près de Québec et aussi une cassette vidéo sur Québec... et sur moi! Comme ça, tu as une idée des activités ici... C'est l'automne à Québec et il fait déjà froid! Heureusement, il y a du soleil, mais il y a du vent. Quel temps est-ce qu'il fait à San Diego? Est-ce qu'il fait froid aussi? J'aime beaucoup Québec. C'est très sympa. Il y a beaucoup de choses à faire. En automne, je fais du patin et de la natation. J'adore le sport. En été, je fais du deltaplane et de la voile. Au printemps, je fais de l'équitation et je joue au tennis. Et en hiver, bien sûr, je fais du ski. C'est super ici pour le ski. Il neige de novembre à avril! Tu imagines? Est-ce qu'il neige à San Diego? Qu'est-ce qu'on fait comme sport? Du ski? Du base-ball? Quand il fait trop froid, je regarde la télévision et j'écoute de la musique. J'adore le rock et la musique québécoise. Et toi? Qu'est-ce que tu écoutes comme musique? Qu'est-ce qu'on fait à San Diego les fins de semaine? J'ai aussi une autre passion : de temps en temps, je fais des films avec un caméscope. C'est l'fun! Tu sais, c'est super, Québec. Et la Californie, c'est comment? C'est l'fun ou pas?

A très bientôt

Emilie

1 Ça, c'est notre café préféré.

2 La musique, c'est super! Tu fais de la musique, toi?

3 Au printemps, on joue au tennis. J'adore!

4 C'est mon copain Michel. En été, on fait du vélo.

5 En automne, on fait de l'équitation.

6 C'est moi! En hiver, on fait du patin.

Cahier d'activités, p. 37, Act. 1

1 Tu as compris?

Answer the following questions about Emilie's letter to Leticia. Don't be afraid to guess.

1. What is Emilie sending to Leticia along with her letter?
2. What are some of Emilie's hobbies and pastimes?
3. What would she like to know about Leticia and San Diego?
4. What does Emilie tell Leticia about the city of Quebec?
5. What else have you learned about Emilie from her letter?

2 C'est Emilie?

Tell whether Emilie would be likely or unlikely to say each of the statements below.

1. «J'adore faire du sport.»
2. «Le ski? Ici on n'aime pas beaucoup ça.»
3. «Pour moi, Québec, c'est barbant en hiver.»
4. «Faire des films avec un caméscope, pour moi, c'est passionnant.»
5. «Je regarde la télé en hiver quand il fait trop froid.»
6. «La musique? Bof! Je n'aime pas beaucoup ça.»

3 Cherche les expressions

In *Nouvelles de Québec,* what does Emilie say to . . .

1. greet Leticia?
2. ask how Leticia is?
3. ask about the weather?
4. tell what she likes?
5. express her opinion about something?
6. inquire about California?
7. say goodbye?

> C'est super.   Comment ça va?   J'adore...
>
> A très bientôt.   J'aime...   C'est très sympa.
>
> Quel temps est-ce qu'il fait?   Salut!
>
> C'est l'fun.   Et la Californie, c'est comment?

4 Les saisons et les sports

D'après la lettre d'Emilie, quels sports est-ce qu'elle fait? En quelle saison? Choisis des sports pour compléter ces phrases.

1. Au printemps, Emilie fait...
2. En hiver, elle fait...
3. En automne, elle fait...
4. En été, elle fait...

> de l'équitation   du ski   de la voile
>
> du deltaplane   du patin   de la natation

5 Et maintenant, à toi

Emilie fait beaucoup de choses! Tu fais les mêmes choses? Pour chaque activité, réponds **Moi aussi** ou **Moi, non.**

1. Emilie fait du ski.
2. Elle écoute de la musique.
3. Emilie fait des films avec un caméscope.
4. Elle fait de l'équitation.
5. Quand il fait trop froid pour sortir, Emilie regarde la télé.
6. Emilie joue au tennis.

Rencontre culturelle

What do you know about Quebec?

What impressions do you get of Quebec when you look at these photos?

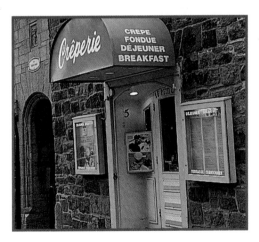

Qu'en penses-tu?

1. What things do you see that are typically American?
2. What do you see in these photos that you might not see in the United States?

Savais-tu que... ?

One of the first things you'll notice about Quebec City is its fascinating blend of styles—old and new, European and North American. Old Quebec (**le Vieux-Québec**) is filled with quaint neighborhood cafés and shops that maintain the old-world flavor of Europe. And yet, it is surrounded by a vibrant, modern city with high-rise hotels, office buildings, and a complex network of freeways. All of these elements together give the city its unique character.

Objective Telling how much you like or dislike something

WA3 QUEBEC CITY-4

Vocabulaire

Sports et activités

jouer au foot(ball)

jouer au football américain

faire de la vidéo

faire du roller en ligne

faire du patin à glace

faire du théâtre

faire de l'athlétisme

faire du vélo

faire de la natation*

You can probably guess what these activities are:

faire de l'aérobic	faire du ski (nautique)	jouer au basket(-ball)
faire du jogging	jouer aux cartes	jouer au golf
faire de la/des photo(s)	jouer au base-ball	jouer au hockey
jouer à des jeux vidéo	jouer au tennis	jouer au volley(-ball)

Cahier d'activités,
p. 38, Act. 4

Travaux pratiques de
grammaire, p. 25, Act. 1–2

*Remember that **nager** also means *to swim.*

6 Pascal à la montagne

Ecoutons Listen to this conversation between Philippe and Pascal. List at least two activities Pascal likes and two he doesn't like.

Grammaire

Expressions with *faire* and *jouer*

You use **faire** (*to make, to do*) followed by the preposition **de** with activities, including sports.

- When the sport is a masculine noun, **de** becomes **du.**

  faire **du** ski   faire **du** patin

- If the activity is plural, **de** becomes **des.**

  faire **des** photos

- The preposition **de** doesn't change before **la** or **l'.**

  faire **de la** natation   faire **de l'**aérobic

You use **jouer** (*to play*) with games or sports that you <u>play</u>. It is followed by the preposition **à.**

- When the game or sport is a masculine noun **à** becomes **au.**

  jouer **au** football

- When the game or sport is plural, **à** becomes **aux.**

  jouer **aux** cartes

- The preposition **à** doesn't change before **la, l'** or **des.**

Grammaire supplémentaire, p. 128, Act. 1–2

Cahier d'activités, p. 38, Act. 3

Travaux pratiques de grammaire, p. 26, Act. 3–4

7   Grammaire en contexte

Ecrivons Ariane et Serge parlent des activités qu'ils aiment faire après l'école. Fais une liste des activités suggérées par les images pour compléter leur conversation.

ARIANE   Qu'est-ce que tu aimes faire après l'école?

SERGE   Moi, j'aime avec mes copains. Et toi?

ARIANE   Moi, j'aime et j'adore 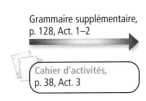 .

SERGE   Tu aimes ? On va jouer à la plage demain. Tu viens?

ARIANE   Non, merci. J'aime mieux  avec des copains.

8   Grammaire en contexte

Parlons You and a Canadian student are discussing what you like to do after school on different days of the week. Create the conversation with one of your classmates.

EXEMPLE   —Qu'est-ce que tu aimes faire le lundi après l'école?
                — J'aime jouer au basket le lundi. Et toi?
                — Moi, j'aime faire du vélo.

Comment dit-on...?

Telling how much you like or dislike something

To tell how much you like something:

J'aime **beaucoup** le sport. *I like . . . a lot!*
J'aime **surtout** faire du ski. *I especially like . . .*

To tell how much you dislike something:

Je n'aime **pas tellement** le football. *I don't like . . . too much.*
Je n'aime **pas beaucoup** le volley-ball. *I don't like . . . very much.*
Je n'aime **pas du tout** la natation. *I don't like . . . at all.*

You can use the expressions in bold type alone as short answers:

—Tu aimes faire du sport?
—Oui, **beaucoup!** or
　Non, **pas tellement.**

Cahier d'activités, p. 39, Act. 5

---

9 **Qu'est-ce qu'ils aiment?**

Ecoutons On a school trip to Quebec, you listen to your classmate talk to a Canadian student. Write down at least one sport or game each speaker likes and one each speaker dislikes.

10 **Pas d'accord!**

Parlons You and a Canadian exchange student want to watch sports on TV, but you can't agree on what to watch. Each time one of you finds something you like, the other doesn't like it and changes the channel. Act this out with a partner.

EXEMPLE　　　—Oh! J'aime bien le football. Et toi, tu aimes?
　　　　　　　　—Pas beaucoup. Regarde, un match de tennis. Tu aimes le tennis?

11 **Qu'est-ce qu'ils aiment faire?**

Parlons The Canadian exchange student is visiting your school. He'd like to get to know your friends better, so he asks you about their interests. Tell him how much each of your friends likes or dislikes the activity pictured, using the cue provided.

EXEMPLE   —Est-ce que Marc aime... ?   —Non, il n'aime pas trop...

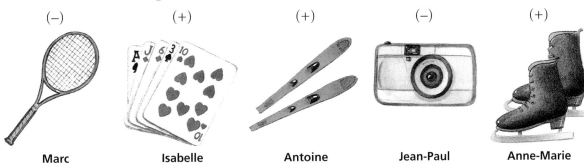

(−)   (+)   (+)   (−)   (+)

Marc   Isabelle   Antoine   Jean-Paul   Anne-Marie

1. Est-ce que Marc aime... ?
2. Est-ce qu'Isabelle aime... ?
3. Et Antoine, est-ce qu'il aime... ?
4. Et Jean-Paul, est-ce qu'il aime... ?
5. Est-ce qu'Anne-Marie aime... ?

Grammaire

Question formation

You've already learned to make a yes-or-no question by raising the pitch of your voice at the end of a sentence. Another way to ask a yes-or-no question is to say **est-ce que** before a statement and raise your voice at the very end.

Est-ce que tu aimes faire du vélo?

Grammaire supplémentaire,
p. 129, Act. 3

Cahier d'activités,
p. 40, Act. 8

Travaux pratiques
de grammaire,
p. 27, Act. 5–6

12 **Grammaire en contexte**

Parlons Avec un camarade, discutez des sports et des passe-temps que vous aimez tous les deux. Posez des questions et répondez à tour de rôle. Variez vos questions.

EXEMPLE   — Est-ce que tu aimes jouer au football américain?
          — Non! J'aime mieux faire de l'aérobic, du théâtre et du roller en ligne.

Vocabulaire à la carte

faire un pique-nique	*to have a picnic*
faire de la randonnée	*to go hiking*
faire des haltères	*to lift weights*
faire de la gymnastique	*to do gymnastics*
faire du surf	*to surf*
faire de la voile	*to go sailing*

13 **Grammaire en contexte**

Parlons Poll five of your classmates about the sports and hobbies they like to do. Which activity is the most popular? Which is the least popular?

Comment dit-on...?

Exchanging information

To find out a friend's interests:

Qu'est-ce que tu fais comme sport?
What sports do you play?
Qu'est-ce que tu fais pour t'amuser?
What do you do to have fun?

To tell about your interests:

Je fais de l'athlétisme. *I do . . .*
Je joue au volley-ball. *I play . . .*
Je ne fais pas de ski. *I don't . . .*
Je ne joue pas au foot. *I don't play . . .*

Note de grammaire

Du, de la, and **de l'** usually become **de** (or **d'**) in a negative sentence.

Je ne fais pas **de** jogging.

Je ne fais pas **d'**athlétisme.

Cahier d'activités, p. 41, Act. 10

Grammaire supplémentaire, p. 129, Act. 4

Travaux pratiques de grammaire, p. 28, Act. 7–8

14 Grammaire en contexte

Parlons With a partner, take turns asking each other about your sports and hobbies.

EXEMPLE
— Qu'est-ce que tu fais pour t'amuser?
— Je fais du jogging et du ski. Et toi?
— Moi, je...

Grammaire

The verb *faire*

The irregular verb **faire** is used in many different expressions.

faire
(to do, to play, or *to make)*

Je	**fais**	Nous	**faisons**
Tu	**fais**	Vous	**faites**
Il/Elle/On	**fait**	Ils/Elles	**font**

Cahier d'activités, p. 41, Act. 11

Grammaire supplémentaire, pp. 129–130, Act. 5–6

Travaux pratiques de grammaire, p. 29, Act. 9–10

15 Grammaire en contexte

Ecrivons Complete the following conversation with the correct forms of the verb **faire.**

— Tu ___1___ quels sports?

— Moi, je ___2___ surtout du ski et du patin.

— Et tes copains, qu'est-ce qu'ils ___3___ comme sport?

— Michel ___4___ de la natation et Hélène ___5___ du roller en ligne.

— Hélène et toi, est-ce que vous ___6___ du sport ensemble?

— Oui, nous ___7___ souvent du vélo.

16 Grammaire en contexte

Parlons Jean and Luc are identical twins. They even enjoy the same activities. Tell what activities they do, based on what you see in their room.

Grammaire

The pronoun *on*

- The subject pronoun **on** is used with the **il/elle** form of the verb. In conversational French, **on** usually means *we.*

    Le samedi, **on** fait du sport. *On Saturdays, we play sports.*

- **On** can mean *they* or *you* when it refers to people in general.

    En France, **on** parle français.

- You will have to use context, the surrounding words and phrases, to tell how a speaker is using **on.**

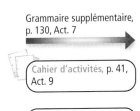

Grammaire supplémentaire, p. 130, Act. 7

Cahier d'activités, p. 41, Act. 9

Travaux pratiques de grammaire, p. 30, Act. 11

17 Grammaire en contexte

Parlons Tell whether you and your friends do or don't do the activities shown in the photos.

   Mes copains et moi, on fait...

1.   2.   3.   4.   5.

Quel temps fait-il?

Il fait beau.

Il fait chaud.

Il fait froid.

Il fait frais.

Il pleut.

Il neige.

Travaux pratiques de grammaire, p. 30, Act. 12

18 ## C'est agréable ou désagréable?

Parlons Is each of these activities pleasant (**agréable**) or unpleasant (**désagréable**)?

1. faire du vélo quand il fait froid
2. faire de la natation quand il fait chaud
3. regarder la télé quand il neige
4. faire du jogging quand il fait frais
5. jouer au football américain quand il pleut

19 ## Et toi?

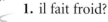

Ecrivons Qu'est-ce que tu aimes faire quand...

1. il fait froid?
2. il pleut?
3. il fait beau?
4. il neige?

Vocabulaire

Les mois de l'année

janvier
février
mars
avril
mai
juin

juillet
août
septembre
octobre
novembre
décembre

Cahier d'activités,
p. 44, Act. 17

Travaux pratiques de
grammaire, p. 31, Act. 13–14

20 Il fait quel temps?

Lisons/Parlons In these months, what is the weather usually like where you live?

1. en mai
2. en février
3. en juillet
4. en octobre
5. en avril
6. en décembre

Il fait froid.   Il fait frais.   Il pleut.

Il neige.

Il fait beau.   Il fait chaud.

Tu te rappelles?

Do you remember the endings that you learned to use with the verb **aimer** in Chapter 1? Those endings are exactly the same for all regular **-er** verbs, which include many French verbs. Here's how the verb **jouer** fits the pattern.

jouer *(to play)*

Je **joue**
Tu **joues**   au tennis.
Il/Elle/On **joue**

Nous **jouons**
Vous **jouez**   au tennis.
Ils/Elles **jouent**

Grammaire supplémentaire,
p. 130, Act. 8

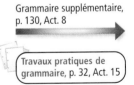

Travaux pratiques de
grammaire, p. 32, Act. 15

21 Qu'est-ce que vous faites en hiver?

Ecoutons Listen as a newspaper reporter asks three Canadian teenagers, Paul, Anne, and Julie, about their hobbies and pastimes. Then, answer the questions below.

1. Which teenagers don't watch TV?
2. Which ones like to listen to music?
3. Which ones play hockey?
4. Which ones like to dance?
5. Which teenagers like to go to the movies?

22 Prisonnier des neiges

Ecrivons Imagine that you're snowed in during a winter storm. Write a note to a friend telling him or her about the weather, what you're doing to pass the time, and how you feel about the situation.

Qu'est-ce que tu fais...

en vacances?

le soir?

le week-end?

Vendredi	Samedi	Dimanche
1	2	3
8	9	10
15	16	17

en automne?

en hiver?

au printemps?

en été?

Cahier d'activités,
p. 42, Act. 12–14

Travaux pratiques de
grammaire, p. 32, Act. 16

23 **Un questionnaire**

Lisons/Parlons To help pair up campers for activities, a camp counselor has sent out the survey you see on the right. Give one answer in each category.

24 **J'aime faire...**

Parlons Dis à tes camarades de classe ce que tu fais à chaque saison et demande-leur ce qu'ils font. Essaie de trouver quelqu'un qui fait au minimum deux des choses que tu fais.

EXEMPLE — **En hiver, je fais du patin à glace. Et toi?**
— **Moi, non! Quand il fait froid, j'écoute de la musique.**

25 **Une lettre**

Ecrivons Tu prépares un voyage au Canada et tu as décidé d'écrire à ton correspondant canadien. Ecris un paragraphe pour lui demander quels sont ses sports et ses passe-temps préférés. Ecris aussi ce que tu fais et ce que tu ne fais pas.

1. **En automne, je...**
a. fais du patin à glace.
b. joue au hockey.
c. écoute de la musique.
d. fais du ski.
e. fais autre chose.

2. **En hiver, je...**
a. joue au football américain.
b. joue au foot.
c. fais du théâtre.
d. joue au volley.
e. fais autre chose.

3. **Au printemps, je...**
a. joue au base-ball.
b. fais de l'athlétisme.
c. fais du vélo.
d. fais de la vidéo.
e. fais autre chose.

4. **En été, je...**
a. fais de la natation.
b. fais du roller en ligne.
c. regarde la télé.
d. fais du ski nautique.
e. fais autre chose.

  VIDEO CD-ROM **1** DVD **1**

Qu'est-ce que tu fais comme sport?

What sports do you play? Where do you go to practice them? We asked some young people about their favorite sports. Here's what they had to say.

Marius,
Côte d'Ivoire

«Je fais beaucoup de sport, mais surtout le football. Je fais le football et le skate, le patin à roulettes et puis j'aime aussi le tennis.»

Aljosa,
France

«Comme sport, j'aime bien faire le tennis. J'aime bien aller à la piscine, voilà. J'aime bien [le] bowling.»

Mélanie,
Québec

«Avec mes amies, moi je fais beaucoup de sport. Je fais partie de l'équipe interscolaire de volley-ball et de badminton de l'école. Je fais de la nata-tion. Je fais du patinage. Je fais de la course. Je fais du tennis aussi souvent l'été. L'hiver, je patine.»

Qu'en penses-tu?

1. Which of these students enjoy the same sports that you do?
2. Which sports that they mention are not played in your area?
3. Can you guess which sports are associated with the following events and places?*

    a. La Coupe du monde   **c.** Le Tour de France

    b. Le Grand Prix de Monaco   **d.** Le stade Roland-Garros

Savais-tu que... ?

While schools in francophone countries do offer extracurricular sports, serious athletes often participate through clubs outside of school. Activities such as swimming, tennis, or volleyball are often organized by parent volunteers or communities. In France, recreation centers (**Maisons des jeunes et de la culture** or **MJC**) sponsor all kinds of social, cultural, and educa-tional activities for young people.

* a. soccer   b. auto racing   c. cycling   d. tennis (the French Open)

Comment dit-on...?

Making, accepting, and turning down suggestions

To make a suggestion:

> **On** fait du patin?
> *How about . . . ?*
> **On** joue au foot?
> *How about . . . ?*

To turn down a suggestion:

> **Désolé(e), mais je ne peux pas.**
> *Sorry, but I can't.*
> **Ça ne me dit rien.**
> *That doesn't interest me.*
> **Non, c'est barbant!**

To accept a suggestion:

> **D'accord.** *OK.*
> **Bonne idée.** *Good idea.*
> **Oui, c'est génial!**
> **Allons-y!** *Let's go!*

Cahier d'activités,
p. 45, Act. 19

---

26 On joue au volley?

Ecoutons Listen as Germain calls his friends Lise, Renaud, Philippe, and Monique to suggest activities for the weekend. Do his friends accept or turn down his suggestions?

27 Qu'est-ce qu'on fait?

Parlons Write down one or two things that you'd like to do this weekend. Then, find three classmates who'd like to join you.

> **EXEMPLE**
> — **On fait du jogging ce week-end?**
> — **Le jogging, c'est barbant!** *or* **D'accord. C'est génial, le jogging.**

Grammaire

Adverbs of frequency

- To tell how often you do something, use **quelquefois** (*sometimes*), **de temps en temps** (*from time to time*), une **fois par semaine** (*. . . time(s) a week*), **souvent** (*often*), **d'habitude** (*usually*), **rarement** (*rarely*), and **ne... jamais** (*never*).

- Short adverbs usually come after the verb. Longer adverbs can be placed at the beginning or the end of a sentence. Put **d'habitude** at the beginning of a sentence and **une fois par semaine** at the end. Put **ne... jamais** around the verb, as you do with **ne... pas.**

> Je fais **souvent** du ski.
> **D'habitude,** je fais du ski au printemps.

> Je fais du ski **une fois par semaine.**
> Je **ne** fais **jamais** de ski.

Grammaire supplémentaire,
p. 131, Act. 9–10

Cahier d'activités,
pp. 45–46, Act. 20–22

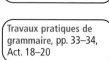

Travaux pratiques de
grammaire, pp. 33–34,
Act. 18–20

Grammaire en contexte

Ecoutons Listen as Emile, a reporter for a school newspaper in Quebec City, interviews his classmates about sports. How often does each person practice sports?

 Grammaire en contexte

Parlons Pauline is an active, French-Canadian teenager. Based on her calendar, take turns with a partner asking about her activities and how often she does them.

EXEMPLE — Est-ce qu'elle fait de l'aérobic?
— Oui, de temps en temps.

N O V E M B R E

DIMANCHE	LUNDI	MARDI	MERCREDI	JEUDI	VENDREDI	SAMEDI
		1 jogging	**2** photo	**3** jogging	**4** théâtre	**5** patin à glace
6 aérobic	**7** jogging	**8** photo	**9**	**10** jogging	**11**	**12** jogging
13 photo	**14** jogging	**15**	**16** aérobic	**17** jogging	**18** théâtre	**19**
20 patin à glace	**21** jogging	**22** jogging	**23** photo	**24** ski	**25**	**26** aérobic
27 jogging	**28**	**29** jogging	**30** photo			

 Grammaire en contexte

Parlons With a partner, discuss your favorite pastimes and how often you do them. Ask questions to keep the conversation going.

EXEMPLE — Qu'est-ce que tu fais pour t'amuser?
— En été, je fais souvent du ski nautique. Et toi?
— Je fais du vélo. Et toi? Tu fais du vélo... ?

le week-end?
en vacances?
en été?
quand il fait froid?
quand il fait beau?

31 Sondage

a. Ecrivons Make a chart like the one shown here. In the left-hand column, list the activities you enjoy. In the middle column, tell when you do them, and in the right-hand column, tell how often.

ACTIVITE	SAISON	FREQUENCE
Je fais du ski. Je fais...	en hiver	de temps en temps

b. Parlons Now, share this information with three other classmates. Ask questions to find out what you have in common and what you don't.

EXEMPLE — Je fais du ski de temps en temps.
— Pas moi! Je ne fais jamais de ski.

32 Le sportif

Lisons/Parlons Your French pen pal Lucien is coming to visit soon. Read his letter and tell whether he would answer **D'accord** or **Ça ne me dit rien** if you were to suggest the following activities.

1. On fait de la vidéo ce week-end?
2. On fait du ski nautique?
3. On joue au foot?

4. On fait de la natation ce soir?
5. On joue au football américain ce week-end?

> Salut!
> J'espère que ça va. Moi, ça va bien. Je fais beaucoup de sport maintenant. Et toi, tu aimes faire du sport? Moi, j'aime jouer au foot, mais je n'aime pas trop le football américain; c'est barbant. D'habitude, le week-end, je joue au tennis ou je fais de la natation. La natation, c'est génial. Mais je n'aime pas faire du ski nautique; c'est nul. Quand il fait froid, je fais de l'aérobic. A part le sport, quelquefois, je fais de la vidéo. Et toi? Qu'est-ce que tu fais le week-end? Ecris-moi vite!
> A bientôt,
> Lucien

33 Cher Lucien, ...

Ecrivons Now, answer Lucien's letter. Be sure to . . .

• tell him what activities you like and why you like them.

• tell him when and how often you do each activity.

• tell him what you don't like to do and why not.

• suggest one or two things you might do together and when.

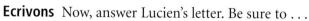

34 De l'école au travail

Ecrivons/Parlons Some well-known athletes from Canada are training in your town for the summer. You've been working as an intern for the local newspaper, and a reporter needs your help to interview one of the French-speaking athletes. Work with a partner to create a list of interview questions in French. You may want to ask what sports he or she likes to do, what the weather is like in Canada during the winter and the summer, and what he or she likes to do for fun. Then, choose the role of interviewer or athlete and practice the interview.

35 Mon journal

Ecrivons Using the information in the chart you made for Activity 31, write about your favorite weekend and after-school activities and how often you do them. Give your opinions of the activities, too.

PRONONCIATION

The sounds [u] and [y]

The sound [u] occurs in such English words as *Sue, shoe,* and *too.* The French [u] is shorter, tenser, and more rounded than the vowel sound in English. Listen to these French words: **tout, nous, vous.** The sound [u] is usually represented by the letter combination **ou.**

The sound [y] is represented in the words s**alut, super,** and **musique.** This sound does not exist in English. To pronounce [y], start by saying [i], as in the English word *me.* Then, round your lips as if you were going to say the English word *moon,* keeping your tongue pressed behind your lower front teeth.

A. A prononcer

Now, practice first the sound [u] and then [y]. Repeat these words.

1. vous	4. rouge	7. tu	10. étude
2. nous	5. cours	8. musique	11. une
3. douze	6. joue	9. nul	12. du

B. A lire

Take turns with a partner reading the following sentences aloud.

1. Salut! Tu t'appelles Louis?
2. J'ai cours aujourd'hui.
3. Tu aimes la trousse rouge?
4. Elle n'aime pas du tout faire du ski.
5. Nous aimons écouter de la musique.
6. Vous jouez souvent au foot?

C. A écrire

You're going to hear a short dialogue. Write down what you hear.

ALLEZ, C'EST A VOUS DE CHOISIR!

A. The title of this selection is **Allez, c'est à vous de choisir!** What do you think this title means? What do you think the article will be about?

B. Look at the organization of the article and the two major headings. What type of information do you think will be included under **Pour les artistes?** What about **Pour les sportifs?** What do you know about the activities in each category?

C. What type of information do you find in each section? Do all the sections have the same type of information? If not, how do they differ?

Pour les artistes

D. Scan the sections titled **La musique, Le théâtre,** and **La danse.** Make a list of the cognates you find. You should find at least ten.

ALLEZ, C'EST A VOUS DE CHOISIR!

Cette année, c'est décidé, vous vous lancez dans une activité! Nous vous en proposons ici quelques exemples, à vous de choisir...

POUR LES ARTISTES

LA MUSIQUE

• Il n'y a pas d'âge pour commencer. L'important, c'est d'être motivé. Et de bien choisir son instrument.

• Vous devez avoir votre instrument. Au début, il est possible de le louer.

• Rythme : en général 1 heure de solfège par semaine et 1/2 h de cours d'instrument. Pour progresser, il faut prévoir 1/4 h de travail chaque jour.

LE THEATRE

• C'est souvent à l'adolescence qu'on commence. On découvre à la fois les joies (et les doutes) de l'improvisation et les grands auteurs.

• Rythme : entre 2 et 3 heures par semaine, plus des textes à apprendre.

• Renseignez-vous auprès de votre mairie ou à l'École de Musique, 4, rue Beaubourg, 75004 Paris. Tél : 01 42 71 25 07.

LA DANSE

• Peu de garçons s'inscrivent au cours de danse et c'est bien dommage car la danse apprend à aimer et maîtriser son corps... et à s'éclater aussi!

• Débutant à tout âge!

• Pour commencer, un caleçon chaud (pour les muscles) et un tee-shirt près du corps (pour que le prof voie vos mouvements) peuvent suffire. Et des chaussures ballerines ou rythmiques.

• Rythme : 1 heure et demie par semaine.

• Fédération française de danse : 12, rue Saint-Germain-d'Auxerrois, 75013 Paris. Tél : 01 42 36 12 61.

POUR LES SPORTIFS

LE TENNIS

- Des matchs sont organisés par les clubs. Ils permettent de se préparer à la compétition.

- Le coût varie selon les clubs et votre niveau. Choisissez un forfait qui comprend les cours et l'accès aux courts.

- Comptez au moins 38 euros pour une raquette de bonne qualité et choisissez des chaussures adaptées, pas les tennis mode que vous portez tous les jours!

- Rythme : 1 heure par semaine, plus les tournois. Si vous jouez beaucoup, faites un autre sport en complément, pour éviter les problèmes de dos.

- Fédération française de tennis : Stade Roland-Garros, 2, avenue Gordon Bennett, 75016 Paris. Tél : 01 47 43 48 00.

LE FOOTBALL

- Avec quelques copains et un ballon, on peut s'amuser presque partout. Mais pour jouer dans les règles de l'art, mieux vaut s'inscrire dans un club.

- Souvent, le short et le maillot sont fournis par le club, mais les chaussures à crampons vissés coûtent entre 23 et 137 euros.

- Rythme : en général 2 heures par semaine. Rencontres entre clubs le samedi ou le dimanche.

- Fédération française de football : 60 bis, avenue d'Iéna, 75763 Paris cédex 16. Tél : 01 44 31 73 00.

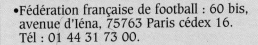

LE KARTING

- Il existe une formule de location de kart avec cours adaptés dès 12 ans.

- Coût : environ 457 euros par an, comprenant les cours et le matériel.

- Rythme : 1 heure par semaine, plus quelques courses (souvent le samedi ou le dimanche).

- Groupement national de karting : 203, rue Lafayette, 75010 Paris. Tél : 01 42 05 09 44.

E. What do you think the word **débutant** means? Can you think of any words in English that are related to this word?

F. At what age do people usually. . .
1. learn how to play an instrument
2. begin drama?
3. learn how to dance?

G. According to the article, how often do you need to practice playing an instrument to improve quickly?

Pour les sportifs

H. What do you think **Rythme** means? How do you know?

I. What do you think **Le Karting** means? Is this an activity that is popular in your area?

J. According to the article, how much does a tennis racket cost?

K. Which of these activities . . .
1. require(s) special shoes?
2. require(s) two or more hours a week?

L. For which activities is it recommended that you join a club?

M. Which activity costs the most to participate in? Why?

N. Conduct a survey among your classmates to see which of these activities are the most and least popular and why. You might also find out in how many of these activities your classmates have participated, which ones are the most interesting, and why. Make a list of questions you need to include in your survey.

Cahier d'activités, p. 47, Act. 24–25

Grammaire supplémentaire

CD-ROM 1
DVD 1

Visit Holt Online
go.hrw.com
KEYWORD: WA3 QUEBEC CITY-4
Jeux interactifs

Première étape   Objective Telling how much you like or dislike something

1 Complète les conversations suivantes avec **faire** ou **jouer**. (**p. 113**)

1. —Corinne, est-ce-que tu aimes _____ au golf?

   —Non. Je préfère _____ du ski.

2. —Frédéric et Arthur, est-ce que vous aimez _____ de la vidéo?

   —Pas tellement. Nous aimons mieux _____ du théâtre.

3. —Et Malika, est-ce qu'elle aime _____ aux cartes?

   —Pas du tout. Mais elle aime _____ de la natation.

4. —Georges, est-ce que tu aimes _____ du jogging?

   —Oui. Mais je préfère _____ au hockey.

2 According to their interests, what do Sandrine and her friends do in their spare time? Write six sentences telling what they do, using the verbs **faire** or **jouer** and an expression from the box in each sentence. Use each expression only once. (**p. 113**)

jeux vidéo	*vélo*	*ski nautique*
tennis	*natation*	*ski*
théâtre	*football*	*patin à glace*

EXEMPLE   Ariane aime la piscine.
Elle aime faire de la natation.

1. Claude aime tellement la plage.
2. Suzanne aime les bicyclettes.
3. Olivier et Victor aiment les ordinateurs.
4. Moi, j'aime la neige.
5. Tu aimes le sport.
6. Marc et moi, nous aimons le foot.
7. Emilie et Michel aiment le hockey.
8. Louise aime Shakespeare et Molière.

3 You have made a list of the activities your classmates like to do. Double-check your list by asking your classmates if your information is correct, using **est-ce que,** and **tu** or **vous** as appropriate. (**p. 115**)

EXEMPLE   Paul et Aurélie aiment faire du ski.
            Est-ce que vous aimez faire du ski?

1. Anne-Marie et Louise aiment jouer au foot.
2. Marc aime jouer à des jeux vidéo.
3. Elodie aime faire de la photo.
4. Jacques et Jules aiment jouer au tennis.
5. Alexandrine aime faire du ski nautique.
6. Véronique et Céline aiment faire de l'athlétisme.
7. Miriam aime faire du vélo.
8. Jean et Françoise aiment jouer aux cartes.

Deuxième étape   Objective Exchanging information

4 You're having a friend over who doesn't like to do anything. Answer the following questions as your friend would, based on the example. (**p. 116**)

EXEMPLE   Tu joues au volley?   **Non, je ne joue pas au volley.**
            Tu fais du ski?   **Non, je ne fais pas de ski.**

1. Tu fais de la natation?
2. Tu joues à des jeux vidéo?
3. Tu fais de l'athlétisme?
4. Tu fais du jogging?
5. Tu joues aux cartes?
6. Tu fais des photos?
7. Tu fais du patin à glace?
8. Tu fais du roller en ligne?

5 Pauline et Louise ont des projets pour la soirée. Complète leur conversation avec les formes correctes de **faire.** (**p. 116**)

LOUISE   Dis, Pauline, on ___1___ de la natation ce soir?

PAULINE   Non. Quand il fait froid, moi, je ne ___2___ pas de natation! J'aime mieux ___3___ du patin à glace! Tu ___4___ du patin à glace, toi?

LOUISE   Non, ça ne me dit rien. En hiver, quand il neige, mes copines et moi, nous ___5___ du ski. C'est génial, le ski!

PAULINE   En été, Gilles et Félix ___6___ du ski nautique. J'adore le ski nautique! Mais ce soir, moi, je ___7___ du patin à glace. C'est décidé!

LOUISE   D'accord. Allons-y!

Grammaire supplémentaire

Visit Holt Online

go.hrw.com

KEYWORD: WA3 QUEBEC CITY-4

Jeux interactifs

6 Odile is asking her friends if they play certain sports. Based on their answers, what are her questions? Remember to use the correct forms of **faire**. (**p. 116**)

EXEMPLE   ODILE   **Vous faites du vélo?**
   JEREMY ET VALENTINE   Oui, on adore faire du vélo.

1. ODILE _____
   SYLVIE   Oui, j'aime beaucoup faire du jogging.

2. ODILE _____
   PIERRE   Oui, Sophie et Marie adorent faire de l'aérobic.

3. ODILE _____
   DAVID   Oui, Arthur aime faire de la natation.

4. ODILE _____
   MARION ET   Oui, nous aimons bien faire du ski.
   FRANCINE

5. ODILE _____
   VANESSA   Oui, Elodie et Jérôme aiment beaucoup faire
   du roller en ligne.

6. ODILE _____
   CHRISTINE   Oui, Thérèse aime faire de la randonnée.

7 Rewrite the following sentences, replacing the subject with the pronoun **on.** Be sure to make any necessary changes. (**p. 117**)

1. Nous adorons le théâtre.
2. Marcel et moi aimons faire de la natation après l'école.
3. Est-ce que vous faites du ski nautique au Texas?
4. Vous jouez aux cartes?
5. Nous faisons de l'aérobic.
6. Est-ce que nous faisons du roller en ligne ce week-end?
7. Est-ce que vous faites du théâtre dans votre école?

8 Complete the following sentences with the activity most appropriate for the weather condition or time of year stated. (**p. 119**)

jouer au football américain   regarder la télé

      jouer au tennis

jouer au hockey   nager   jouer à des jeux vidéo

1. En automne, mon frère _____.
2. Quand il fait chaud, les enfants _____.
3. Quand il neige, Jacqueline _____.
4. Quand il pleut, je _____.
5. Quand il fait frais, mon frère et moi _____.

9 François is asking Janine how often she plays certain sports. Rewrite their conversation, using the fragments below. Remember to use the correct form of the verb and to put the adverb in the correct position. (**p. 122**)

FRANÇOIS tu/est-ce que/souvent/faire/de la natation

JANINE faire/de la natation/je/souvent/au printemps/oui

FRANÇOIS faire/du ski/de temps en temps/tu/est-ce que

JANINE faire/du ski/oui/je/quand il neige

FRANÇOIS quelquefois/tu/est-ce que/jouer/au foot

JANINE ne...jamais/jouer/non/au foot/je

10 Vanessa has taken a survey to find out how often teenagers play certain sports. Rewrite her notes, using the adverbs from the box. The meaning of the sentences should remain the same. Use each adverb only once. (**p. 122**)

EXEMPLE   Camille fait du vélo trois fois par semaine.
Camille fait souvent du vélo.

> ne ... jamais   d'habitude   quelquefois
> souvent   une fois par semaine

1. Koffi joue au tennis de temps en temps.
2. Estelle et Olivia font du patin à glace le samedi matin.
3. Quand il pleut, Fatima ne fait pas de jogging.
4. Sébastien joue au golf tous les jours au printemps.

CD-ROM **1** DVD **1**

1 Listen to this radio commercial for the **Village des Sports,** a resort in Quebec. List at least one activity offered in each season.

2 You've decided to spend part of your vacation at the **Village des Sports.** Read the information you've received about the resort. Then, answer the questions that follow.

Village des Sports

c'est l'fun fun fun!

en hiver comme en été

Le plus grand centre du sport au Canada offre du plaisir pour toute la famille.
Services d'accueil, de restauration et de location sur place.

EN ETE
- le tennis
- le volley
- l'athlétisme
- le base-ball
- le roller en ligne
- le ski nautique
- la natation
- l'équitation
- la voile

EN AUTOMNE
- le football
- l'équitation
- la randonnée
- le volley

EN HIVER
- le hockey
- le ski
- le patin à glace
- la luge

AU PRINTEMPS
- le base-ball
- la randonnée
- le roller en ligne
- le tennis

Village des Sports
1860, boul. Valcartier
(418) 844-3725
à 24 km du centre-ville de Québec via
la route 371 Nord

1. Would the **Village des Sports** be good for a family vacation? Why or why not?

2. According to the brochure, in what season(s) can you go . . .
   a. in-line skating?
   c. hiking?
   b. water skiing?
   d. horseback riding?

3. You have a friend who doesn't like cold weather. What three activities could your friend do at the **Village des Sports?**

3
a. You've arrived at the **Village des Sports.** You meet your three roommates, get to know them, and ask them about the activities they enjoy.

b. You and your roommates decide to participate in an activity together. Each of you suggests an activity until you all agree on one.

4 What differences are there between the way students in your area and students in Quebec spend their free time?

5 ## Ecrivons!

You're going to write a letter to your French class back home describing your activities at the **Village des Sports.** Organizing your ideas using the strategy below will help you create your letter.

Stratégie pour écrire

Arranging ideas logically is a helpful way to organize your ideas before you begin writing.

1. Divide a sheet of paper into three separate columns.
2. Label the first column on your paper **J'aime... ,** the next column **Je n'aime pas... ,** and the third column **Le temps.**
3. In the first column, list the activities that you like to participate in at the **Village des Sports.** In the next column, list the activities you dislike, and in the third column, tell what the weather is like there.
4. Now you are ready to write your letter.

J'aime	Je n'aime pas	Le temps
faire du ski		Il fait froid.

6 ## Jeu de rôle

You're a famous Canadian athlete. Your partner, a reporter for the local television station, will interview you about your busy training routine. Tell the interviewer what you do at different times of the year, in various weather conditions, and how often. Then, take the role of the reporter and interview your partner, who will assume the identity of a different Canadian athlete.

Que sais-je?

Can you use what you've learned in this chapter?

Can you tell how much you like or dislike something?
p. 114

1 Can you tell someone how much you like or dislike these activities?

1.　　　2.　　　3.　　　4.　　　5.

2 Can you tell someone which sports and activities you enjoy a lot? Which ones you don't enjoy at all?

Can you exchange information?
p. 116

3 How would you tell someone about a few of your sports and hobbies, using the verbs **jouer** and **faire?**

4 How would you find out if someone plays these games?

1.　　　2.　　　3.

5 How would you tell someone in French . . .
1. what you do in a certain season?
2. what you like to do in a certain month?
3. what you do in certain weather?
4. what you like to do at a certain time of day?

Can you make, accept, and turn down suggestions?
p. 122

6 How would you suggest that . . .
1. you and a friend go waterskiing?
2. you and your friends play baseball?

7 If a friend asked you to go jogging, how would you accept the suggestion? How would you turn it down?

Telling how much you like or dislike something

Beaucoup.	A lot.
surtout	especially
Pas tellement.	Not too much.
Pas beaucoup.	Not very much.
Pas du tout.	Not at all.

Sports and hobbies

faire de l'aérobic	to do aerobics
de l'athlétisme	to do track and field
du jogging	to jog
de la natation	to swim
du patin à glace	to ice-skate
de la photo	to do photography
des photos	to take pictures
du roller en ligne	to in-line skate
du ski	to ski
du ski nautique	to water-ski
du théâtre	to do drama
du vélo	to bike
de la vidéo	to make videos
jouer au base-ball	to play baseball
au basket(-ball)	to play basketball
au foot(ball)	to play soccer
au football américain	to play football
au golf	to play golf
au hockey	to play hockey
à des jeux vidéo	to play video games
au tennis	to play tennis
au volley(-ball)	to play volleyball
aux cartes	to play cards

Other useful expressions

Est-ce que	(introduces a yes-or-no question)

Deuxième étape

Exchanging information

Qu'est-ce que tu fais comme sport?	What sports do you play?
Qu'est-ce que tu fais pour t'amuser?	What do you do to have fun?
Je fais...	I play/do . . .
Je joue...	I play . . .
Je ne fais pas de...	I don't play/do . . .
Je ne joue pas...	I don't play . . .
faire	to do, to play, to make
jouer	to play

Weather

Quel temps fait-il?	What's the weather like?
Il fait beau.	It's nice weather.
Il fait chaud.	It's hot.
Il fait frais.	It's cool.
Il fait froid.	It's cold.
Il pleut.	It's raining.
Il neige.	It's snowing.

Seasons, months, and times

Qu'est-ce que tu fais...	What do you do . . .
le week-end?	on weekends?
le soir?	in the evening?
en vacances?	on vacation?
au printemps?	in the spring?
en été?	in the summer?
en automne?	in the fall?
en hiver?	in the winter?
en janvier?	in January?
en février?	in February?
en mars?	in March?
en avril?	in April?
en mai?	in May?
en juin?	in June?
en juillet?	in July?
en août?	in August?
en septembre?	in September?
en octobre?	in October?
en novembre?	in November?
en décembre?	in December?

Other useful expressions

on	we, they, you

Troisième étape

Making, accepting, and turning down suggestions

On...?	How about . . . ?
D'accord.	OK.
Bonne idée.	Good idea.
Allons-y!	Let's go!
Oui, c'est...	Yes, it's . . .
Désolé(e), mais je ne peux pas.	Sorry, but I can't.
Ça ne me dit rien.	That doesn't interest me.
Non, c'est...	No, it's (that's) . . .

Expressions of frequency

quelquefois	sometimes
...fois par semaine	. . . time(s) a week
de temps en temps	from time to time
souvent	often
rarement	rarely
ne... jamais	never
d'habitude	usually

Allez, viens à Paris!

Capitale de la France

Population : plus de 2.150.000; région parisienne : plus de 10.000.000

Points d'intérêt : la tour Eiffel, l'Arc de triomphe, la cathédrale Notre-Dame, le centre Georges Pompidou, la basilique du Sacré-Cœur

Musées : l'Orangerie, le musée du Louvre, le musée d'Orsay, le musée de l'Homme, le musée Rodin

Parcs et jardins : le jardin du Luxembourg, le Champ-de-Mars, les Tuileries

Parisiens célèbres : Charles Baudelaire, Colette, Victor Hugo, Edith Piaf, Auguste Rodin, Jean-Paul Sartre

Industries : haute couture, finance, technologie, transport, tourisme

go.hrw.com
WA3 PARIS

VIDEO

CD-ROM 2
DVD 1

L'avenue des Champs-Elysées et l'Arc de triomphe ▶

Paris

Paris is a city that has no equal. It is the intellectual and cultural capital of the French-speaking world and also the largest city in Europe, if you include the greater Parisian area. Whether you like to visit museums, go to the theater, sit in cafés, or stroll along tree-lined boulevards, there's something for everyone here. Paris is one of the world's most beautiful and exciting cities!

Visit Holt Online

go.hrw.com

KEYWORD: WA3 PARIS

Activités Internet

1 **Le centre Georges Pompidou**
The public space Parisians call **Beaubourg** houses a major library and the National Museum of Modern Art. Outside, you can see jugglers, magicians, and all kinds of entertainers. It is one of Paris's most popular tourist attractions.

2 **Montmartre**
Many of the streets in this district are lined with artists who sell their work and will even paint your portrait.

3 **La cathédrale Notre-Dame**
In the shadow of this cathedral, booksellers, called **bouquinistes,** sell rare books and posters along the banks of the river Seine.

 Les cafés
In Paris, the terrace of a café is a wonderful place to sit and watch the world go by.

In chapters 5, 6, and 7, you'll meet some Parisians. Paris is a very old city; it is thought to be named after a tribe called the Parisii that settled there 2,300 years ago. Many of the buildings around Paris are several hundred years old, giving it a special character completely different from that of most American cities. At the same time, Paris has all the amenities of a large modern city—a transportation system that is the envy of the world, well-maintained public phones, and streets that are cleaned every morning, for example.

5 La tour Eiffel
This iron skyscraper was erected as a temporary exhibit for the Centennial Exposition in 1889 and has been the object of controversy ever since. It is 320.75 meters tall, including the television antenna added in 1957. To reach the top platform, ride one of the hydraulic elevators or climb the 1,792 stairs!

6 Le stade Roland-Garros
The famous French Open tennis tournament takes place in this stadium every summer.

7 Le métro
The Paris subway is one of the world's most efficient mass-transit systems.

5

On va au café?

Objectives

In this chapter you will learn to

Première étape

- make suggestions
- make excuses
- make a recommendation

Deuxième étape

- get someone's attention
- order food and beverages

Troisième étape

- inquire about and express likes and dislikes
- pay the check

Visit Holt Online

go.hrw.com

KEYWORD: WA3 PARIS-5

Online Edition

◄ On va au café?

MISE EN TRAIN · *Qu'est-ce qu'on prend?*

DVD VIDEO

Stratégie
pour comprendre
Where does this story take place? What do you expect Chloé, Cécile, Thomas, and Sébastien to talk about in that setting? What could happen at the end to make them upset?

Chloé **Thomas** **Cécile** **Le serveur**

1

Chloé : Allô? Sébastien? Salut. C'est Chloé. Dis, on va au café. Tu viens avec nous?

2

Chloé : Sébastien ne peut pas venir avec nous. Il a des devoirs à faire. Bon. On y va?

3

Thomas : Qu'est-ce que vous prenez?
Cécile : Je vais prendre une menthe à l'eau.
Chloé : Euh... je ne sais pas.
Thomas : Moi, je vais prendre une glace.

4

Thomas : C'est combien, les coupes Melba?
Chloé : Trois trente-cinq.

5 **Le serveur :** Vous avez choisi?

Cécile : Apportez-moi une menthe à l'eau, s'il vous plaît.

6 **Thomas :** Tu aimes le fromage?

Chloé : Oui.

Thomas : Prends un croque-monsieur.

Chloé : D'accord. Un croque-monsieur pour moi, s'il vous plaît!

7 **Chloé :** Qu'est-ce que vous avez comme jus de fruit?

Le serveur : Nous avons du jus d'orange, du jus de pomme...

Chloé : Un jus d'orange, s'il vous plaît.

8 **Le serveur :** Une coupe Melba, une coupe Melba, une menthe à l'eau, une eau minérale, un croque-monsieur et un jus d'orange. Bon appétit!

A B C D e

9 **Thomas :** Monsieur! L'addition, s'il vous plaît.

Le serveur : Tout de suite.

10 **Chloé :** Eh, je ne trouve pas mon porte-monnaie! Je n'ai pas d'argent!

Cécile : C'est pas vrai!

Cahier d'activités, p. 49, Act. 1

1 Tu as compris?

Answer the following questions about *Qu'est-ce qu'on prend?*

1. What is the relationship between the teenagers in *Qu'est-ce qu'on prend?*
2. Where are they at the beginning of the story?
3. Where do they decide to go?
4. Who has trouble deciding what to order?
5. What is the problem at the end of the story?

2 Mets en ordre

Mets les phrases suivantes en ordre d'après *Qu'est-ce qu'on prend?*

1. Cécile commande une menthe à l'eau.
2. Thomas demande l'addition.
3. Chloé invite Sébastien à aller au café.
4. Chloé ne retrouve pas son argent.
5. Le serveur dit «Bon appétit!».
6. Chloé commande un jus d'orange.

3 Les deux font la paire

Choisis la bonne réponse d'après *Qu'est-ce qu'on prend?*

1. On va au café?
2. Qu'est-ce que vous prenez?
3. C'est combien, les coupes Melba?
4. Qu'est-ce que vous avez comme jus de fruit?

a. Nous avons du jus d'orange, du jus de pomme...
b. Je vais prendre une menthe à l'eau.
c. Désolé. J'ai des devoirs à faire.
d. Trois trente-cinq.

4 Cherche les expressions

Look back at *Qu'est-ce qu'on prend?* What do the students say to . . .

1. give an excuse for someone?
2. ask if someone's ready to order?
3. order food?
4. ask what kind of fruit juice the restaurant serves?
5. ask how much something costs?
6. ask for the check?

Apportez-moi...	Vous avez choisi?
Il a des devoirs à faire.	L'addition, s'il vous plaît.
Je vais prendre...	
C'est combien,... ?	Qu'est-ce que vous avez comme jus de fruit?

5 Et maintenant, à toi

Chloé is in an embarrassing situation. What do you think she is going to do? Take turns with a partner suggesting ways Chloé and her friends might resolve their problem.

Comment dit-on...?

Making suggestions; making excuses

To make suggestions:

On va au café? *How about going to the café?*
On fait du ski?
On joue au base-ball?

To make excuses:

Désolé(e). J'ai des devoirs à faire. *Sorry. I have homework to do.*
J'ai des courses à faire. *I have errands to do.*
J'ai des trucs à faire. *I have some things to do.*
J'ai des tas de choses à faire. *I have lots of things to do.*
Je ne peux pas parce que... *I can't because . . .*

Cahier d'activités,
pp. 51–52, Act. 6–8

6 **Qu'est-ce que tu as envie de faire?**

Ecoutons Listen to the following dialogues. Do the speakers accept or turn down
the suggestions?

Do you remember the following ways to accept a suggestion?

> **D'accord.**
> **Bonne idée.**

Do you remember the following ways to turn down a suggestion?

> **Ça ne me dit rien. J'aime mieux...**
> **Désolé(e), mais je ne peux pas.**

7 **Qu'est-ce qu'on fait?**

Parlons Suggest to your friends that you all do these activities after class. They will either accept your suggestions or turn them down and make excuses. Take turns making suggestions.

EXEMPLE —On... ?
—**D'accord,...** *or* **Désolé(e),...**

1.

2.

3.

4.

5.

8 **Un petit mot**

Ecrivons You and your friend have agreed to go to the café on Saturday. You can't make it. Write your friend a note. Say that you can't go, make an excuse, and suggest another activity at another time.

Mon ami (e),
Je suis désolé(e), mais...

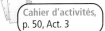

Cahier d'activités,
p. 50, Act. 3

Travaux pratiques de grammaire,
pp. 35–36, Act. 1–4

J'ai soif. Je voudrais...

un jus de pomme

un coca

un citron pressé

un jus d'orange

un sirop de
fraise à l'eau

une eau minérale

un chocolat

une limonade

un café

J'ai faim! Je voudrais...

des crêpes

un croque-monsieur

un sandwich au jambon

un sandwich au saucisson

de la quiche

une omelette

un steak-frites

un sandwich au fromage

un hot-dog

9 Qu'est-ce qu'il commande?

Ecoutons Look at the picture. As the boys tell the waiter what they would like, decide which boy is ordering.

Didier   Minh   Paul   Mamadou   Nabil

10 Vous désirez?

Ecrivons Now, take the role of the server in Activity 9. Write down each boy's order.

11 La fête internationale

Ecrivons Your French class is going to participate in an international food fair at school. You've been assigned to poll your classmates about the types of food and drink they would like to have at the fair. Make a list of five questions you might ask.

Comment dit-on...?

Making a recommendation

To recommend something to eat or drink:

Prends une limonade. (informal) *Have* . . .
Prenez un sandwich. (formal) *Have* . . .

Travaux pratiques de grammaire, p. 36, Act. 5

The verb *prendre*

Prendre is an irregular verb.

prendre *(to take; to have food or drink)*

Je	**prends**	Nous	**prenons**
Tu	**prends**	Vous	**prenez**
Il/Elle/On	**prend**	Ils/Elles	**prennent**

Tu **prends** des frites?

Nous **prenons** un croque-monsieur.

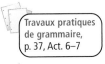

Travaux pratiques
de grammaire,
p. 37, Act. 6–7

Grammaire supplémentaire,
p. 160, Act. 1–2

Cahier d'activités, p. 51, Act. 5; p. 52, Act. 9

12 **Grammaire en contexte**

Ecrivons You and your friends are deciding what to have in a café. Complete the conversation with the appropriate forms of the verb **prendre.**

—Alors, qu'est-ce que vous ___1___ ?

—Moi, j'ai très faim, je ___2___ un steak-frites.

—Et toi, Anne, qu'est-ce que tu ___3___ ?

—Michel et moi, nous ___4___ une pizza.

—Et Isabelle, qu'est-ce qu'elle ___5___ ?

—Isabelle et Sylvie n'ont pas faim, mais elles ont très soif. Alors elles ___6___ un coca.

DE BONS CONSEILS

Resist the temptation to match English with French word-for-word. In many cases, it doesn't work. For example, in English you say *I am hungry,* while in French you say **J'ai faim** (literally, *I have hunger*).

13 **Au café**

Parlons What are these people having?

Paul et Julie

Sandrine

Eric

Michel

Fabienne

PANORAMA CULTUREL

Où retrouves-tu tes amis?

Where do you go to meet with your friends? Here's what some francophone students had to say about where they go and what they do.

Clémentine,
France

«Nous allons dans des cafés ou chez d'autres amis. Quand il fait beau, [on va] à la piscine. Ça dépend du temps qu'il fait.»

Armande,
Côte d'Ivoire

«Je vais à la maison, soit chez moi, ou bien chez eux [mes amis]. Puis on va à l'Alocodrome, enfin pour prendre un peu d'aloco, puis on revient à la maison.»

Déjan,
France

«J'aime bien aller au café après l'école. On va jouer un peu au baby, au flipper et après, je rentre chez moi faire les devoirs. On a un parc à côté de chez nous et on rencontre tous nos amis.»

Qu'en penses-tu?

1. Where do these students go to meet their friends?
2. Do you and your friends like to go to the same places and do the same things as these teenagers? Where do you go? What do you do?

Savais-tu que... ?

Many cultures have a particular kind of place where people gather. In many francophone countries, a café is more than just a place to eat; it's a social institution! Cafés primarily serve beverages. They may also serve bread (**pain**) or flaky crescent rolls (**croissants**) in the morning, and some cafés serve lunch. If you order something, you may stay in most cafés as long as you like. In some African countries, people like to go to open-air restaurants called **maquis.** They usually open only in the evening and serve traditional snack foods such as fried plantains (**aloco**), as well as full meals.

Comment dit-on...?

Getting someone's attention; ordering food and beverages

To get the server's attention:

Excusez-moi.
Monsieur! Madame! Mademoiselle!
La carte, s'il vous plaît. *The menu, please.*

The server may ask:

Vous avez choisi? *Have you decided/chosen?*
Vous prenez? *What are you having?*

You might want to ask:

Vous avez des jus de fruit?
Qu'est-ce que vous avez comme boissons? *What kind of drinks do you have?*
Qu'est-ce qu'il y a à boire? *What is there to drink?*

To order:

Je voudrais un hamburger.
Je vais prendre un coca, **s'il vous plaît.** *I'll have . . . , please.*
Un sandwich, **s'il vous plaît.** . . . , *please.*
Donnez-moi un hot-dog, **s'il vous plaît.** *Please give me . . .*
Apportez-moi une limonade, **s'il vous plaît.** *Please bring me . . .*

Cahier d'activités, p. 53, Act. 10–12;
p. 54, Act. 14; p. 55, Act. 16–17

14 C'est le serveur ou le client?

Ecoutons Listen to these remarks and decide whether the server (**le serveur/la serveuse**) or the customer (**le client/la cliente**) is speaking.

15 Méli-mélo!

Lisons/Parlons Unscramble the following conversation between a server and a customer. Then, act it out with a partner.

—Qu'est-ce qu'il y a comme sandwiches?
—Bien sûr.
—Eh bien, donnez-moi un sandwich au fromage, s'il vous plaît.
—Vous avez choisi?
—Il y a des sandwiches au jambon, au saucisson, au fromage...

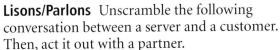

A la française

If you need time to think during a conversation, you can say **Eh bien...** and pause for a moment before you continue speaking.

—**Vous prenez, mademoiselle?**
—**Eh bien... un steak-frites, s'il vous plaît.**

At first you'll have to make a conscious effort to do this. The more you practice, the more natural it will become.

16 On prend un sandwich?

 **Lisons/Parlons** You've stopped at a café for lunch. Get the server's attention, look at the menu, and order. Take turns playing the role of the server.

LA MAISON DU SANDWICH

NOS SANDWICHES

au jambon de Paris	3,00€	au gruyère	3,00€
au jambon de pays	3,50€	au camembert	3,00€
au saucisson	3,00€	au saumon	4,50€
au pâté	3,50€	au crabe	4,00€
mixte (jambon et gruyère)	3,50€	végétarien	3,50€

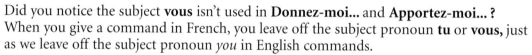

Grammaire

The imperative

Did you notice the subject **vous** isn't used in **Donnez-moi...** and **Apportez-moi...** ? When you give a command in French, you leave off the subject pronoun **tu** or **vous,** just as we leave off the subject pronoun *you* in English commands.

• When you write the **tu** form of a regular **-er** verb as a command, drop the final **s** of the usual verb ending.

> Tu écoutes... → **Ecoute!**
>
> Tu regardes... → **Regarde!**

• If the verb isn't a regular **-er** verb, the spelling of the command form doesn't change.

> Tu fais... → **Fais** les devoirs!
>
> Tu prends... → **Prends** un hot-dog, Paul!

• Remember to use the **tu** form when you talk with family members and people your own age or younger. Use the **vous** form when you talk with people older than you or with more than one person.

> **Prenez** un coca, Marc et Eve.

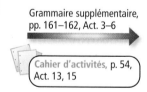

Grammaire supplémentaire, pp. 161–162, Act. 3–6

Cahier d'activités, p. 54, Act. 13, 15

Travaux pratiques de grammaire, p. 38, Act. 8–10

17 Grammaire en contexte

Parlons Your friends can't decide how they want to spend their Saturday afternoon. You're the one they always turn to for advice. Respond to each of their statements below by telling them what they should do.

EXEMPLE —Nous avons faim.

—**Prenez un sandwich.**

1. Nous avons soif.
2. J'aime beaucoup la musique.
3. Il fait beau aujourd'hui.
4. Nous avons un examen demain.
5. Il fait frais.
6. Je voudrais faire du sport.

18 Grammaire en contexte

Parlons You don't know what to order at the café. The server makes some suggestions for you, but you don't like the suggestions. Take turns playing the server.

EXEMPLE —**Prenez un sandwich au fromage.**

—**Non, je n'aime pas le fromage.**

—**Alors, prenez un sandwich au jambon.**

—**Non, apportez-moi un hot-dog, s'il vous plaît.**

Note culturelle

In France, waiters and waitresses are considered professionals. In better restaurants, waiters and waitresses must not only be good servers but they must also be knowledgeable about food and wine. Even in simple restaurants or cafés, servers take great pride in their work. Contrary to what you may have seen in American movies, it is impolite to address a waiter as **Garçon.** It is more polite to say **Monsieur** to a waiter, and **Madame** or **Mademoiselle** to a waitress. It is expected that diners will take time to enjoy their food, so service in French restaurants may seem slow to Americans. It is not uncommon for a meal to last several hours.

19 A la crêperie

Lisons/Parlons You and some friends get together at a **crêperie.** Look at the menu and order. Take turns playing the server.

La Crêperie Normande

Crêpes salées :
Jambon - fromage . . . . 4,50€

Epinards - crème fraîche . . . . 4,50€

Champignons . . . . 5,00€

Crêpes sucrées :
Sucre . . . . 3,50€

Banane - Chantilly . . . . 4,50€

Chocolat . . . . 4,00€

Glace vanille - sauce noisette . . . . 5,00€

20 Mon journal

Ecrivons Make a list of the foods and drinks you like to have when you go out with your friends. Then, mention several items you'd try if you were at a café in France.

DEUXIEME ETAPE   *cent cinquante-trois* **153**

Comment dit-on...?

Inquiring about and expressing likes and dislikes

To ask how someone likes the food or drink:

Comment tu trouves ça? *How do you like it?*

To say you like your food/drink:

C'est... *It's . . .*
   bon! *good!*
   excellent! *excellent!*
   délicieux! *delicious!*
   pas mauvais. *pretty good.*

To say you don't like your food/drink:

C'est... *It's . . .*
   pas bon. *not good.*
   pas terrible. *not so great.*
   dégoûtant. *gross.*
   mauvais. *bad.*

Cahier d'activités, pp. 56–57, Act. 19–21

Travaux pratiques de grammaire, p. 39, Act. 11–12

21 C'est bon, ça?

Ecoutons Listen to the following remarks. Do the speakers like or dislike the food they've been served?

Note culturelle

French speakers have a tendency to use understatement **(la litote).** For instance, if the food were bad, they might say **C'est pas terrible.** Similarly, rather than saying something is good, they would say **C'est pas mauvais.**

22 A mon avis...

Parlons The school cafeteria is thinking of adding some items to the menu. A poll is being taken among the students. Discuss each of the items below with a partner.

1.

2.

3.

4.

23 **Ça, c'est bon.**

Parlons You and your partner are in a café. Ask if your partner has decided what to order and tell what you think of his or her choice.

> EXEMPLE   — Tu as choisi? Qu'est-ce que tu vas prendre?
>
> — Euh... je vais prendre un hot-dog.
>
> — Un hot-dog? C'est dégoûtant! *or* Bonne idée. C'est délicieux.

 24 **Chère correspondante**

Ecrivons Your French pen pal Cécile asked you what teenagers in America eat or drink when they get together. Write a brief note in French telling her what you and your friends have when you go out and what you think of each item.

Comment dit-on...?

Paying the check

> L'addition, s'il vous plaît.
>
> Tout de suite, madame.

CD-ROM **2**
DVD **1**

To ask for the check:

L'addition, s'il vous plaît.
The check, please.

The server might answer:

Oui, tout de suite. *Yes, right away.*
Un moment, s'il vous plaît.

To ask how much something is:

C'est combien, un sandwich?
Ça fait combien, s'il vous plaît?
How much is it, . . . ? (total)

C'est huit **euros.**
Ça fait cinquante **euros.**
It's . . . euros. (total)

Cahier d'activités, pp. 57–58, Act. 23–24

Grammaire supplémentaire, p. 163, Act. 9

 25 **Au restaurant**

Ecoutons Listen to the following remarks. Are the speakers ordering or getting ready to pay the check?

Tu te rappelles?

Do you remember the numbers from 20–100?

20 **vingt**	50 **cinquante**	80 **quatre-vingts**
30 **trente**	60 **soixante**	90 **quatre-vingt-dix**
40 **quarante**	70 **soixante-dix**	100 **cent**

Travaux pratiques de grammaire, pp. 39–40, Act. 13–14

Grammaire supplémentaire, p. 163, Act. 7–8

26 Ça fait combien?

Parlons You and your friend have just finished eating at a café. Look at this check, tell what you had (**Moi, j'ai pris...**), and figure out how much each of you owes.

EXEMPLE   —Moi, j'ai pris...
          —Ça fait... euros.

Note culturelle

In cafés and restaurants, a 15% tip is included in the check if the words **service compris** are posted or written on the menu. If you're not sure, it's acceptable to ask **Le service est compris?** It's customary, however, to leave a little extra if the service is particularly good.

```
        LA  GIRAFE
      Port de Cavalaire
    Tél : 04 94 64 40 31

  28-09-02

  CROQUE-MONSIEUR     3,50€
  STEAK-FRITES        4,50€
  EAU MINERALE        1,50€
  COCA                2,00€

  TOTAL              11,50€

  La Direction souhaite
  que cet instant de
  détente vous ait été
      AGREABLE
```

27 Qu'est-ce qu'on dit?

Ecrivons Write what you think the people in this scene are saying. Then, with a partner, compare what you both have written.

28

De l'école au travail

Parlons During the summer you found a job as a waitperson at the Café Sport. Ask your customers if they have decided what to order and what they would like to eat and drink. They'll tell you what they like to eat and you'll suggest dishes according to their tastes. At the end, tell them how much they have to pay and hand them the check.

CAFE SPORT

Sandwiches		BOISSONS	
Fromage	2,50 €	Jus de fruit	2,00 €
Jambon	3,00 €	orange, pomme, pamplemousse	
Saucisson	3,00 €		
Hamburger	3,50 €	Limonade	1,50 €
Hot-dog	2,50 €	Café	1,50 €
Steak-frites	5,00 €	Cola	2,00 €
Croque-monsieur	3,50 €	Eau minérale	1,50 €
Pizza	3,50 €	Chocolat	2,50 €
Frites	1,50 €		
Glace	1,50 €		

The nasal sound [ã]

Listen carefully to the vowel sounds in the following words: **ans, en.** These words contain the nasal sound [ã]. It's called a nasal sound because part of the air goes through the back of your mouth and nose when you make the sound. Listen to the English word *sandwich,* and the French **sandwich.** Is the first syllable pronounced the same in the two words? The sound in French is a pure nasal sound, with no trace of the *n* sound in it. In English you say *envy,* but in French you say **envie.** The nasal sound [ã] has four possible spellings: **an, am, en,** and **em.**

These letter combinations don't always represent a nasal sound. If another vowel follows the **n** or the **m,** or if the **n** or **m** is doubled, there may not be a nasal sound. You'll have to learn the pronunciation when you learn the word.

Listen to the following pairs of words and compare the sounds.

France/*ani*mal   pr*en*d/pr*en*ez   *jam*bon/*ami*   *en*vie/*en*nemi

A. A prononcer

Repeat the following words.

en France	attendez	comment	soixante
anglais	dimanche	jambon	temps
orange	tellement	vent	souvent

B. A lire

Take turns with a partner reading the following sentences aloud.

1. Il a cent francs.
2. J'ai un excellent roman allemand.
3. Elle a danse et sciences nat vendredi.
4. Moi, je vais prendre un sandwich au jambon.

C. A écrire

You're going to hear a short dialogue. Write down what you hear.

Des menus de cafés

A. When you look at menus, what information are you usually looking for? Can you find this type of information on these menus?

B. French cuisine is enjoyed the world over. However, you can often find dishes from other cultures at French cafés and restaurants.

   1. Which items on the menus are typical American dishes?

   2. What French words might you find on American menus?

   3. What other French words do you know that are related to food and restaurants?

C. In the Café des Lauriers, what ingredients do the **salade niçoise,** the **salade mexicaine,** and the **salade sicilienne** have in common?

SNACK • BAR Café DES LAURIERS

Salade verte	3,00€
Salade niçoise	5,75€
(salade verte, tomates, œufs, haricots verts, thon, olives)	
Salade mexicaine	6,00€
(salade verte, tomates, maïs, poivrons, thon, olives)	
Salade sicilienne	6,00€
(salade verte, tomates, basilic, mozzarella, huile d'olive)	
Assiette anglaise	6,75€
(jambon blanc, saucisson, rôti de porc, beurre)	
Sandwiches	
jambon blanc	.4,25€
saucisson	4,25€
pâté	4,50€
fromage	4,00€
Croque-monsieur	4,00€
Portion fromage	2,75€
Pizza	4,50€
Quiche	4,50€
Hamburger	.4,50€

FONTAINE ELYSÉE

SANDWICHES

Jambon cru	4,50€
Jambon de Paris	4,00€
Pâté	4,00€
Mixte	5,50€
Roquefort aux noix	4,50€

OMELETTES

Jambon	5,50€
Fromage	5,50€
Mixte	6,00€

PLATS DIVERS

Croque-monsieur	4,50€
Escargots (les 6)	7,75€
Hot-Dog 1 Saucisse	4,50€
Hot-Dog 2 Saucisses	8,50€

BOISSONS CHAUDES

Café express	2,25€
Décaféiné	2,25€
Café ou chocolat viennois	4,50€
Café crème	4,00€
Cappuccino	4,75€

BOISSONS FRAICHES

Eau minérale, limonade	4,25€
Cola	4,50€
Jus de fruit	4,50€
raisin, poire, abricot, pamplemousse, ananas	

SPECIALITES

COUPE CHAMPS-ELYSEES :
Chocolat - Pistache - Caramel - Sauce Chocolat - Mandarine Impériale - Chantilly — 8,00€

BANANA SPLIT :
Glace -Vanille - Chocolat - Banane Fruit - Sauce Chocolat - Chantilly — 6,25€

COUPE MELBA :
Vanille - Pêche Fruit - Chantilly - Sauce Fraise — 6,25€

D. Which café lists the beverages served? Do you recognize any of them? What is the difference between **BOISSONS FRAICHES** and **BOISSONS CHAUDES?**

E. How many different cognates can you find on the menus? (You should be able to find at least ten!)

F. Read the following statements about your friends' likes and dislikes. Which café would you recommend to each one?

1. **Chantal a soif, mais elle n'a pas faim. Elle aime les jus de fruit.**
2. **Michel adore la glace.**
3. **Jean-Paul est végétarien.**
4. **Mai voudrait une omelette.**
5. **Alain aime les quiches.**

G. Judging from the menus, what are the differences between the two cafés? What are the specialties of each one?

H. If you were invited to go out and were given a choice, which café would you choose? Why? Which one would you choose if you had to pay?

I. If you had 15 € to spend, what would you order?

J. Now, make your own menu. Plan what you want to serve and how you want the menu to look. Will you have any illustrations? Don't forget to include prices.

Cahier d'activités, p. 59, Act. 26

CD-ROM 2
DVD 1

Visit Holt Online

go.hrw.com

KEYWORD: WA3 PARIS-5

Jeux interactifs

Première étape

Objectives Making suggestions; making excuses; making a recommendation

1 Choose the appropriate completion for each sentence. (**p. 149**)

1. Guillaume et Ludovic...
2. Paul...
3. Anne et Lucie...
4. Marie-Lise et toi...
5. André et moi...
6. Alice...
7. Moi, je...

    a. prend un jus de pomme; elle a soif.
    b. prenons des hot-dogs.
    c. prenez un chocolat.
    d. prennent du jus d'orange; elles ont très soif.
    e. prends un croque-monsieur.
    f. prennent un sandwich.
    g. prend un steak-frites; il a faim.

2 You and your friends are deciding what to order in a café. Complete the sentences that follow with the correct forms of **prendre.** (**p. 149**)

1. Tu _____ un jus de pomme?
2. Eric _____ un hot-dog.
3. Vous _____ un café?
4. Moi, je _____ une limonade.
5. Elles _____ des sandwiches.
6. Nous _____ des cocas.
7. Jean et Alphonse _____ un steak-frites.
8. Le professeur _____ un croque-monsieur.

3 You and your friends are browsing through a basket full of items on sale. Tell your friends what to get (**prendre**) based on what they tell you about their favorite colors. (**p. 152**)

> un jean noir   des baskets bleues
>
> des sweat-shirts orange   un tee-shirt rouge
>
> des pull-overs verts
>
> un short blanc   un bracelet rose

EXEMPLE   Céline : J'aime le rouge. **Prends le tee-shirt rouge!**

1. Valentine et Sophie : On adore l'orange.
2. Jérôme : Moi, j'aime bien le noir.
3. Clément : Moi, j'aime le blanc.
4. Anne et Lydie : On aime bien le bleu.
5. Aurélie : Moi, j'aime le rose.
6. Marcel et Pascal : On adore le vert.

4 A physical education teacher is encouraging her students to exercise. Based on their objections, write what she had told them to do. (**p. 152**)

EXEMPLE   —**Faites du sport!**
                 —Mais on n'aime pas faire du sport!

1. —Mais je n'aime pas faire de la natation!
2. —Mais on n'aime pas faire du jogging!
3. —Mais on n'aime pas jouer au basket!
4. —Mais je n'aime pas jouer au tennis!
5. —Mais nous n'aimons pas jouer au football!
6. —Mais je n'aime pas faire du roller en ligne!

GRAMMAIRE SUPPLÉMENTAIRE   *cent soixante et un*   **161**

5 Rewrite the following requests, using the imperative of the verbs in parentheses followed by **-moi.** (**p. 152**)

    EXEMPLE   —Monsieur, je voudrais un café, s'il vous plaît. (apporter)

                 —**Apportez-moi un café,** s'il vous plaît.

1. —Maman, je voudrais une limonade, s'il te plaît. (apporter)

   —_____, s'il te plaît.

2. —Jérémy, je voudrais un sandwich au fromage, s'il te plaît. (donner)

   —_____, s'il te plaît.

3. —Monsieur, je voudrais une eau minérale, s'il vous plaît. (donner)

   —_____, s'il vous plaît.

4. —Mademoiselle, je voudrais un coca, s'il vous plaît. (apporter)

   —_____, s'il vous plaît.

5. —Bérénice, je voudrais un chocolat, s'il te plaît. (apporter)

   —_____, s'il te plaît.

6 Mr. and Mrs. Laforge are in a restaurant with their two children. Complete their conversation below with the correct forms of the verbs in parentheses. (**pp. 149, 151, 152**)

ERIC	Maman, j'___**1**___ (avoir) faim. Est-ce que je peux ___**2**___ (prendre) une pizza?
MME LAFORGE	Oui, c'est une bonne idée. Et toi, Emilie, tu ___**3**___ (avoir) faim?
EMILIE	Non, mais j'___**4**___ (avoir) soif. Est-ce que je peux ___**5**___ (prendre) un coca?
MME LAFORGE	Non. ___**6**___ (Prendre) un jus de fruit, ils sont délicieux ici. Et toi, Marc, tu ___**7**___ (prendre) un croque-monsieur ou tu ___**8**___ (préférer) un sandwich au fromage?
M. LAFORGE	Un sandwich au fromage. Et toi, Marie?
MME LAFORGE	Moi, j'___**9**___ (adore) les œufs. Je ___**10**___ (prendre) une omelette.
LE SERVEUR	Vous ___**11**___ (avoir) choisi?
M. LAFORGE	Oui, ___**12**___ (apporter)-nous une pizza, une omelette, un sandwich au fromage, deux jus d'orange et deux eaux minérales, s'il vous plaît.

7 Maud would like to know how much the following items cost. Write the waiter's answers to her questions. The prices are given in parentheses. Write out the amounts in French. (**p. 155**)

EXEMPLE   C'est combien, la pizza suprême? (10, 50 €) **C'est dix euros cinquante.**

1. C'est combien, le steak-frites? (6,50 €)
2. C'est combien, l'omelette au jambon? (5,75 €)
3. C'est combien, la salade niçoise? (7,75 €)
4. C'est combien, trois sandwiches au rosbif? (13,25 €)
5. C'est combien, le couscous? (11,50 €)
6. C'est combien, le croque-monsieur et le café? (9,75 €)

8 Write out in French the number that would come next in each of the series below. (**p. 155**)

1. vingt-deux, quarante-quatre, soixante-six...
2. seize, trente-deux, quarante-huit...
3. onze, trente et un, cinquante et un...
4. quatre-vingt-quinze, quatre-vingt-dix, quatre-vingt-cinq...
5. soixante-dix, quatre-vingts, quatre-vingt-dix...
6. vingt-cinq, trente-cinq, quarante-cinq...

9 Choose the correct form of the verb. (**pp. 151, 152, 155**)

1. C' _____ combien un hamburger?
   a. est
   b. a
   c. es

2. Mathieu, _____ ton hot-dog.
   a. manges
   b. mange
   c. mangez

3. Sabine et Laure, _____ une pizza.
   a. prends
   b. prenez
   c. prendre

4. _____-moi un coca, s'il vous plaît.
   a. Apportez
   b. Apportes
   c. Apporter

5. Comment tu _____ ça?
   a. trouves
   b. trouve
   c. trouvez

6. Ça _____ combien?
   a. fait
   b. fais
   c. faire

Mise en pratique

CD-ROM **2**
DVD **1**

Visit Holt Online
go.hrw.com
KEYWORD: WA3 PARIS-5
Self-Test

1 In which café would you most likely hear these conversations?

Café de Paris

15, Place du Palais - 75004 Paris
Téléphone 01-43-54-20-21

Nos *glaces*

Coupe Melba 7,50
Coupe Nougat 7,00
Banana Split 6,50

Nos *boissons*

Eau minérale 2,00
Jus de fruit 2,25
Café 1,75
Thé 1,25

SERVICE COMPRIS 15%

87, Avenue Victor Hugo -
75017 Paris
Tél. 01-45-62-52-53

Sandwiches

Croque-monsieur	4,50
Sandwich au jambon	3,75
Sandwich au fromage	3,00
Sandwich au rosbif	3,75

Boissons

Orangina, Coca	1,50
Eau minérale	1,75
Café	1,25
Jus de fruit	2,00

Café Américain

135, Boulevard d'Argençon • 75008 Paris
• Téléphone 01-44-15-30-33

★ **Pizzas** ★

Trois fromages . . . 7,50
Suprême 9,75

★ **Plats** ★

Couscous 7,50
Steak-frites 6,75

★ **Boissons** ★

Coca 2,00
Limonade 2,25
Eau minérale 2,50

S E R V I C E   C O M P R I S   1 5 %

2 You and your partner are hungry. Suggest that you go to a café, decide what you both want to eat, and choose one of the cafés above.

3 From what you know about French cafés, are these statements true or false?

1. If you don't see **service compris** on the menu, you should leave a tip.

2. To call the waiter, you should say **Garçon!**

3. It is usually acceptable to stay in a French café for a long time, as long as you've ordered something to eat or drink.

4. If a French person says **C'est pas mauvais,** he or she doesn't like the food.

4 # Ecrivons!

The French Club at your school is going to have a picnic to raise money. Plan the picnic with two classmates and then create your own poster announcing it.

First, create a name and catchy slogan to attract attention to your event. Determine the time and place of the picnic, the food, and the activities planned. Include a brief description of the purpose of the event. You should also decide how much each item will cost. Jot down all of your decisions.

Stratégie pour écrire

Arranging ideas spatially is a useful way to organize information before you write. It's a way of creating a type of blueprint to show how your finished product will look.

Now, you're ready to create your blueprint. On a sheet of paper, draw a box for each item that you will include on your poster (title, slogan, date, time, place, food, and so on) in the place where you want the information to appear. Label each box with the type of information that will go in that space.

Next, using the blueprint you've developed, create your poster promoting the French Club picnic. Use what you've learned in this chapter, such as commands. You might add drawings or magazine cutouts to illustrate your poster.

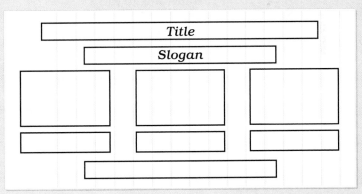

5 # Jeu de rôle

The day of the French Club picnic has arrived. One person in your group will act as host, the others will be the guests. The host will ask people what they want. Guests will tell what they want and talk about how they like the food and drink. After eating, suggest activities and decide which one you'll participate in.

Que sais-je?

Can you use what you've learned in this chapter?

Can you make suggestions, excuses, and recommendations?
pp. 145, 148

1 How would you suggest to a friend that you . . .
1. go to the café?   2. play tennis?

2 How would you turn down a suggestion and make an excuse?

3 How would you recommend to a friend something . . .
1. to eat?   2. to drink?

Can you get someone's attention and order food and beverages?
p. 151

4 In a café, how would you . . .
1. get the server's attention?
2. ask what kinds of sandwiches they serve?
3. ask what there is to drink?

5 How would you say that you're . . .
1. hungry?   2. thirsty?

6 How would you order . . .
1. something to eat?   2. something to drink?

7 How would you tell what people are having, using the verb **prendre**?

1. il   2. tu   3. nous   4. ils

Can you inquire about and express likes and dislikes?
p. 154

8 How would you ask a friend how he or she likes a certain food?

9 How would you tell someone what you think of these items?

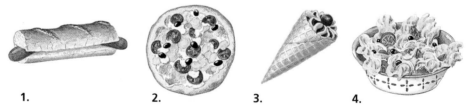

1.   2.   3.   4.

Can you pay the check?
p. 155

10 How would you ask how much each item in number 9 costs?

11 How would you ask for the check?

12 How would you ask what the total is?

Première étape

Making suggestions; making excuses

On va au café?	How about going to the café?
On... ?	How about . . . ?
Désolé(e). J'ai des devoirs à faire.	Sorry. I have homework to do.
J'ai des courses à faire.	I have errands to do.
J'ai des trucs à faire.	I have some things to do.
J'ai des tas de choses à faire.	I have lots of things to do.
Je ne peux pas parce que...	I can't because . . .

Foods and beverages

un croque-monsieur	toasted ham and cheese sandwich
un sandwich au jambon	ham sandwich
au saucisson	salami sandwich
au fromage	cheese sandwich
un hot-dog	hot dog
un steak-frites	steak and French fries
une quiche	quiche
une omelette	omelet
une crêpe	very thin pancake
une eau minérale	mineral water
une limonade	lemon soda
un citron pressé	lemonade
un sirop de fraise (à l'eau)	water with strawberry syrup
un coca	cola
un jus d'orange	orange juice
un jus de pomme	apple juice
un café	coffee
un chocolat	hot chocolate

Making a recommendation

Prends/Prenez... prendre	Have . . . to take; to have food or drink

Other useful expressions

avoir soif	to be thirsty
avoir faim	to be hungry

Deuxième étape

Getting someone's attention

Excusez-moi.	Excuse me.
Monsieur!	Waiter!
Madame!	Waitress!
Mademoiselle!	Waitress!
La carte, s'il vous plaît.	The menu, please.

Ordering food and beverages

Vous avez choisi?	Have you decided/chosen?
Vous prenez?	What are you having?
Vous avez... ?	Do you have . . . ?
Qu'est-ce que vous avez comme boissons?	What do you have to drink?
Qu'est-ce qu'il y a à boire?	What is there to drink?
Je voudrais...	I'd like . . .
Je vais prendre... , s'il vous plaît.	I'll have . . . , please.
... , s'il vous plaît.	. . . , please.
Donnez-moi... , s'il vous plaît.	Please give me . . .
Apportez-moi... , s'il vous plaît.	Please bring me . . .

Troisième étape

Inquiring about and expressing likes and dislikes

Comment tu trouves ça?	How do you like it?
C'est...	It's . . .
bon!	good!
excellent!	excellent!
délicieux!	delicious!
pas mauvais!	pretty good!
pas bon.	not good.
pas terrible.	not so great.
dégoûtant.	gross.
mauvais.	bad.

Paying the check

L'addition, s'il vous plaît.	The check, please.
Oui, tout de suite.	Yes, right away.
Un moment, s'il vous plaît.	One moment, please.
C'est combien,... ?	How much is . . . ?
Ça fait combien, s'il vous plaît?	How much is it, please?
C'est... euros.	It's . . . euros.
Ça fait... euros.	It's . . . euros.

6
Amusons-nous!

Objectives

In this chapter you will learn to

Première étape

• make plans

Deuxième étape

• extend and respond to invitations

Troisième étape

• arrange to meet someone

Visit Holt Online

go.hrw.com

KEYWORD: WA3 PARIS-6

Online Edition

▶ Ici, les Parisiens se relaxent dans le jardin devant le palais du Luxembourg.

cent soixante-neuf **169**

MISE EN TRAIN • *Projets de week-end*

Stratégie pour comprendre
What do you think the title of this episode means? What do you think Mathieu and Isabelle are talking about? Can you guess from what you see in the photos?

Isabelle   **Mathieu**

Vendredi après-midi...

1

Mathieu : Salut, Isabelle. Dis, qu'est-ce que tu vas faire demain?

Isabelle : Oh, pas grand-chose. Le matin, je vais aller à mon cours de danse. L'après-midi, je vais faire les magasins. Mais le soir, je suis libre.

2

Mathieu : Il y a un concert super à Bercy : Patrick Bruel. J'aimerais bien y aller. Tu veux venir avec moi?

Isabelle : Oh non, je n'ai pas envie d'aller à un concert.

Mathieu : Ah, dommage...

3

Mathieu : Et dimanche après-midi, tu es libre?

Isabelle : Dimanche? Oui, je n'ai rien de prévu.

Mathieu : Tu veux aller au zoo?

Isabelle : Ah, non, je déteste les zoos.

4

Mathieu : Alors, allons au Louvre.

Isabelle : Non, je n'aime pas trop les musées.

5   **Mathieu :**   Qu'est-ce que tu veux faire, alors?

6   **Isabelle :**   S'il fait beau, on peut faire une promenade au palais de Chaillot. On peut même monter au sommet de la tour Eiffel.
   Mathieu :   Bof.

7   **Isabelle :**   J'ai une idée! Tu ne veux pas aller faire un tour dans un bateau-mouche?
   Mathieu :   Ça, non. C'est pas terrible.

8   **Isabelle :**   On va au Sacré-Cœur?
   Mathieu :   Non, je n'ai pas envie.

9   **Mathieu :**   On peut tout simplement aller au cinéma. Tu veux?
   Isabelle :   D'accord. Je veux bien. Qu'est-ce que tu veux voir comme film?
   Mathieu :   Moi, je propose *Dracula*. Ça passe à 16h40 et à 18h55.

10   **Isabelle :**   Oh non, je n'aime pas les films d'horreur. Je préfère aller voir un film comique.
   Mathieu :   Oh non! Encore un film comique?! Tu sais, c'est bizarre. On n'est jamais d'accord!

Cahier d'activités, p. 61, Act. 1–2

1 Tu as compris?

Answer the following questions according to *Projets de week-end.* Don't be afraid to guess.

1. What are Isabelle's plans for tomorrow?
2. What day and time of day is it?
3. Can you name three places where Mathieu suggests they go?
4. Can you name three things that Isabelle prefers to do?
5. What do they finally agree to do? What problem remains?

2 Vrai ou faux?

1. Isabelle aime aller au zoo.
2. Isabelle a un cours de danse.
3. Mathieu aime la musique de Patrick Bruel.
4. Isabelle aime bien les musées.
5. Isabelle veut voir un film d'horreur dimanche après-midi.

3 Mets en ordre

Mets les phrases en ordre d'après *Projets de week-end.*

1. Isabelle propose d'aller au palais de Chaillot.
2. Mathieu propose d'aller au zoo.
3. Isabelle propose d'aller au Sacré-Cœur.
4. Mathieu ne veut pas faire de promenade.
5. Isabelle refuse d'aller au concert.
6. Isabelle accepte d'aller au cinéma.

4 Où est-ce qu'on veut aller?

Choisis les activités qu'Isabelle veut faire et les activités que Mathieu préfère.

aller voir un film comique	aller voir un film d'horreur	faire une promenade au palais de Chaillot
aller à un concert		aller au musée
aller au zoo	faire un tour en bateau	aller au Sacré-Cœur

5 Invitations et refus

Match Mathieu's suggestions for weekend activities with Isabelle's refusals.

Tu veux...

1. aller au concert de Patrick Bruel?
2. aller au Louvre?
3. aller au zoo?
4. aller voir *Dracula?*

Désolée, mais...

a. je déteste les zoos.
b. je préfère aller voir un film comique.
c. je n'aime pas trop les musées.
d. je n'ai pas envie.

6 Et maintenant, à toi

How would you react to Mathieu and Isabelle's suggestions for the weekend? Which would you choose to do? Why? Compare your answers with a partner's.

Comment dit-on...?

Making plans

To ask what a friend's planning to do:

> **Qu'est-ce que tu vas faire** demain? *What are you going to do . . . ?*
> **Tu vas faire quoi** ce week-end? *What are you going to do . . . ?*

To tell what you're going to do:

> Vendredi, **je vais** faire du vélo.
> Samedi après-midi, **je vais** aller au café. } *I'm going to . . .*
> Dimanche, **je vais** regarder la télé.
> **Pas grand-chose.** *Not much.*
> **Rien de spécial.** *Nothing special.*

7 Les projets de Thérèse

Ecoutons Listen as Sophie asks Thérèse about her plans for the weekend. Write down at least three things Thérèse plans to do.

Vocabulaire

regarder un match	*to watch a game (on TV)*
manger quelque chose	*to eat something*
voir un film	*to see a movie*
aller voir un match	*to go see a game*
voir une pièce	*to see a play*
faire une promenade	*to go for a walk*
faire les vitrines	*to window-shop*
faire un pique-nique	*to have a picnic*
aller à une boum	*to go to a party*

Travaux pratiques de grammaire, p. 41, Act. 1–2

Note de grammaire

If you want to say that you do an activity regularly on a certain day of the week, use the article **le** before the day of the week.

> Je fais du patin à glace **le mercredi** *(on Wednesdays)*.

To say that you are doing something only on one particular day, use the day of the week without an article before it.

> Je vais faire du patin à glace **mercredi** *(on Wednesday)*.

Travaux pratiques de grammaire, p. 42, Act. 3–4

Grammaire supplémentaire, p. 190, Act. 1–2

8 Grammaire en contexte

a. Ecrivons Ecris trois activités que tu vas faire cette semaine.

b. Parlons Maintenant, dis à ton/ta camarade ce que tu vas faire et demande-lui ce qu'il/elle va faire.

> **EXEMPLE**
> Cette semaine, je vais faire de l'athlétisme et jouer au football. Vendredi soir, je vais voir un film. Et toi, qu'est-ce que tu vas faire?

Grammaire

The verb *aller*

Aller is an irregular verb.

aller *(to go)*

Je	**vais**	Nous	**allons**
Tu	**vas**	Vous	**allez**
Il/Elle/On	**va**	Ils/Elles	**vont**

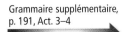
Grammaire supplémentaire, p. 191, Act. 3–4

- You can use a form of the verb **aller** with the infinitive of another verb to say that you're *going to do something* in the future.

    Je vais jouer au base-ball demain.

Cahier d'activités, p. 63, Act. 7

- To say that you're not going to do something in the near future, put **ne... pas** around the conjugated form of the verb **aller.**

    Je ne vais pas jouer au base-ball demain.

Travaux pratiques de grammaire, p. 43, Act. 5–6

---

9 **Grammaire en contexte**

Ecoutons Listen to the following sentences and decide whether the people are talking about what they're doing or what they're going to do.

10 **Grammaire en contexte**

Parlons You have a busy weekend planned! Tell what you're going to do and on what day you plan to do it.

1.

2.

3.

4.

5.

6.

⑪ Qu'est-ce qu'ils vont faire?

Parlons/Ecrivons What are these people going to do?

1. Elles

2. Ils

3. Je

4. Nous

5. Vous

6. Elle

A la française

The French often use the present tense of a verb to say that something will happen in the near future, just as we do in English.

Samedi matin, je vais jouer au tennis. *Saturday morning, I'm going to play tennis.*

Samedi matin, je joue au tennis. *Saturday morning, I'm playing tennis.*

---

⑫ Enquête

Parlons Ask the members of your group what they're going to do this weekend and tell them what you're planning. Then, tell the class what you're all planning to do.

EXEMPLE
—Qu'est-ce que tu fais ce week-end, Nicole?

—Samedi, je vais faire du ski nautique. Et toi?

—Moi, je vais à une boum.

—Je vais à une boum et Nicole va faire du ski nautique samedi.
(to the class)

Where do you and your friends like to go in your spare time?

au restaurant

au cinéma

au parc

au stade

au zoo

au centre commercial

à la plage

à la piscine

au musée

à la Maison des jeunes

au théâtre

à la bibliothèque

Cahier d'activités, pp. 63–64, Act. 6, 8   Travaux pratiques de grammaire, pp. 44–45, Act. 7–9

13 Où vas-tu?

Lisons Où est-ce que tu vas pour faire ces activités?

1. Je vais faire de la natation...
2. Je vais faire les vitrines...
3. Je vais voir un film...
4. Je vais manger quelque chose...
5. Je vais voir un match...
6. Je vais voir une pièce...

a. au cinéma.
b. au théâtre.
c. au centre commercial.
d. à la piscine.
e. au café.
f. au stade.

Contractions with *à*

The preposition **à** usually means *to* or *at*.
When you use **à** before **le** or **les,** make the following contractions:

à + le = au   Je vais **au** stade.

à + les = aux   Martine va aller **aux** Tuileries.

The preposition **à** doesn't contract with **l'** or **la:**

Cet après-midi, on ne va pas **à la** Maison des jeunes. On va **à l'**école.

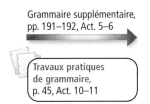

Grammaire supplémentaire,
pp. 191–192, Act. 5–6

Travaux pratiques
de grammaire,
p. 45, Act. 10–11

---

14 **Grammaire en contexte**

Lisons/Ecrivons Christine et Alain parlent des endroits où ils aiment aller le week-end. Regarde les images et complète leur conversation.

CHRISTINE   Moi, j'adore aller avec mes copains. Après, on va

souvent . Et toi?

ALAIN   Moi, j'aime mieux aller  . J'adore le sport. J'aime bien

aller aussi. On y joue souvent au foot.

CHRISTINE   Qu'est-ce que tu vas faire ce week-end? On va ?

ALAIN   Ah, non, je n'aime pas trop nager. Tu veux aller ?

---

15 **Qu'est-ce qu'on fait?**

Parlons You're trying to decide what to do after school. With a partner, take turns suggesting places to go. Then, accept or reject each other's suggestions.

le café	le musée	la piscine	le parc
la piscine	la Maison des jeunes		le zoo
la bibliothèque	le centre commercial		

---

16 **Mon journal**

Ecrivons Tu as des projets pour le week-end? Qu'est-ce que tu vas faire? Où vas-tu? Quand?

EXEMPLE   **Vendredi après-midi, je vais faire mes devoirs. Samedi, je...**

PANORAMA CULTUREL

Qu'est-ce que tu fais quand tu sors?

When you go out with your friends, where do you go? What do you do? We asked some French-speaking students what they like to do on weekends with their friends. Here's what they said.

Julie,
Côte d'Ivoire

«Quand je sors, je me balade. Je vais manger un peu. Souvent, on va jouer de la musique. On joue au tennis... souvent, au basket aussi.»

Arnaud,
France

«Je vais au cinéma. Je vais dans une discothèque. J'achète des disques.»

Céline,
Viêt-nam

«Je vais à la patinoire, ou [je vais] faire les boutiques, ou [je vais] au restaurant, enfin dans les fast-foods, ou alors je vais faire du sport, du tennis. Je vais nager.»

Qu'en penses-tu?

1. Do you and your friends like to do any of the things these teenagers mentioned?
2. Do they mention anything that you wouldn't do? Why wouldn't you do these things?
3. What do you and your friends like to do that these teenagers haven't mentioned?

Savais-tu que...?

Teenagers around the world generally like to do the same things. They usually have favorite places where they go to meet with their friends, just as you do. In most towns, students can find films, plays, concerts, and **discothèques** to go to in their free time. Dance parties (**boums**) are very popular. Most cities in France also have a **Maison des jeunes et de la culture (la MJC)** where a variety of activities, such as photography, music, dance, drama, arts and crafts, and computer science, is available to young people.

Comment dit-on...?

Extending and responding to invitations

To extend an invitation:

Allons au parc! *Let's go . . . !*
Tu veux aller au café **avec moi?** *Do you want to . . . with me?*
Je voudrais aller faire du vélo. **Tu viens?** *Will you come?*
On peut faire du ski. *We can . . .*

To accept an invitation:

D'accord.
Bonne idée.
Je veux bien. *I'd really like to.*
Pourquoi pas? *Why not?*

To refuse an invitation:

Ça ne me dit rien.
J'ai des trucs à faire.
Désolé(e), je ne peux pas.
Désolé(e), je suis occupé(e).
Sorry, I'm busy.

Cahier d'activités, pp. 65–66, Act. 11–14

Les loisirs préférés	15-25 ans
Cinéma	90
Discothèque	69
Fête foraine	58
Concert de rock	42
Parc d'attractions	37
Match (payant)	36
Monument historique	31
Bal public	30
Musée	27
Théâtre	17
Concert de jazz	11
Cirque	10
Concert classique	6
Spectacle de danse	5
Opéra	3

17 On accepte ou on refuse?

Ecoutons Ecoute ces dialogues. Est-ce qu'on accepte ou refuse l'invitation?

18 **Et toi? Tu veux?**

Lisons Choisis la bonne réponse.

1. J'ai faim.
2. Je voudrais faire un pique-nique.
3. Tu ne viens pas?
4. Je voudrais voir un match de foot.
5. Tu veux voir une pièce?

a. Allons au parc!
b. J'ai des trucs à faire.
c. Pourquoi pas? Allons au théâtre!
d. Tu veux aller au café?
e. Allons au stade!

19 **Tu acceptes?**

Parlons Your partner will invite you to participate in some of the following activities. Accept or refuse, telling where you're going or what you're going to do instead. Then, reverse roles.

1.

2.

3.

4.

5.

6.

Grammaire

The verb *vouloir*

Vouloir is an irregular verb.

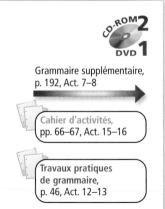

vouloir *(to want)*			
Je	**veux**	Nous	**voulons**
Tu	**veux**	Vous	**voulez**
Il/Elle/On	**veut**	Ils/Elles	**veulent**

Je voudrais *(I would like)* is a more polite form of **je veux.**

Grammaire supplémentaire, p. 192, Act. 7–8

Cahier d'activités, pp. 66–67, Act. 15–16

Travaux pratiques de grammaire, p. 46, Act. 12–13

20 Grammaire en contexte

Parlons Qu'est-ce qu'on veut faire ce soir?

1. Pierre et Marc

2. Alain

3. Moi, je...

4. Elodie et Guy

5. Mes copains et moi, nous...

6. David et Monique

21 Invitations pour le week-end

Parlons You're making plans for the upcoming weekend. Take turns with a partner suggesting activities and accepting or politely refusing the suggestions.

22 Vous voulez faire quoi?

Parlons You and your friends can't decide what to do this weekend. Each of you makes a suggestion, and the others react to it. See if you can find three things you'd all like to do.

EXEMPLE
—Vous voulez faire du vélo?
—Oui, je veux bien.
—Moi, je ne veux pas. Je n'aime pas faire du vélo.

23 A la boum!

Lisons/Parlons Le Cercle Français organise une fête. Tu vas inviter trois camarades. Avant d'accepter ou de refuser ton invitation, ils veulent savoir quelles activités tu veux faire. Dis-leur ce que tu veux faire et tes camarades vont accepter ou refuser.

danser

parler français avec des copains

manger des escargots

écouter de la musique québécoise

voir un film français

L'ambiance sera extra!

Le Cercle Français
t'invite
à une fête
le 10 mai
de 7h à 10h

Si tu viens, ce sera plus sympa!

Rencontre culturelle

Qu'en penses-tu?

1. Judging from these photos, how would you describe a typical date in France?
2. Do American teenagers usually go out on dates in groups or in couples? Which do you think is preferable? Why?
3. What do you think is the best age to begin dating? Why?

Savais-tu que... ?

French teenagers tend to go out in groups. They usually do not "date" in the same way American teenagers do. They do not generally pair off into couples until they are older. Those who do have a boyfriend or girlfriend still go out with a group — but they almost always pay their own way.

Comment dit-on...?

Arranging to meet someone

To ask when:

> **Quand?**
> **Quand ça?**

To tell when:

> **Lundi./Demain matin./Ce week-end.**
> **Tout de suite.** *Right away.*

To ask where:

> **Où?**
>
> **Où ça?**

To tell where:

> **Au** café. *At the . . .*
> **Devant** le cinéma. *In front of . . .*
> **Dans** le café. *In . . .*
> **Au métro** Saint-Michel. *At the . . . subway stop.*
> **Chez** moi. *At . . . house.*

To ask with whom:

> **Avec qui?**

To tell with whom:

> **Avec** Ahmed et Nathalie.

To ask at what time:

> **A quelle heure?**

To tell at what time:

> **A dix heures du matin.** *At ten in the morning.*
> **A cinq heures de l'après-midi.** *At five in the afternoon.*
> **A cinq heures et quart.** *At quarter past five.*
> **A cinq heures et demie.** *At half past five.*
> **Vers six heures.** *About six o'clock.*

To ask the time:

> **Quelle heure est-il?** *What time is it?*

To give the time:

> **Il est six heures.** *It's six o'clock.*
> **Il est six heures moins le quart.**
> *It's a quarter to six.*
> **Il est six heures dix.** *It's ten after six.*
> **Il est midi.** *It's noon.*
> **Il est minuit.** *It's midnight.*

To confirm:

> **Bon, on se retrouve** à trois heures.
> *OK, we'll meet . . .*
> **Rendez-vous** mardi au café. *We'll meet . . .*
> **Entendu.** *OK.*

Cahier d'activités, pp. 68–69, Act. 19–20

Travaux pratiques de grammaire, pp. 47–48, Act. 14–17

24 **L'invitation de Sylvie**

Ecoutons While you're waiting to use a public phone in Paris, you overhear a young woman inviting a friend to go out. Listen to the conversation and then choose the correct answers to these questions.

1. Sylvie parle avec qui?

    a. Marc   **b.** Anna   **c.** Paul

2. Elle va où?

    a. au musée   **b.** au parc   **c.** au stade

3. A quelle heure?

    a. 1h30   **b.** 10h15   **c.** 12h00

4. Où est-ce qu'ils se retrouvent?

    a. au métro Solférino   **b.** dans un café   **c.** devant le musée

Note culturelle

You've already learned that train, airline, school, and other official schedules use a 24-hour system called **l'heure officielle.** When you look in an entertainment guide such as *Pariscope,* you may see that a movie starts at 20h00, which is 8:00 P.M. In everyday conversation, however, people use a 12-hour system. For example, for 1:30 P.M., you may hear, **une heure et demie de l'après-midi,** rather than **treize heures trente.** Expressions such as **et demie, et quart,** and **moins le quart** are used only in conversational time, never in official time.

25 **A quelle heure?**

Parlons Où est-ce que Christian et Noëlle vont aujourd'hui? Qu'est-ce qu'ils vont faire? A quelle heure?

   1. 9h00   2. 12h00   3. 5h45   4. 8h30

26 **Qui et où?**

 Ecoutons Listen to these three messages on your answering machine and write down who they're from and where you're being invited to go. Listen a second time and write down the meeting time and place.

27 **Qu'est-ce que tu vas faire ce soir?**

a. Ecrivons Fais une liste de trois choses que tu vas faire ce soir. Dis à quelle heure et où tu vas les faire.

b. Parlons Maintenant, demande à ton/ta camarade ce qu'il/elle va faire ce soir. Ensuite, continue à lui poser des questions sur ses projets.

Grammaire

Information questions

There are several ways to ask information questions in French.

• People often ask information questions using only a question word or phrase. They will sometimes add **ça** after the question word to make it sound less abrupt.

Où ça?
Quand ça?

• Another way to ask an information question is to attach the question word or phrase at the end of a statement.

Tu vas **où?**
Tu veux faire **quoi?**
Tu vas au cinéma **à quelle heure?**
Tu vas au parc **avec qui?**

• Still another way is to begin an information question with the question word or phrase, followed by **est-ce que (qu').**

Où est-ce que tu vas?
Qu'est-ce que tu veux faire ce soir?
Avec qui est-ce que tu vas au cinéma?
A quelle heure est-ce qu'on se retrouve?

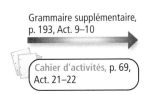

Grammaire supplémentaire, p. 193, Act. 9–10

Cahier d'activités, p. 69, Act. 21–22

Travaux pratiques de grammaire, pp. 49–50, Act. 18–21

28 **Grammaire en contexte**

Parlons Some friends are inviting you to join them. Ask questions to get more information about their plans. Complete the conversation with the appropriate question words or phrases.

— Tu veux aller au cinéma?

—

— Demain soir.

—

— Vers six heures.

—

— Au cinéma Gaumont.

—

— Avec Catherine et Michel.

— D'accord!

— Bon, on se retrouve...

29 Grammaire en contexte

Ecrivons You'd like to find out more about what teenagers in France normally do. Write down at least six questions to ask your pen pal about his or her classes, activities, and hobbies.

30 Allons au cinéma!

Parlons Look at the movie schedule below. Choose a movie you want to see and invite your partner to go with you. When you've agreed on a movie to see, decide at which time you want to go and arrange a time and place to meet.

Le Beaumont 15, Bd des Italiens • 75002 PARIS

- **Astérix chez les Bretons**, *v.f. Séances : 12h, 14h15, 16h30, 18h45, 21h00*
- **Les Randonneurs**, *v.f. Séances : 11h55, 13h55, 15h55*
- **Roméo et Juliette**, *v.f. Séances : 13h40, 16h15, 18h55, 21h30*
- **La Guerre des étoiles**, *v.o. Séances : 11h30, 14h, 16h30, 19h, 21h30*
- **Mon chien Skip**, *v.f. Séances : 13h30, 15h, 16h30*
- **Les 101 Dalmatiens**, *v.o. Séances : 11h05, 13h45, 16h20, 19h, 21h35*
- **Hercule**, *v.f. Séance : 21h*
- **Les Visiteurs**, *v.f. Séances : 13h30, 16h30*
- **Le Journal d'Anne Frank**, *v.f. Séances : 12h30, 14h, 16h*
- **Casablanca**, *v.o. Séances : 16h30, 19h*

31 Ça te dit?

Ecrivons A friend has written you this note suggesting some things to do this weekend. Write an answer, accepting the invitations or making suggestions of your own.

> Salut! Ça va? Tu veux faire quoi ce week-end? Moi, je voudrais faire les magasins vendredi soir et jouer au tennis samedi après-midi. On va au ciné samedi soir vers huit heures et demie. Tu viens? Et dimanche matin, tu veux aller au café? Qu'est-ce que tu en penses? Fabienne

 Parlons This summer you're working as a camp counselor. You're trying to set up a group meeting some time during the evening this week, and you need to find out when is a good time and place for everyone to meet. Work with a partner and find out what he or she is planning on doing each evening and at what time. Agree on a possible day and time to schedule the meeting.

PRONONCIATION

The vowel sounds [ø] and [œ]

The vowel sound [ø] in **veux** is represented by the letter combination **eu.** It is pronounced with the lips rounded and the tongue pressed against the back of the lower front teeth. To produce this sound, first make the sound **è,** as in **algèbre,** and hold it. Then, round the lips slightly to the position for closed **o,** as in **photo.** Repeat these words.

jeudi	veux	peu	deux

The vowel sound [œ] in the word **heure** is similar to the sound in **veux** and is also represented by the letters **eu.** This sound is more open, however, and occurs when these letters are followed by a consonant sound in the same syllable. To produce this sound, first make the sound **è,** as in **algèbre,** and hold it. Then, round the lips slightly to the position for open **o,** as in **short.** Repeat these words.

classeur	feuille	heure

A. A prononcer

Repeat the following words.

1. jeudi	déjeuner	peux
2. deux	veut	mieux
3. ordinateur	jeunes	heure
4. feuille	classeur	veulent

B. A lire

Take turns with a partner reading each of the following sentences aloud.

1. Tu as deux ordinateurs? On peut étudier chez toi jeudi?

2. Tu veux manger des escargots? C'est délicieux!

3. On va à la Maison des jeunes? A quelle heure?

4. Tu as une feuille de papier? Je n'ai pas mon classeur.

C. A écrire

You're going to hear a short dialogue. Write down what you hear.

Lisons!

$\mathcal{P}$arcs d'attractions

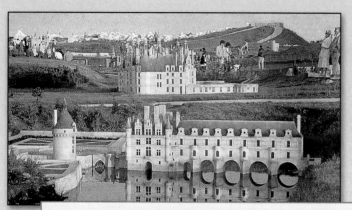

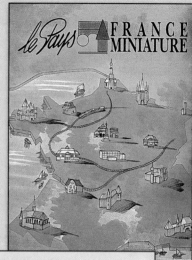

Le Pays FRANCE MINIATURE, c'est la France comme vous ne l'avez jamais vue! Sur une immense carte en relief, sont regroupées les plus belles richesses de notre patrimoine : 166 monuments historiques, 15 villages typiques de nos régions, les paysages et les scènes de la vie quotidienne à l'échelle 1/30ème... au cœur d'un environnement naturel extraordinaire.

CALENDRIER :
Ouverture : 15 mars au 15 novembre.
Tous les jours de 10h à 19h.

TARIFS :
Individuels : Adultes : 12 €.
Enfants : 8 € (de 11 à 16 ans).

RESTAURATION
Deux restaurants de 300 places chacun et 2 kiosques proposent des menus de différentes régions de France (un restaurant ouvert le samedi soir).
Aire de pique-nique aménagée.

$\mathcal{P}$arcs d'attractions

Stratégie pour lire

When you run across a word you don't know, use context to guess the meaning of the word. You automatically use this strategy in your own language. For example, you may not know the English word *dingo*, but when you see it in a sentence, you can make an intelligent guess about what it means. Read this sentence: *He thought that the kangaroos and the koala bears were cute, but that the dingos were mean-looking.* You can guess that a dingo is a possibly vicious animal found in Australia. It is, in fact, a wild dog.

Where do you like to go on the weekend? Look at these brochures to see where Parisians go for fun.

A. What kinds of places do these brochures describe?

B. One of your friends visited **France Miniature** and told you about it. Check the brochure to see if what he said was accurate or not.

1. "I saw more than 150 monuments!"
2. "There were twenty villages represented."
3. "The size of everything was on a scale of 1/25."
4. "It was more expensive than **Parc Astérix.**"
5. "We stayed until midnight."
6. "We went on my birthday, June 15th."

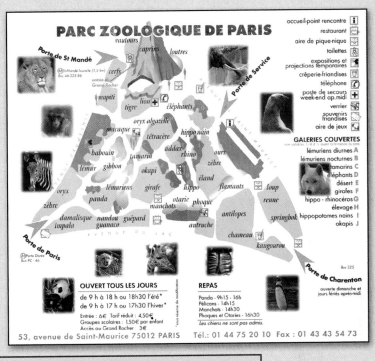

PARC ZOOLOGIQUE DE PARIS

vautours
Porte de St Mandé
caprins *loutres*
cerfs
(M)St-Mandé-Tourelle (1,5 km)
Bus 46-325-96
entrée du Grand Rocher
Porte de Service
wapiti
lion +
tigre *éléphants*
oryx algazelle
macaque *tétracère*
hippo nain
babouin *tamarin* *addax* *rhino* *ours*
lemur *gibbon* *okapi* *zèbre*
éland
oryx *lémuriens* *girafe* *hippo* *flamants* *loup*
zèbre *panda* *otarie* *phoque* *renne*
manchots
damalisque *nandon* *guépard* *antilopes* *springbok*
impala *guanaco* *autruche*
Porte de Paris
(M)Porte Dorée
Bus PC - 46
chameau
kangourou
Porte de Charenton
Bus 325
AVENUE DU LAC

accueil-point rencontre [i]
restaurant
aire de pique-nique
toilettes
expositions et projections temporaires
crêperie-friandises
téléphone
poste de secours week-end ap. midi
verrier
souvenirs friandises
aire de jeux

GALERIES COUVERTES

lémuriens diurnes A
lémuriens nocturnes B
tamarins C
éléphants D
désert E
girafes F
hippo - rhinocéros G
élevage H
hippopotames nains I
okapis J

ouverte dimanche et jours fériés après-midi

OUVERT TOUS LES JOURS
de 9 h à 18 h ou 18h30 l'été*
de 9 h à 17 h ou 17h30 l'hiver*

Entrée : 6€ Tarif réduit : 4,50€
Groupes scolaires : 1,50€ par enfant
Accès au Grand Rocher   3€

*tous réserve de modification

REPAS
Panda - 9h15 - 16h
Pélicans - 14h15
Manchots - 14h30
Phoques et Otaries - 16h30
Les chiens ne sont pas admis.

53, avenue de Saint-Maurice 75012 PARIS   Tél.: 01 44 75 20 10 Fax : 01 43 43 54 73

Parc ASTERIX

Bienvenue
Welcome
Welkom

PARC ASTERIX

Bienvenue en Gaule pour une journée mémorable!

Pour passer une journée partagée entre l'émotion et l'aventure. Pour retrouver cette bonne humeur légendaire et communicative. Pour faire un voyage mémorable en Gaule, au pays du bien-vivre et de l'histoire...

Venez au Parc Astérix! Astérix et tous ses amis vous y attendent...

Départ de Paris les mercredis et samedis à 9h, du 10 avril au 2 octobre. Retour du site à 18h et arrivée à Paris vers 19h30.

Prix par personne : 52 €
Enfants de 3 à 11 ans inclus : 40 €
Le prix inclut l'hébergement.

C. Look at the brochure for **Parc Astérix** and answer the following questions.

1. During which months would you not be able to go on this trip?

2. On which days of the week can you take this trip to **Parc Astérix?**

3. If you took the trip in the advertisement, at what time would you leave Paris?

4. At what time would you leave the park for the trip back?

5. If you go with three friends and one of you brings your ten-year-old sister, how much will it cost?

D. Imagine you and a friend want to go to the **Parc zoologique de Paris.**

1. Is the park open on Sundays? Is there a restaurant?

2. How much is it going to cost? Will it make a difference if you're students?

3. How late can you stay in the summer? In the winter?

4. What are some of the animals you'll get to see?

5. At what time do the pelicans eat? The pandas?

6. How many picnic areas are there? What is near the first-aid station? Where can you buy a gift?

E. Which of these places would you like to go to most? Why?

Cahier d'activités, p. 71, Act. 24

Grammaire supplémentaire

Première étape Objective Making plans

1 Malika is leaving a message on Axel's answering machine. Complete her message with **le** when appropriate. Be careful! In some cases, you won't need to add anything. (**p. 173**)

Salut, Axel! C'est moi, Malika! Ça va? Ecoute! On va au Café Américain ___1___ lundi soir. Tu viens? On va souvent à la crêperie ___2___ lundi, mais cette semaine, on va aller au café. Bonne idée, non? ___3___ mercredi après-midi, on va aller voir une pièce. On va quelquefois au théâtre ___4___ mercredi. C'est super, le théâtre! Est-ce que tu peux venir? Ah, oui, ___5___ samedi, on va à la boum de Nadine. Qu'est-ce que tu fais d'habitude ___6___ samedi soir? Tu veux venir avec nous? Eh bien, à bientôt peut-être. Tchao!

2 Véronique and Elodie are trying to choose a convenient time to go to the movies. Complete Elodie's responses according to her schedule below. (**p. 173**)

LUNDI	MARDI	MERCREDI	JEUDI	VENDREDI	SAMEDI	DIMANCHE
sortie de l'école 17h15	sortie de l'école 16h00	sortie de l'école 12h15	sortie de l'école 17h15	sortie de l'école 16h00	sortie de l'école 11h15	
devoirs! étudier pour l'examen	18h00– 19h30 danse	14h00– 16h00 natation	18h00– 19h30 danse	20h00 dîner au restaurant	14h00– 16h00 natation	
					20h00 boum de Michèle	20h30 concert de I AM

1. J'ai danse _____ et _____ de 18h00 à 19h30.

2. _____ soir, j'ai des devoirs à faire.

3. _____ la sortie de l'école est à 12h15, mais j'ai natation à 14h00.

4. _____ et _____, j'ai natation de 14h00 à 16h00.

5. Je vais au restaurant _____ soir.

6. _____ soir, il y a le concert de I AM.

7. Tu es libre _____ après-midi?

3 Fernand and Michèle are discussing what to do this coming Saturday. Complete their conversation with the correct forms of **aller.** (**p. 174**)

FERNAND   Dis, Michèle, tu ___1___ faire quoi demain?

MICHELE   Bof. Rien de spécial. D'habitude, le samedi, je fais les vitrines.

FERNAND   Eric et moi, on ___2___ faire un pique-nique. Tu viens avec nous?

MICHELE   Désolée, mais ça ne me dit rien, les pique-niques.

FERNAND   Mais écoute, Michèle! Les pique-niques, c'est génial! Tous les copains ___3___ venir! On ___4___ jouer au foot! Julien et Juliette ___5___ apporter des hot-dogs! Nous ___6___ nous amuser!

MICHELE   D'accord. Pourquoi pas? On se retrouve où?

FERNAND   Devant la MJC. Vers trois heures.

MICHELE   Entendu. Je ___7___ passer chez toi vers deux heures et demie.

4 Fais une phrase avec les mots proposés. Utilise la forme correcte du verbe **aller.** (**p. 174**)

EXEMPLE   Marc et Li/faire les vitrines   **Marc et Li vont faire les vitrines.**

1. Toi, tu/aller au café
2. Moi, je/aller au théâtre
3. Marc/voir un film
4. Simone et moi, nous/voir un match
5. Pascal et Maurice, vous/faire une promenade
6. Michèle et François/aller à une boum
7. Nous/faire un pique-nique
8. Vous/manger quelque chose

5 Christelle and Alain are talking about what they like to do during their free time. Complete the following sentences according to the photos. (**p. 177**)

1. Je vais  pour faire du jogging.

2. J'aime aller  pour nager.

3. En été, j'aime aller  .

4. Mes amis et moi, nous aimons aller  .

WA3 PARIS-6

6 Imagine que tu vas faire un voyage à Paris avec tes amis cet été. Utilise **à, à la, au,** et **aux** pour compléter les phrases suivantes. (**p. 177**)

1. Christine va aller ____ cathédrale (f.).
2. Nous allons aller ____ théâtre et ____ restaurant.
3. Marc va aller ____ concerts de rock du festival de la musique.
4. Moi, je vais ____ Maison des jeunes.
5. Les garçons ne vont pas aller ____ centre commercial.
6. Je vais voir un film français ____ cinéma.
7. Et Mark et Jeanne vont voir un match de foot ____ stade.

Deuxième étape   Objective Extending and responding to invitations

7 Complète les phrases suivantes avec la forme correcte du verbe **vouloir.** (**p. 180**)

1. Mes copines _____ aller au restaurant.
2. Mais moi, je _____ aller au café.
3. Et vous, vous _____ manger quelque chose?
4. Non. Nous _____ voir un film.
5. Et toi, Eric, tu _____ faire quoi?
6. Patricia et moi, on _____ faire les vitrines.

8 Based on their preferences, write what the following students want to do. Be sure to use the appropriate subject pronoun, the correct form of **vouloir,** and an expression from the box. Use each expression only once. (**p. 180**)

voir un film	regarder un match de foot à la télé	voir une pièce	manger quelque chose
aller à une boum		aller à la bibliothèque	aller à la piscine

EXEMPLE   Marianne a faim. **Elle veut manger quelque chose.**

1. Suzanne et Monique adorent nager.
2. J'aime lire.
3. Vous adorez le théâtre.
4. Gilles aime bien le cinéma.
5. Anne et moi, nous aimons danser.
6. Tu aimes le football.

9 Complète la conversation suivante avec la réponse correcte. (**p. 185**)

> Avec Lise.   A sept heures et demie.
>
> Chez moi.   Ce soir.

DIANE   Tu viens manger avec nous, Isabelle?

ISABELLE   Oui. Je veux bien. Quand ça?

DIANE   ____1____

ISABELLE   Où est-ce qu'on se retrouve?

DIANE   ____2____

ISABELLE   Avec qui on va manger?

DIANE   ____3____

ISABELLE   On se retrouve à quelle heure?

DIANE   ____4____

10 Fais correspondre la réponse de la colonne A à la question posée dans la colonne B. (**p. 185**)

A	B
1. Mireille et Matthieu.	**a.** Où est-ce qu'on se retrouve?
2. On va voir *Les Randonneurs.*	**b.** Qu'est-ce tu vas voir?
3. Demain, à deux heures et demie.	**c.** Tu vas avec qui?
4. Je vais voir un film.	**d.** Quand ça?
5. Au cinéma Beaubourg.	**e.** Qu'est-ce que tu vas faire ce week-end?

La tour Eiffel est le monument parisien le plus connu au monde. Elle a été construite pour l'Exposition universelle de 1889. Jusqu'à la construction de l'Empire State Building de New York en 1931, la tour Eiffel était la plus haute tour du monde avec ses 320 mètres, antenne comprise. La tour a trois étages. Il y a un restaurant au premier et au deuxième étages. Le troisième étage offre un superbe point de vue sur la ville. Horaires : 9h30 à 23h. Tarifs : 3 € à 8,50 €.

Le musée d'Orsay a été installé dans l'ancienne gare d'Orsay, construite par Victor Laloux et inaugurée en 1900 au moment de l'Exposition universelle. C'est en 1977 qu'un Conseil des ministres a décidé de transformer la gare et son hôtel en un musée consacré à la création artistique du XIXe siècle (1848-1914). Collections : Arts Décoratifs, Histoire, Littérature, Mobilier, Peinture, Photographie, Sculpture. L'intérieur a été réalisé par l'architecte italienne Gae Aulenti. 1, rue de Bellechasse, 7e. Tél. : 01 40 49 48 14. Métro : Solférino. Horaires : tous les jours sauf le lundi de 10h-18h, le jeudi jusqu'à 21h45. Tarifs : 5,50 €.

Notre-Dame de Paris est un chef-d'œuvre de l'art gothique français, construite entre 1163 et 1330. La façade principale est composée de trois gigantesques portails. Visite guidée et gratuite de la cathédrale tous les jours : à 12h du lundi au vendredi, à 14h30 le samedi, à 14h le dimanche. Visite payante des tours tous les jours de 10h à 17h30. Concerts gratuits tous les dimanches à 17h45. Pas de visite les jours fériés.
Tél : 01 42 34 56 10.
Tarifs : Visite des tours : 5 €.

1 Look over the advertisements and answer the questions below.

1. Which place(s) offer(s) a view of Paris?

2. Where can you go to a free concert? On what day?

3. Are any of these places open in the evening? If so, which ones?

4. Where can you see nineteenth-century French art?

5. Which attraction is closed on holidays?

6. Which places list their prices?

7. Which attraction is closed on Mondays?

8. Which attraction costs the most to visit?

9. At which place can you buy something to eat?

2 Your French friends are discussing which Paris attraction to visit. Listen to their conversation and write down the attraction they decide on. Listen again and tell when and where they agree to meet.

3 Using what you've learned about French culture, answer the following questions.

1. Where do French teenagers like to go to have fun?

2. Would a French teenager be surprised at American dating customs? Why?

4

Ecrivons!

You have one day in Paris to do whatever you like. Write a note to your French class back home telling everyone what you plan to do during your day in Paris.

> ### Stratégie pour écrire
> Arranging your ideas chronologically is helpful when planning activities for the day. To do this, take a sheet of paper, turn it sideways, and divide it into five columns. Label the first column **de 8h à 10h**, the second column **de 10h à midi**, and so on, in two-hour increments up to 6:00 in the evening. Next, decide what you would like to do at these times and write the information in the appropriate columns.

de 8h à 10h	de 10h à midi	de midi à 2h
aller au café	aller au zoo	
faire une promenade dans le jardin des Tuileries.		

Now, using the information from the chart you've prepared, write the note to your French class. Tell everyone what you plan to see and do throughout the day. Here are some connecting words that may help your writing flow more smoothly: **d'abord** *(first)*, **ensuite** *(next)*, and **après ça** *(after that)*.

5 Jeu de rôle

Get together with some classmates. Choose one place in Paris you'd all like to visit and decide on a meeting time and place. Make sure that the Paris attraction you choose to visit will be open when you plan to go. Act this out with your group.

Que sais-je?

WA3 PARIS-6

Can you use what you've learned in this chapter?

Can you make plans?
p. 173

1 How would you say that these people are going to these places?

1. Je   2. Nous   3. Anne et Etienne

2 How would you tell what you're planning to do this weekend?

Can you extend and respond to invitations?
p. 179

3 How would you invite a friend to . . .
1. go window shopping?
2. go for a walk?
3. go see a basketball game?
4. go to the café?

4 How would you accept the following invitations? How would you refuse them?
1. Je voudrais aller faire du ski. Tu viens?
2. Allons à la Maison des jeunes!
3. On va au restaurant. Tu viens?
4. Tu veux aller au cinéma?

5 How would you say that the following people want to go to these places?

1. Ahmed   2. Isabelle et Ferdinand   3. Mon amie et moi

Can you arrange to meet someone?
p. 183

6 If someone invited you to go to the movies, what are three questions you might ask to find out more information?

7 What are some possible answers to the following questions?
1. Où ça?
2. Avec qui?
3. A quelle heure?
4. Quand ça?

Making plans

Qu'est-ce que tu vas faire... ?	What are you going to do . . . ?
Tu vas faire quoi...?	What are you going to do . . . ?
Je vais...	I'm going . . .
Pas grand-chose.	Not much.
Rien de spécial.	Nothing special.

Things to do

aller à une boum	to go to a party
faire une ` promenade	to go for a walk
faire un pique-nique	to have a picnic
faire les vitrines	to window-shop
manger quelque chose	to eat something
regarder un match	to watch a game (on TV)
voir un film	to see a movie
aller voir un match	to go see a game
voir une pièce	to see a play

Places to go

la bibliothèque	library
le centre commercial	mall
le cinéma	movie theater
la Maison des jeunes et de la culture (MJC)	recreation center
le musée	museum
le parc	park
la piscine	swimming pool
la plage	beach
le restaurant	restaurant
le stade	stadium
le théâtre	theater
le zoo	zoo

Other useful expressions

aller	to go
au/à la/à l'/aux	to, at

Deuxième étape

Extending invitations

Allons... !	Let's go . . . !
Tu veux... avec moi?	Do you want . . . with me?
Tu viens?	Will you come?
On peut...	We can . . .

Accepting invitations

D'accord.	OK.
Bonne idée.	Good idea.
Je veux bien.	I'd really like to.
Pourquoi pas?	Why not?

Refusing invitations

Ça ne me dit rien.	I don't feel like it.
J'ai des trucs à faire.	I've got things to do.
Désolé(e), je ne peux pas.	Sorry, I can't.
Désolé(e), je suis occupé(e).	Sorry, I'm busy.

Other useful expressions

je voudrais...	I'd like . . .
vouloir	to want

Troisième étape

Arranging to meet someone

Quand (ça)?	When?
tout de suite	right away
Où (ça)?	Where?
dans	in
devant	in front of
au (métro)...	at the . . . (metro stop)
chez...	at . . . ('s) house
Avec qui?	With whom?
avec...	with . . .
A quelle heure?	At what time?
A cinq heures.	At five o'clock.
et demie	half past
et quart	quarter past
moins le quart	quarter to
moins cinq	five to
Quelle heure est-il?	What time is it?
Il est midi.	It's noon.
Il est minuit.	It's midnight.
Il est midi (minuit) et demi.	It's half past noon (midnight).
vers	about
Bon, on se retrouve...	OK, we'll meet . . .
Rendez-vous...	We'll meet . . .
Entendu.	OK.

Other useful expressions

ce week-end	this weekend
demain	tomorrow
est-ce que	(introduces a yes-no question)

Reference Section

Function is another word for the way in which you use language for a specific purpose. When you find yourself in specific situations, such as in a restaurant, in a grocery store, or at school, you'll want to communicate with those around you. In order to communicate in French, you have to "function" in the language.

Each chapter in this book focuses on language functions. You can easily find them in boxes labeled **Comment dit-on... ?** The other features in the chapter—grammar, vocabulary, culture notes—support the functions you're learning.

Here is a list of functions and the French expressions presented in this book. You'll need them in order to communicate in a wide range of situations. Following each function entry, you will find the chapter and page number where each function is presented.

Socializing

Greeting people **Ch. 1, p. 22**
Bonjour.
Salut.

Saying goodbye **Ch. 1, p. 22**
Salut.   A bientôt.
Au revoir.   A demain.
A tout à l'heure.   Tchao.

Asking how people are and telling how you are **Ch. 1, p. 23**
(Comment) ça va?   Bof.
Ça va.   Pas mal.
Super!   Pas terrible.
Très bien.   Et toi?
Comme ci comme ça.

Expressing and responding to thanks **Ch. 3, p. 90**
Merci.
A votre service.

Extending invitations **Ch. 6, p. 179**
Allons... !
Tu veux... avec moi?
Tu viens?
On peut...

Accepting invitations **Ch. 6, p. 179**
Je veux bien.   D'accord.
Pourquoi pas?   Bonne idée.

Refusing invitations **Ch. 6, p. 179**
Désolé(e), je suis occupé(e).
Ça ne me dit rien.
J'ai des trucs à faire.
Désolé(e), je ne peux pas.

Identifying people **Ch. 7, p. 203**
C'est...
Ce sont...
Voici...
Voilà...

Introducing people **Ch. 7, p. 207**
C'est...
Je te/vous présente...
Très heureux (heureuse). (FORMAL)

Inquiring about past events **Ch. 9, p. 270**
Qu'est-ce que tu as fait... ?
Tu es allé(e) où?
Et après?
Qu'est-ce qui s'est passé?

Relating past events **Ch. 9, p. 270**
D'abord,...
Ensuite,...
Après,...
Je suis allé(e)...
Et après ça,...
Finalement,/Enfin,...

Inquiring about future plans **Ch. 11, p. 329**
Qu'est-ce que tu vas faire... ?
Où est-ce que tu vas aller... ?

Sharing future plans **Ch. 11, p. 329**
J'ai l'intention de...
Je vais...

Seeing someone off **Ch. 11, p. 336**
Bon voyage!
Bonnes vacances!
Amuse-toi bien!
Bonne chance!

Exchanging Information

Asking someone's name and giving yours
Ch. 1, p. 24
> Tu t'appelles comment?
> Je m'appelle...

Asking and giving someone else's name Ch. 1, p. 24
> Il/Elle s'appelle comment?
> Il/Elle s'appelle...

Asking someone's age and giving yours Ch. 1, p. 25
> Tu as quel âge?
> J'ai... ans.

Asking for information Ch. 2, p. 55
> Tu as quels cours... ?
> Tu as quoi... ?
> Vous avez... ?
> Tu as... à quelle heure?

Giving information Ch. 2, p. 55
> Nous avons...
> J'ai...

Telling when you have class Ch. 2, p. 58
> à... heure(s)
> à... heure(s) quinze
> à... heure(s) trente
> à... heure(s) quarante-cinq

Making requests Ch. 3, p. 80
> Tu as... ?
> Vous avez... ?

Responding to requests Ch. 3, p. 80
> Voilà.
> Je regrette.
> Je n'ai pas de...

Asking others what they need and telling what you need Ch. 3, p. 82
> Qu'est-ce qu'il te faut pour... ?
> Qu'est-ce qu'il vous faut pour... ?
> Il me faut...

Expressing need Ch. 8, p. 238; Ch. 10, p. 301
> Qu'est-ce qu'il te faut?
> Il me faut...
> De quoi est-ce que tu as besoin?
> J'ai besoin de...
> Oui, il me faut...
> Oui, vous avez... ?
> Je cherche quelque chose pour...
> J'aimerais... pour aller avec...

Asking for information Ch. 3, p. 90
> C'est combien?

Getting someone's attention
Ch. 3, p. 90; Ch. 5, p. 151
> Pardon...
> Excusez-moi.
> ... , s'il vous plaît.
> Monsieur!
> Madame!
> Mademoiselle!

Exchanging information Ch. 4, p. 116
> Qu'est-ce que tu fais comme sport?
> Qu'est-ce que tu fais pour t'amuser?
> Je fais...
> Je ne fais pas de...
> Je (ne) joue (pas)...

Ordering food and beverages Ch. 5, p. 151
> Vous avez choisi?
> Vous prenez?
> Je voudrais...
> Je vais prendre..., s'il vous plaît.
> ... , s'il vous plaît.
> Donnez-moi... , s'il vous plaît.
> Apportez-moi... , s'il vous plaît.
> Vous avez... ?
> Qu'est-ce que vous avez comme boissons?
> Qu'est-ce qu'il y a à boire?

Paying the check Ch. 5, p. 155
> L'addition, s'il vous plaît.
> Oui, tout de suite.
> Un moment, s'il vous plaît.
> Ça fait combien, s'il vous plaît?
> Ça fait... euros.
> C'est combien, ... ?
> C'est... euros.

Making plans Ch. 6, p. 173
> Qu'est-ce que tu vas faire... ?
> Tu vas faire quoi... ?
> Je vais...
> Pas grand-chose.
> Rien de spécial.

Arranging to meet someone Ch. 6, p. 183
> Quand (ça)?   et quart
> Tout de suite.   moins le quart
> Où (ça)?   moins cinq
> Devant...   midi (et demi)
> Au métro...   minuit (et demi)
> Chez...   Vers...
> Dans...   Quelle heure est-il?
> Avec qui?   Il est...
> A quelle heure?   On se retrouve...
> A cinq heures...   Rendez-vous...
> et demie   Entendu.

Describing and characterizing people Ch. 7, p. 209

Il est comment?
Elle est comment?
Ils/Elles sont comment?
Il/Elle est...
Ils/Elles sont...
Il/Elle n'est ni... ni...

Making a telephone call Ch. 9, p. 276

Bonjour.
Je suis bien chez... ?
C'est...
(Est-ce que)... est là, s'il vous plaît?
(Est-ce que) je peux parler à... ?
Je peux laisser un message?
Vous pouvez lui dire que j'ai téléphoné?
Ça ne répond pas.
C'est occupé.

Answering a telephone call Ch. 9, p. 276

Allô?
Qui est à l'appareil?
Une seconde, s'il vous plaît.
D'accord.
Bien sûr.
Vous pouvez rappeler plus tard?
Ne quittez pas.

Inquiring Ch. 10, p. 301

(Est-ce que) je peux vous aider?
Vous désirez?
Je peux l'(les) essayer?
Je peux essayer... ?
C'est combien, ... ?
Ça fait combien?
Vous avez ça en... ?

Pointing out places and things Ch. 12, p. 361

Là, tu vois, c'est...
Ça, c'est...
Regarde, voilà...
Là, c'est...
Voici...

Asking for advice Ch. 12, p. 366

Comment est-ce qu'on y va?

Making suggestions Ch. 12, p. 366

On peut y aller...
On peut prendre...

Asking for directions Ch. 12, p. 371

Pardon, ..., s'il vous plaît?
Pardon, ... Où est..., s'il vous plaît?
Pardon, ... Je cherche..., s'il vous plaît.

Giving directions Ch. 12, p. 371

Vous continuez jusqu'au prochain feu rouge.
Vous tournez...
Vous allez tout droit jusqu'à...
Prenez la rue..., puis traversez la rue...
Vous passez...
C'est tout de suite à...

Expressing Feelings and Emotions

Expressing likes, dislikes, and preferences Ch. 1, pp. 26, 32

J'aime (bien)...	J'aime mieux...
Je n'aime pas...	J'adore...
Je préfère...	

Ch. 5, p. 154

C'est...	
excellent!	bon!
pas mauvais!	délicieux!
pas terrible!	pas bon!
mauvais!	dégoûtant!

Telling what you'd like and what you'd like to do Ch. 3, p. 85

Je voudrais...
Je voudrais acheter...

Telling how much you like or dislike something Ch. 4, p. 114

Beaucoup.	Pas du tout.
Pas beaucoup.	surtout
Pas tellement.	

Inquiring about likes and dislikes Ch. 1, p. 26

Tu aimes... ?

Ch. 5, p. 154

Comment tu trouves ça?

Sharing confidences Ch. 9, p. 279

J'ai un petit problème.
Je peux te parler?
Tu as une minute?

Consoling others Ch. 9, p. 279

Je t'écoute.
Ne t'en fais pas!
Ça va aller mieux!
Qu'est-ce que je peux faire?

Making a decision Ch. 10, p. 310

Vous avez décidé de prendre... ?
Vous avez choisi?
Vous le/la/les prenez?
Je le/la/les prends.
C'est trop cher.

Hesitating Ch. 10, p. 310
  Euh... J'hésite.
  Je ne sais pas.
  Il/Elle me plaît, mais il/elle est...

Expressing indecision Ch. 11, p. 329
  J'hésite.
  Je ne sais pas.
  Je n'en sais rien.
  Je n'ai rien de prévu.

Expressing wishes Ch. 11, p. 329
  J'ai envie de...
  Je voudrais bien...

Expressing Attitudes and Opinions

Agreeing Ch. 2, p. 54
  Oui, beaucoup.
  Moi aussi.
  Moi non plus.

Disagreeing Ch. 2, p. 54
  Moi, non.
  Non, pas trop.
  Moi, si.
  Pas moi.

Asking for opinions Ch. 2, p. 61
  Comment tu trouves... ?
  Comment tu trouves ça?

Ch. 9, p. 269
  Tu as passé un bon week-end?

Ch. 10, p. 306
  Il/Elle me va?
  Il/Elle te/vous plaît?
  Tu aimes mieux... ou... ?

Ch. 11, p. 337
  Tu as passé un bon... ?
  Tu t'es bien amusé(e)?
  Ça s'est bien passé?

Expressing opinions Ch. 2, p. 61
  C'est...

facile.	pas terrible.
génial.	pas super.
super.	zéro.
cool.	barbant.
intéressant.	nul.
passionnant.	pas mal.
difficile.	

  Ça va.

Ch. 9, p. 269
  Oui, très chouette.

Oui, excellent.
Oui, très bon.
Oui, ça a été.
Oh, pas mauvais.
C'était épouvantable.
Très mauvais.

Ch. 11, p. 337
  C'était formidable!
  Non, pas vraiment.
  C'était ennuyeux.
  C'était un véritable cauchemar!

Paying a compliment Ch. 10, p. 306
  C'est tout à fait ton/ votre style.
  Il/Elle te/vous va très bien.
  Il/Elle va très bien avec...
  Je le/la/les trouve...
  C'est parfait.

Criticizing Ch. 10, p. 306
  Il/Elle ne te/vous va pas du tout.
  Il/Elle ne va pas du tout avec...
  Il/Elle est (Ils/Elles sont) trop...
  Je le/la/les trouve...

Persuading

Making suggestions Ch. 4, p. 122
  On... ?
  On fait... ?
  On joue... ?

Ch. 5, p. 145
  On va... ?

Accepting suggestions Ch. 4, p. 122
  D'accord.
  Bonne idée.
  Oui, c'est...
  Allons-y!

Turning down suggestions; making excuses
Ch. 4, p. 122
  Non, c'est...
  Ça ne me dit rien.
  Désolé(e), mais je ne peux pas.

Ch. 5, p. 145
  Désolé(e). J'ai des devoirs à faire.
        J'ai des courses à faire.
        J'ai des trucs à faire.
        J'ai des tas de choses à faire.
        Je ne peux pas parce que...

Making a recommendation Ch. 5, p. 148
  Prends...
  Prenez...

Asking for permission Ch. 7, p. 213
> Tu es d'accord?
> (Est-ce que) je peux... ?

Giving permission Ch. 7, p. 213
> Oui, si tu veux.
> Pourquoi pas?
> D'accord, si tu... d'abord...
> Oui, bien sûr.

Refusing permission Ch. 7, p. 213
> Pas question!
> Non, c'est impossible.
> Non, tu dois...
> Pas ce soir.

Making requests Ch. 8, p. 240
> Tu peux (aller faire les courses)?
> Tu me rapportes... ?

Ch. 12, p. 364
> Est-ce que tu peux... ?
> Tu pourrais passer à... ?

Accepting requests Ch. 8, p. 240
> Pourquoi pas?
> Bon, d'accord.
> Je veux bien.
> J'y vais tout de suite.

Ch. 12, p. 364
> D'accord.
> Si tu veux.

Declining requests Ch. 8, p. 240
> Je ne peux pas maintenant.
> Je regrette, mais je n'ai pas le temps.
> J'ai des tas de choses (trucs) à faire.

Ch. 12, p. 364
> Je suis désolé(e), mais je n'ai pas le temps.

Telling someone what to do Ch. 8, p. 240
> Rapporte(-moi)...
> Prends...
> Achète(-moi)...
> N'oublie pas de...

Offering food Ch. 8, p. 247
> Tu veux... ?
> Vous voulez... ?
> Vous prenez... ?
> Tu prends... ?
> Encore... ?

Accepting food Ch. 8, p. 247
> Oui, s'il vous/te plaît.
> Oui, avec plaisir.
> Oui, j'en veux bien.

Refusing food Ch. 8, p. 247
> Non, merci.
> Non, merci. Je n'ai plus faim.
> Je n'en veux plus.

Asking for advice Ch. 9, p. 279
> A ton avis, qu'est-ce que je fais?
> Qu'est-ce que tu me conseilles?

Ch. 10, p. 300
> Je ne sais pas quoi mettre pour...
> Qu'est-ce que je mets?

Giving advice Ch. 9, p. 279
> Oublie-le/-la/-les!
> Téléphone-lui/-leur!
> Tu devrais...
> Pourquoi tu ne... pas?

Ch. 10, p. 300
> Pourquoi est-ce que tu ne mets pas... ?
> Mets...

Reminding Ch. 11, p. 333
> N'oublie pas...
> Tu n'as pas oublié... ?
> Tu ne peux pas partir sans...
> Tu prends... ?

Reassuring Ch. 11, p. 333
> Ne t'en fais pas.
> J'ai pensé à tout.
> Je n'ai rien oublié.

This list presents additional vocabulary you may want to use when you're working on the activities in the textbook and in the workbooks. It also includes the optional vocabulary labeled **Vocabulaire à la carte** that appears in several chapters. If you can't find the words you need here, try the French-English and English-French vocabulary lists beginning on page R31.

Adjectives

absurd	*absurde*
awesome (impressive)	*impressionnant(e)*
boring	*ennuyeux/ennuyeuse*
chilly (weather)	*froid, frais*
colorful (thing)	*vif/vive*
despicable	*ignoble*
eccentric	*excentrique*
incredible	*incroyable*
tasteful (remark, object)	*de bon goût*
tasteless (flavor)	*insipide;* (remark, object) *de mauvais goût*
terrifying	*terrifiant(e)*
threatening	*menaçant(e)*
tremendous (excellent)	*formidable*
unforgettable	*inoubliable*
unique	*unique*

Clothing

blazer	*un blazer*
button	*un bouton*
coat	*un manteau*
collar	*un col*
eyeglasses	*des lunettes* (f.)
gloves	*des gants* (m.)
handkerchief	*un mouchoir*
high-heeled shoes	*des chaussures* (f.) *à talons*
lace	*de la dentelle*
linen	*du lin*
necklace	*un collier*
nylon	*du nylon*
pajamas	*un pyjama*
polyester	*du polyester*
raincoat	*un imperméable*
rayon	*de la rayonne*
ring	*une bague*
sale (discount)	*des soldes* (m.)
silk	*de la soie*
sleeve	*une manche*
slippers	*des pantoufles* (f.)
suit (man's)	*un costume;* (woman's) *un tailleur*
suspenders	*des bretelles* (f.)
velvet	*du velours*
vest	*un gilet*
wool	*de la laine*
zipper	*une fermeture éclair®*

Colors and Patterns

beige	*beige*
checked	*à carreaux*
colorful	*coloré(e), vif/vive*
dark blue	*bleu foncé*
dark-colored	*foncé(e)*
flowered	*à fleurs*
gold (adj.)	*d'or, doré(e)*
light blue	*bleu clair*
light-colored	*clair(e)*
patterned	*à motifs*
polka-dotted	*à pois*
striped	*à rayures*
turquoise	*turquoise*

Computers

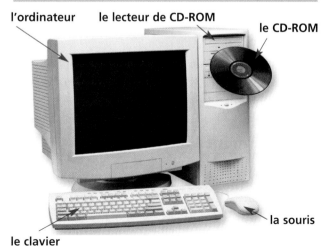

l'ordinateur   le lecteur de CD-ROM   le CD-ROM

la souris

le clavier

CD-ROM	*le CD-ROM, le disque optique compact*
CD-ROM drive	*le lecteur de CD-ROM, l'unité* (f.) *de CD-ROM*
to click	*cliquer*
computer	*l'ordinateur* (m.)
delete key	*la touche d'effacement*
disk drive	*le lecteur de disquette, l'unité de disquettes* (f.)
diskette, floppy disk	*la disquette, la disquette souple*
to drag	*glisser, déplacer*
e-mail	*le courrier électronique, la messagerie électronique*
file	*le dossier*
file (folder)	*le fichier*
hard drive	*le disque dur*
homepage	*la page d'accueil*
Internet	*Internet* (m.)
keyboard	*le clavier*
keyword	*le mot-clé*
log on	*l'ouverture* (f.) *de session*
modem	*le modem*
monitor	*le moniteur, le logimètre*
mouse	*la souris*

password	*le mot de passe*
to print	*imprimer*
printer	*l'imprimante* (f.)
to quit	*quitter*
to record	*enregistrer*
return key	*la touche de retour*
to save	*sauvegarder, enregistrer*
screen	*l'écran* (m.)
to search	*chercher, rechercher*
search engine	*le moteur de recherche, l'outil* (m.) *de recherche*
to send	*envoyer*
software	*le logiciel*
Web site	*le site du Web, le site W3*
World Wide Web	*le World Wide Web, le Web, le W3*

Entertainment

blues	*le blues*
CD player	*le lecteur de CD*
camera flash	*le flash*
folk music	*la musique folklorique*
headphones	*les écouteurs*

hit (song)	*le tube*
lens	*l'objectif* (m.)
microphone	*le micro(phone)*
opera	*l'opéra* (m.)
pop music	*la musique pop*
reggae	*le reggae*
roll of film	*la pellicule (photo)*
screen	*l'écran* (m.)
speakers	*les enceintes* (f.), *les baffles* (m.)
to turn off	*éteindre*
to turn on	*allumer*
turntable	*la platine*
walkman	*le balladeur*

Family

adopted	*adopté(e), adoptif/adoptive*
brother-in-law	*le beau-frère*
child	*un(e) enfant*
couple	*un couple*
daughter-in-law	*la belle-fille*
divorced	*divorcé(e)*
engaged	*fiancé(e)*
goddaughter	*la filleule*
godfather	*le parrain*
godmother	*la marraine*
godson	*le filleul*
grandchildren	*les petits-enfants*
granddaughter	*la petite-fille*
grandson	*le petit-fils*
great-granddaughter	*l'arrière-petite-fille* (f.)
great-grandfather	*l'arrière-grand-père* (m.)
great-grandmother	*l'arrière-grand-mère* (f.)
great-grandson	*l'arrière-petit-fils* (m.)
half-brother	*le demi-frère*
half-sister	*la demi-sœur*
mother-in-law	*la belle-mère*
only child	*un/une enfant unique*
single	*célibataire*
sister-in-law	*la belle-sœur*

son-in-law	le gendre; le beau-fils
stepbrother	le demi-frère
stepdaughter	la belle-fille
stepfather	le beau-père
stepmother	la belle-mère
stepsister	la demi-sœur
stepson	le beau-fils
widow	la veuve
widower	le veuf

Foods and Beverages

appetizer	une entrée
apricot	un abricot
asparagus	des asperges (f.)
bacon	du bacon
bowl	un bol
Brussels sprouts	des choux (m.) de Bruxelles
cabbage	du chou
cauliflower	du chou-fleur
cereal	des céréales (f.)
chestnut	un marron
cookie	un biscuit
cucumber	un concombre
cutlet	une escalope
fried egg	un œuf au plat; **hard-boiled egg** un œuf dur; **scrambled eggs** des œufs brouillés; **soft-boiled egg** un œuf à la coque

eggplant	une aubergine
French bread	une baguette
garlic	de l'ail (m.)
grapefruit	un pamplemousse
honey	du miel
liver	du foie
margarine	de la margarine
marshmallow	une guimauve
mayonnaise	de la mayonnaise
melon	un melon
mustard	de la moutarde
nuts	des noix (f.)
peanut butter	du beurre de cacahouètes
pepper (spice)	du poivre; (vegetable) un poivron
popcorn	du pop-corn
potato chips	des chips (f.)
raspberry	une framboise

salmon	du saumon
salt	du sel
shellfish	des fruits (m.) de mer
soup	de la soupe
spinach	des épinards (m.)
spoon	une cuillère
syrup	du sirop
veal	du veau
watermelon	une pastèque
zucchini	une courgette
bland	doux (douce)
hot (spicy)	épicé(e)
juicy (fruit)	juteux/juteuse; (meat) tendre
rare (cooked)	saignant(e)
medium (cooked)	à point
spicy	épicé(e)
well-done (cooked)	bien cuit(e)
tasty	savoureux/savoureuse

Housework

to clean	nettoyer
to dry	faire sécher
to dust	faire la poussière
to fold	plier
to hang	pendre
to iron	repasser
to put away	ranger
to rake	ratisser
to shovel	enlever à la pelle
to sweep	balayer

Pets

bird	un oiseau
cow	une vache
frog	une grenouille
goldfish	un poisson rouge
guinea pig	un cochon d'Inde
hamster	un hamster
horse	un cheval
kitten	un chaton
lizard	un lézard
mouse	une souris
parrot	un perroquet
pig	un cochon
puppy	un chiot
rabbit	un lapin
turtle	une tortue

Places Around Town

airport	*l'aéroport* (m.)
beauty shop	*le salon de coiffure*
bridge	*le pont*
church	*l'église* (f.)
consulate	*le consulat*
hospital	*l'hôpital* (m.)
mosque	*la mosquée*
police station	*le commissariat de police*
synagogue	*la synagogue*
tourist office	*l'office de tourisme* (m.)
town hall	*l'hôtel* (m.) *de ville*

Professions

Note: If only one form is given, that form is used for both men and women. Note that you can also say **une femme banquier, une femme médecin,** and so forth.

archaeologist	*un(e) archéologue*
architect	*un(e) architecte*
athlete	*un(e) athlète*
banker	*un banquier*
businessman/ businesswoman	*un homme d'affaires (une femme d'affaires)*
dancer	*un danseur (une danseuse)*
dentist	*un(e) dentiste*
doctor	*un médecin*
editor	*un rédacteur (une rédactrice)*
engineer	*un ingénieur*
fashion designer	*un(e) styliste de mode*
fashion model	*un mannequin*
hairdresser	*un coiffeur (une coiffeuse)*
homemaker	*un homme au foyer (une femme au foyer)*
lawyer	*un(e) avocat(e)*

manager (company)	*un directeur (une directrice);* (**store, restaurant**) *un gérant (une gérante)*
mechanic	*un mécanicien (une mécanicienne)*
painter (art)	*un peintre;* (**buildings**) *un peintre en bâtiment*
pilot	*un pilote*
plumber	*un plombier*
scientist	*un(e) scientifique*
secretary	*un(e) secrétaire*
social worker	*un assistant social (une assistante sociale)*
taxi driver	*un chauffeur de taxi*
technician	*un technicien (une technicienne)*
truck driver	*un routier*
veterinarian	*un(e) vétérinaire*
worker	*un ouvrier (une ouvrière)*
writer	*un écrivain*

School Subjects

accounting	*la comptabilité*
business	*le commerce*
foreign languages	*les langues* (f.) *étrangères*
home economics	*les arts* (m.) *ménagers*
marching band	*la fanfare*
orchestra	*l'orchestre* (m.)
social studies	*les sciences* (f.) *sociales*
typing	*la dactylographie*
woodworking	*la menuiserie*
world history	*l'histoire* (f.) *mondiale*

School Supplies

calendar	*un calendrier*
colored pencils	*des crayons* (m.) *de couleur*
compass	*un compas*
correction fluid	*du liquide correcteur*
glue	*de la colle*
gym uniform	*une tenue de gymnastique*
marker	*un feutre*
rubber band	*un élastique*
scissors	*des ciseaux* (m.)
staple	*une agrafe*
stapler	*une agrafeuse*
transparent tape	*du ruban adhésif*

Sports and Interests

badminton	*le badminton*
boxing	*la boxe*

fishing rod	*la canne à pêche*
foot race	*la course à pied*
to go for a ride	*faire une promenade,*
(by bike, car,	*faire un tour (à bicyclette,*
motorcycle, moped)	*en voiture, à moto, à*
	vélomoteur)
to do gymnastics	*faire de la gymnastique*
hunting	*la chasse*
to lift weights	*faire des haltères*
mountain climbing	*l'alpinisme* (m.)
to play checkers	*jouer aux dames*
to play chess	*jouer aux échecs*

to ride a skateboard	*faire de la planche à*
	roulettes
to sew	*coudre; faire de la*
	couture
speed skating	*le patinage de vitesse*
to surf	*faire du surf*

Weather

barometer	*le baromètre*
blizzard	*la tempête de neige*
cloudy	*nuageux*
drizzle	*la bruine*
fog	*le brouillard*
frost	*la gelée*
hail	*la grêle*
to hail	*grêler*
heat wave	*la canicule*
hurricane	*l'ouragan* (m.)
ice (on the road)	*le verglas*
It's pouring.	*Il pleut à verse.*
It's sleeting.	*Il tombe de la neige*
	fondue.
It's sunny.	*Il fait du soleil.*
lightning bolt	*l'éclair* (m.)
mist	*la brume*
shower (rain)	*l'averse* (f.)
storm	*la tempête*
thermometer	*le thermomètre*
thunder	*le tonnerre*
thunderstorm	*l'orage* (m.)
tornado	*la tornade*

Cities

Algiers	*Alger*
Brussels	*Bruxelles*
Cairo	*Le Caire*
Geneva	*Genève*
Lisbon	*Lisbonne*
London	*Londres*
Montreal	*Montréal*
Moscow	*Moscou*
New Orleans	*La Nouvelle-Orléans*
Quebec City	*Québec*
Tangier	*Tanger*
Venice	*Venise*
Vienna	*Vienne*

The Continents

Africa	*l'Afrique* (f.)
Antarctica	*l'Antarctique* (f.)
Asia	*l'Asie* (f.)
Australia	*l'Océanie* (f.)
Europe	*l'Europe* (f.)
North America	*l'Amérique* (f.) *du Nord*
South America	*l'Amérique* (f.) *du Sud*

Countries

Algeria	*l'Algérie* (f.)
Argentina	*l'Argentine* (f.)
Australia	*l'Australie* (f.)
Austria	*l'Autriche* (f.)
Belgium	*la Belgique*
Brazil	*le Brésil*
Canada	*le Canada*
China	*la Chine*
Côte d'Ivoire	*la République de Côte*
	d'Ivoire
Egypt	*l'Egypte* (f.)
England	*l'Angleterre* (f.)
France	*la France*
Germany	*l'Allemagne* (f.)

Greece	*la Grèce*
Holland	*la Hollande*
India	*l'Inde* (f.)
Ireland	*l'Irlande* (f.)
Israel	*Israël* (m.)
Italy	*l'Italie* (f.)
Jamaica	*la Jamaïque*
Japan	*le Japon*
Jordan	*la Jordanie*
Lebanon	*le Liban*
Libya	*la Libye*
Luxembourg	*le Luxembourg*
Mexico	*le Mexique*
Monaco	*Monaco* (f.)
Morocco	*le Maroc*
Netherlands	*les Pays-Bas* (m.)
North Korea	*la Corée du Nord*
Peru	*le Pérou*
Philippines	*les Philippines* (f.)
Poland	*la Pologne*
Portugal	*le Portugal*
Russia	*la Russie*
Senegal	*le Sénégal*
South Korea	*la Corée du Sud*
Spain	*l'Espagne* (f.)
Switzerland	*la Suisse*
Syria	*la Syrie*
Tunisia	*la Tunisie*
Turkey	*la Turquie*
United States	*les Etats-Unis* (m.)
Vietnam	*le Viêt-nam*

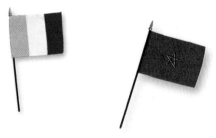

States

California	*la Californie*
Florida	*la Floride*
Georgia	*la Géorgie*
Louisiana	*la Louisiane*
New Mexico	*le Nouveau Mexique*
North Carolina	*la Caroline du Nord*
Pennsylvania	*la Pennsylvanie*
South Carolina	*la Caroline du Sud*
Texas	*le Texas*
Virginia	*la Virginie*

Oceans and Seas

Atlantic Ocean	*l'Atlantique* (m.), *l'océan* (m.) *Atlantique*
Caribbean Sea	*la mer des Caraïbes*
English Channel	*la Manche*
Indian Ocean	*l'océan* (m.) *Indien*
Mediterranean Sea	*la mer Méditerranée*
Pacific Ocean	*le Pacifique, l'océan* (m.) *Pacifique*

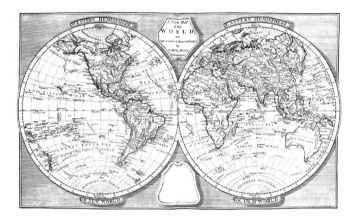

Other Geographical Terms

Alps	*les Alpes* (f.)
border	*la frontière*
capital	*la capitale*
continent	*le continent*
country	*le pays*
hill	*la colline*
lake	*le lac*
latitude	*la latitude*
longitude	*la longitude*
North Africa	*l'Afrique* (f.) *du Nord*
ocean	*l'océan* (m.)
plain	*la plaine*
Pyrenees	*les Pyrénées* (f.)
river	*la rivière, le fleuve*
sea	*la mer*
state	*l'état* (m.)
the North Pole	*le pôle Nord*
the South Pole	*le pôle Sud*
valley	*la vallée*

ADJECTIVES

REGULAR ADJECTIVES

In French, adjectives agree in gender and number with the nouns that they modify. A regular adjective has four forms: masculine singular, feminine singular, masculine plural, and feminine plural. To make a regular adjective agree with a feminine noun, add an **-e** to the masculine singular form of the adjective. To make one agree with a plural noun, add an **-s** to the masculine singular form. To make one adjective agree with a feminine plural noun, add **-es** to the masculine singular form. Adjectives ending in **-é**, like **désolé,** also follow these rules.

	SINGULAR	PLURAL
MASCULINE	un jean **vert**	des jeans **verts**
FEMININE	une ceinture **verte**	des ceintures **vertes**

ADJECTIVES THAT END IN AN UNACCENTED -E

When an adjective ends in an unaccented **-e,** the masculine singular and the feminine singular forms are the same. To form the plural of these adjectives, add an **-s** to the singular forms.

	SINGULAR	PLURAL
MASCULINE	un cahier **rouge**	des cahiers **rouges**
FEMININE	une trousse **rouge**	des trousses **rouges**

ADJECTIVES THAT END IN -S

When the masculine singular form of an adjective ends in an **-s,** the masculine plural form does not change. The feminine forms follow the regular adjective rules.

	SINGULAR	PLURAL
MASCULINE	un sac **gris**	des sacs **gris**
FEMININE	une robe **grise**	des robes **grises**

ADJECTIVES THAT END IN -EUX

Adjectives that end in **-eux** do not change in the masculine plural. The feminine singular form of these adjectives is made by replacing the **-x** with **-se.** To form the feminine plural, replace the **-x** with **-ses.**

	SINGULAR	PLURAL
MASCULINE	un garçon **heureux**	des garçons **heureux**
FEMININE	une fille **heureuse**	des filles **heureuses**

ADJECTIVES THAT END IN -IF

To make the feminine singular form of adjectives that end in **-if,** replace **-if** with **-ive.** To make the plural forms of these adjectives, add an **-s** to the singular forms.

	SINGULAR	PLURAL
MASCULINE	un garçon **sportif**	des garçons **sportifs**
FEMININE	une fille **sportive**	des filles **sportives**

ADJECTIVES THAT END IN -IEN

To make the feminine singular and feminine plural forms of adjectives that end in **-ien** in their masculine singular form, add **-ne** and **-nes.** Add an **-s** to form the masculine plural.

	SINGULAR	PLURAL
MASCULINE	un garçon **canadien**	des garçons **canadiens**
FEMININE	une fille **canadienne**	des filles **canadiennes**

ADJECTIVES THAT DOUBLE THE LAST CONSONANT

To make the adjectives **bon, gentil, gros, mignon, nul,** and **violet** agree with a feminine noun, double the last consonant and add an **-e.** To make the plural forms, add an **-s** to the singular forms. Note that with **gros,** the masculine singular and masculine plural forms are the same.

	SINGULAR					
MASCULINE	bon	gentil	gros	mignon	nul	violet
FEMININE	bonne	gentille	grosse	mignonne	nulle	violette

	PLURAL					
MASCULINE	bons	gentils	gros	mignons	nuls	violets
FEMININE	bonnes	gentilles	grosses	mignonnes	nulles	violettes

INVARIABLE ADJECTIVES

Some adjectives are invariable. They never change form. **Cool, marron, orange,** and **super** are examples of invariable adjectives.

> Il me faut une montre **marron** et des baskets **orange.**

IRREGULAR ADJECTIVES

The forms of some adjectives must simply be memorized. This is the case for **blanc, sympa,** and **roux.**

Note that **sympathique,** the long form of the adjective, follows the rules for adjectives that end in an unaccented -**e,** like **rouge.**

	SINGULAR	PLURAL
MASCULINE	blanc	blancs
FEMININE	blanche	blanches

	SINGULAR	PLURAL
MASCULINE	roux	roux
FEMININE	rousse	rousses

	SINGULAR	PLURAL
MASCULINE	sympa	sympas
FEMININE	sympa	sympas

POSITION OF ADJECTIVES

In French, adjectives are usually placed after the noun that they modify.

> C'est une femme **intelligente.**

Certain adjectives precede the noun. Some of these are **bon, jeune, joli, grand,** and **petit.**

> C'est un **petit** village.

DEMONSTRATIVE ADJECTIVES

This, that, these, and *those* are demonstrative adjectives. There are two masculine singular forms of these adjectives in French: **ce** and **cet. Cet** is used with masculine singular nouns that begin with a vowel sound. Some examples are **cet ordinateur** and **cet homme.** Demonstrative adjectives always precede the noun that they modify.

	Singular Before a Consonant	Singular Before a Vowel Sound	Plural
MASCULINE	ce livre	cet ordinateur	ces posters
FEMININE	cette montre	cette école	ces gommes

POSSESSIVE ADJECTIVES

Possessive adjectives come before the noun that they modify and agree in gender and number with that noun. All nouns that begin with a vowel sound use the masculine singular form, for example **mon ami(e), ton ami(e), son ami(e).**

	Masculine Singular	Feminine Singular	Masc./Fem. Singular Before a Vowel Sound	Masc./Fem. Plural
my	**mon** père	**ma** mère	**mon** oncle	**mes** cousines
your	**ton** livre	**ta** montre	**ton** écharpe	**tes** cahiers
his, her, its	**son** chien	**sa** sœur	**son** école	**ses** cours

The possessive adjectives for *our, your,* and *their* have only two forms, singular and plural.

	Masc./Fem. Singular	Masc./Fem. Plural
our	**notre** frère	**nos** tantes
your	**votre** classeur	**vos** amis
their	**leur** copain	**leurs** trousses

ADJECTIVES AS NOUNS

To use an adjective as a noun, add a definite article before the adjective. The article that you use agrees in gender and number with the noun that the adjective is replacing.

> —Tu aimes les chemises rouges ou **les blanches?**
>> *Do you like the red shirts or the white ones?*
> —J'aime **les blanches.**
>> *I like the white ones.*

ADVERBS

POSITION OF ADVERBS

Most adverbs follow the conjugated verb. In the **passé composé,** they usually precede the past participle.

> Nathalie fait **souvent** des photos.   Je n'ai pas **bien** mangé ce matin.

Adverbs that are made up of more than one word can be placed at the beginning or at the end of a sentence. When you use **ne (n')... jamais,** place it around the conjugated verb.

> **D'habitude,** je fais du tennis le soir.
> J'aime faire de l'aérobic **deux fois par semaine.**
> Je **n'**ai **jamais** fait de ski.

ARTICLES

DEFINITE ARTICLES

French has four definite articles: **le, la, l',** and **les.** The form that you use depends on the gender and number of the noun it modifies. Use **le** with masculine singular nouns, **le livre; la** with feminine singular nouns, **la chemise;** and **les** with both masculine and feminine nouns that are plural, **les crayons.** The form **l'** is used with both masculine and feminine nouns that begin with a vowel sound: **l'ami, l'amie, l'homme.** In French, you sometimes use a definite article when no article is required in English.

J'aime **le** chocolat et toi, tu préfères **le** café.

	Singular Before a Consonant	Singular Before a Vowel Sound	Plural
MASCULINE	**le** professeur	**l'**ami	**les** livres
FEMININE	**la** pharmacie	**l'**école	**les** pommes

INDEFINITE ARTICLES

In English, there are three indefinite articles: *a, an,* and *some.* In French there are also three: **un, une,** and **des.** The indefinite articles agree in number and gender with the nouns they modify.

	SINGULAR	PLURAL
MASCULINE	**un** poisson	**des** chats
FEMININE	**une** orange	**des** lunettes

PARTITIVE ARTICLES

To say that you want *part* or *some* of an item, use the partitive articles. Use **du** with a masculine noun and **de la** with a feminine noun. Use **de l'** with singular nouns that begin with a vowel sound whether they are masculine or feminine.

Je veux **de la** tarte aux pommes. *I want some apple pie.*

To indicate the whole as opposed to a part of the item, use the indefinite articles **un, une,** and **des.**

Pour la fête, il me faut **des** tartes. *I need (some) pies for the party.*

NEGATION AND THE ARTICLES

When the main verb of a sentence is negated, the indefinite and the partitive articles change to **de/d'.** Definite articles remain the same after a negative verb.

J'ai **le** livre de maths.   —> Je n'ai pas **le** livre de maths.

J'ai **des** stylos.   —> Je n'ai pas **de** stylos.

J'ai mangé **de la** pizza.   —> Je n'ai pas mangé **de** pizza.

INTERROGATIVES

QUESTION FORMATION

There are several ways to ask yes-no questions. One of these is to raise the pitch of your voice at the end of a statement. The other is to place **est-ce que** in front of a statement.

Tu aimes le chocolat. —> **Tu aimes le chocolat?** (intonation) *or*
Est-ce que tu aimes le chocolat?

NEGATIVE QUESTIONS

The answer to a yes-no question depends on the way the question was stated. If the verb in a question is positive, then the answer is **oui** if you agree, and **non** if you don't. If the verb in a question is negative, then **non** is used to agree with the question and **si** to disagree.

Question	Agreeing with the Question	Disagreeing with the Question
Tu aimes lire?	**Oui,** j'aime lire.	**Non,** je n'aime pas lire.
Tu n'aimes pas lire?	**Non,** je n'aime pas lire.	**Si,** j'aime lire.

INFORMATION QUESTIONS

To ask for specific kinds of information, use the following question words:

A quelle heure?   *At what time?*   **Où?**   *Where?*
Avec qui?   *With whom?*   **Quand?**   *When?*

These words can be used by themselves, at the beginning of a question, at the beginning of a question, followed by **est-ce que,** or at the end of a question.

Avec qui?   **Avec qui** est-ce qu'on va au cinéma?
Avec qui on va au cinéma?   On va au cinéma **avec qui?**

NOUNS

PLURAL FORMS OF NOUNS

In French, you make most nouns plural by adding an **-s** to the end of the word, unless they already end in **-s** or **-x.** Nouns that end in **-eau** are made plural by adding an **-x,** and nouns that end in **-al** are generally made plural by replacing the **-al** with **-aux.**

	Regular Nouns	-s or -x	-eau	-al
SINGULAR	table	bus	manteau	hôpital
PLURAL	tables	bus	manteaux	hôpitaux

PREPOSITIONS

THE PREPOSITIONS A AND DE

The preposition **à** means *to, at,* or *in,* and **de** means *from* or *of.* When **à** and **de** are used in front of the definite articles **le** and **les,** they form contractions. If they precede any other definite article, there is no contraction.

> Il va **à l'**école et **au** musée. *He's going to school and to the museum.*

> Nous sommes loin **du** musée. *We are far from the museum.*

	Masculine Article	Feminine Article	Vowel Sound	Plural
à	à + le = **au**	à + la = **à la**	à + l' = **à l'**	à + les = **aux**
de	de + le = **du**	de + la = **de la**	de + l' = **de l'**	de + les = **des**

De can also indicate possession or ownership.

> C'est le livre **de** Laurent. *It's Laurent's book.*

> C'est le stylo **du** prof. *It's the professor's pen.*

PREPOSITIONS AND PLACES

To say that you are at or going to a place, you need to use a preposition. With cities, use the preposition **à : à Paris.** One notable exception is **en Arles.** When speaking about masculine countries, use **au : au Maroc.** With plural names of countries, use **aux : aux Etats-Unis.** Most countries ending in **-e** are feminine; in these cases, use **en : en France.** **Le Mexique** is an exception. If a country begins with a vowel, like **Israël,** use **en : en Israël.**

Cities	Masculine Countries	Feminine Countries or Masculine Countries that Begin with a Vowel	Plural Countries
à Nantes à Paris en Arles	au Canada au Maroc au Mexique	en Italie en Espagne en Israël	aux Etats-Unis aux Philippines aux Pays-Bas

PRONOUNS

In French, as in English, a pronoun can refer to a person, place, or thing. Pronouns are used to avoid repetition. In French, pronouns agree in gender and number with the noun that they replace.

SUBJECT PRONOUNS

Subject pronouns replace the subject in a sentence.

je (j')	*I*	nous	*we*
tu	*you* (familiar)	vous	*you* (plural or formal)
il	*he / it*	ils	*they*
elle	*she / it*	elles	*they*
on	*we / one / they*		

THE IMPERSONAL PRONOUN IL

Many statements in French begin with the personal pronoun **il**. In these statements, **il** does not refer to any particular person or thing. For this reason, these statements are called impersonal statements.

Il fait beau. *It's nice out.*

Il est huit heures. *It's eight o'clock.*

Il me/te faut... *I/You need . . .*

Il y a... *There is/are . . .*

DIRECT OBJECT PRONOUNS: LE, LA, LES

A direct object is a noun that receives the action of the verb. It answers the questions *What?* or *Whom?* To say *him, her, it,* or *them,* use the pronouns **le, la,** and **les.** In French, you place the direct object pronoun in front of the conjugated verb.

Il regarde **la télé.** —> Il **la** regarde.

If there is an infinitive in the sentence, the direct object pronoun comes before the infinitive.

Je vais attendre **Pierre.** —> Je vais l'attendre.

In an affirmative command, the direct object pronoun follows the verb and is connected to it with a hyphen.

Regarde **la télévision.** —> Regarde-**la**!

	SINGULAR	PLURAL
MASCULINE	le / l'	les
FEMININE	la / l'	les

INDIRECT OBJECT PRONOUNS: LUI, LEUR

The indirect object answers the question *To whom?* and refers only to people. In French an indirect object follows the preposition **à**: **Il parle à Marie.** The indirect object pronoun replaces the prepositional phrase **à** + **a person,** and precedes the conjugated verb.

> Nous téléphonons **à Mireille.** —> Nous **lui** téléphonons.

If there is an infinitive in the sentence, the indirect object pronoun comes before the infinitive.

> Il n'aime pas parler **à ses parents.** —> Il n'aime pas **leur** parler.

In an affirmative command, the indirect object pronoun follows the verb and is connected to it with a hyphen.

> Téléphone **à ta sœur.** —> Téléphone-**lui**!

THE PRONOUN Y

To replace a phrase meaning *to, on, at,* or *in* any place that has already been mentioned, you can use the pronoun **y.** It can replace phrases beginning with prepositions of location such as **à, sur, chez, dans,** and **en** + **a place or thing.** Place **y** before the conjugated verb.

> Elle va **à la pharmacie.** —> Elle **y** va.

If there is an infinitive, place **y** before the infinitive.

> Elle va aller **à la poste** demain. —> Elle va **y** aller demain.

THE PRONOUN EN

The pronoun **en** replaces a phrase beginning with **de, du, de la, de l',** or **des.** It usually means *about it, some (of it/of them),* or simply *it/them,* and is placed before the conjugated verb.

> Tu achètes **des haricots verts?** —> Oui, j'**en** achète pour le dîner.

En in a negative sentence means *not any* or *none.*

> Tu ne bois pas **de café.** —> Tu n'**en** bois pas.

En is placed before the conjugated verb.

> Je parle **de mes vacances.** —> J'**en** parle.

If there is an infinitive, place **en** before the infinitive.

> Vous aimez manger **des fruits.** —> Vous aimez **en** manger.

Notice that with the **passé composé, en** precedes the helping verb.

> Il a mangé **du pain.** —> Il **en** a mangé.

VERBS

THE PRESENT TENSE OF REGULAR VERBS

To conjugate a verb in French, use the following formulas. Which formula you choose depends on the ending of the infinitive. There are three major verb categories: **-er, -ir,** and **-re.** Each one has a different conjugation. Within these categories, there are regular and irregular verbs. To conjugate regular verbs, you drop the infinitive endings and add these endings.

Subject	aimer (to love, to like) Stem	Ending	choisir (to choose) Stem	Ending	vendre (to sell) Stem	Ending
je/j'		-e		-is		-s
tu		-es		-is		-s
il/elle/on	aim	-e	chois	-it	vend	—
nous		-ons		-issons		-ons
vous		-ez		-issez		-ez
ils/elles		-ent		-issent		-ent

VERBS WITH STEM AND SPELLING CHANGES

Verbs listed in this section are not irregular, but they do have some stem and spelling changes.

With **acheter** and **promener**, add an **accent grave** over the second-to-last **e** for all forms except **nous** and **vous**. Notice that the accent on the second **e** in **préférer** changes from **é** to **è** in all forms except the **nous** and **vous** forms.

	acheter (to buy)	préférer (to prefer)	promener (to walk (an animal))
je/j'	achète	préfère	promène
tu	achètes	préfères	promènes
il/elle/on	achète	préfère	promène
nous	achetons	préférons	promenons
vous	achetez	préférez	promenez
ils/elles	achètent	préfèrent	promènent
Past Participle	acheté	préféré	promené

The following verbs have different stems for **nous** and **vous.**

	appeler *(to call)*	essayer *(to try)*
je/j'	appelle	essaie
tu	appelles	essaies
il/elle/on	appelle	essaie
nous	appelons	essayons
vous	appelez	essayez
ils/elles	appellent	essaient
Past Participle	appelé	essayé

The following verbs show a difference only in the **nous** form.

	commencer *(to start)*	manger *(to eat)*
je/j'	commence	mange
tu	commences	manges
il/elle/on	commence	mange
nous	commençons	mangeons
vous	commencez	mangez
ils/elles	commencent	mangent
Past Participle	commencé	mangé

	nager *(to swim)*	voyager *(to travel)*
je/j'	nage	voyage
tu	nages	voyages
il/elle/on	nage	voyage
nous	nageons	voyageons
vous	nagez	voyagez
ils/elles	nagent	voyagent
Past Participle	nagé	voyagé

VERBS LIKE DORMIR

These verbs follow a different pattern from the one you learned for regular -**ir** verbs.
These verbs have two stems: one for the singular subjects, and one for the plural ones.

	dormir (to sleep)	**partir** (to leave)	**sortir** (to go out, to take out)
je/j'	dors	pars	sors
tu	dors	pars	sors
il/elle/on	dort	part	sort
nous	dorm**ons**	part**ons**	sort**ons**
vous	dorm**ez**	part**ez**	sort**ez**
ils/elles	dorm**ent**	part**ent**	sort**ent**

VERBS WITH IRREGULAR FORMS

Verbs listed in this section do not follow the pattern of verbs like **aimer, choisir,** or **vendre.** Therefore, they are called *irregular verbs.* The following four irregular verbs are used frequently.

	aller (to go)	**avoir** (to have)
je/j'	vais	ai
tu	vas	as
il/elle/on	va	a
nous	allons	avons
vous	allez	avez
ils/elles	vont	ont

	être (to be)	**faire** (to do, to make, to play)
je/j'	suis	fais
tu	es	fais
il/elle/on	est	fait
nous	sommes	faisons
vous	êtes	faites
ils/elles	sont	font

Devoir, pouvoir, and vouloir are also irregular. They are usually followed by an infinitive.

Je peux chanter. *I can sing.*

	devoir *(must, to have to)*	**pouvoir** *(to be able to, can)*	**vouloir** *(to want)*
je/j'	dois	peux	veux
tu	dois	peux	veux
il/elle/on	doit	peut	veut
nous	devons	pouvons	voulons
vous	devez	pouvez	voulez
ils/elles	doivent	peuvent	veulent

These verbs also have irregular forms.

	dire *(to say)*	**écrire** *(to write)*	**lire** *(to read)*
je/j'	dis	écris	lis
tu	dis	écris	lis
il/elle/on	dit	écrit	lit
nous	disons	écrivons	lisons
vous	dites	écrivez	lisez
ils/elles	disent	écrivent	lisent
Past Participle	dit	écrit	lu

	mettre *(to put, to put on, to wear)*	**prendre** *(to take, to have food or drink)*	**voir** *(to see)*
je/j'	mets	prends	vois
tu	mets	prends	vois
il/elle/on	met	prend	voit
nous	mettons	prenons	voyons
vous	mettez	prenez	voyez
ils/elles	mettent	prennent	voient
Past Participle	mis	pris	vu

THE NEAR FUTURE (FUTUR PROCHE)

Like the past tense, the near future is made of two parts. The future tense of a verb consists of the present tense of **aller** plus the infinitive:

Vous **allez sortir** avec vos copains demain. *You're going to go out with your friends tomorrow.*

THE PAST TENSE (PASSE COMPOSE)

The past tense of most verbs is formed with two parts: the present tense form of the helping verb **avoir** and the past participle of the main verb. To form the past participle, use the formulas below. To make a sentence negative in the past, place the **ne... pas** around the helping verb **avoir.**

INFINITIVE	aimer (to love, to like)		choisir (to choose)		vendre (to sell)	
	Stem	**Ending**	**Stem**	**Ending**	**Stem**	**Ending**
PAST PARTICIPLE	aim aimé	-é	chois choisi	-i	vend vendu	-u
PASSE COMPOSE	j'ai aimé		j'ai choisi		j'ai vendu	

J'**ai mangé** de la pizza.   Nous **avons choisi** le livre.

Elle n'**a pas vendu** sa voiture.   Nous n'**avons** pas **mangé** de pizza.

Some verbs have irregular past participles.

faire —> fait	prendre —> pris	avoir —> eu
lire —> lu	voir —> vu	mettre —> mis

With some verbs, such as **aller,** you use the helping verb **être** instead of **avoir.** The past participle of these verbs agrees in gender and number with the subject of the sentence.

Je **suis allé(e)** à l'école.   Ils **sont allés** à la poste.   Elle **est allée** au café.

THE IMPERATIVE (COMMANDS)

To make a request or a command of most verbs, use the **tu, nous,** or **vous** form of the present tense of the verb without the subject. Remember to drop the final **-s** in the **tu** form of an **-er** verb.

Mange!

Ecoute le professeur!

Faites vos devoirs!

Prenons un sandwich!

aimer (to love, to like)		choisir (to choose)		vendre (to sell)	
Stem	**Ending**	**Stem**	**Ending**	**Stem**	**Ending**
aim	-e -ons -ez	chois	-is -issons -issez	vend	-s -ons -ez

Chapter	Letter Combination	IPA Symbol	Example
Ch. 1, p. 35 Intonation			
Ch. 2, p. 63 Liaison			vous‿avez des‿amis
Ch. 3, p. 91 The **r** sound	the letter **r**	/ʀ/	rouge vert
Ch. 4, p. 125 The sounds [y] and [u]	the letter **u** the letter combination **ou**	/y/ /u/	une nous
Ch. 5, p. 157 The nasal sound [ɑ̃]	the letter combination **an** the letter combination **am** the letter combination **en** the letter combination **em**	/ɑ̃/	anglais jambon comment temps
Ch. 6, p. 187 The vowel sounds [ø] and [œ]	the letter combination **eu** the letter combination **eu**	/ø/ /œ/	deux heure
Ch. 7, p. 215 The nasal sounds [ɔ̃], [ɛ̃], and [œ̃]	the letter combination **on** the letter combination **om** the letter combination **in** the letter combination **im** the letter combination **ain** the letter combination **aim** the letter combination **(i)en** the letter combination **un** the letter combination **um**	/ɔ̃/ /ɛ̃/ /œ̃/	pardon nombre cousin impossible copain faim bien lundi humble
Ch. 8, p. 249 The sounds [o] and [ɔ]	the letter combination **au** the letter combination **eau** the letter **ô** the letter **o**	/o/ /ɔ/	jaune beau rôle carotte
Ch. 9, p. 281 The vowel sounds [e] and [ɛ]	the letter combination **ez** the letter combination **er** the letter combination **ait** the letter combination **ais** the letter combination **ei** the letter **ê**	/e/ /ɛ/	apportez trouver fait français neige bête
Ch. 10, p. 311 The glides [j], [w], and [ɥ]	the letter **i** the letter combination **ill** the letter combination **oi** the letter combination **oui** the letter combination **ui**	/j/ /w/ /ɥ/	mieux maillot moi Louis huit
Ch. 11, p. 339 **h aspiré, th, ch,** and **gn**	the letter **h** the letter combination **th** the letter combination **ch** the letter combination **gn**	/ʔ/ /t/ /ʃ/ /ɲ/	les halls théâtre chocolat oignon
Ch. 12, p. 373 Review			

Numbers

LES NOMBRES CARDINAUX

0	zéro	20	vingt	80	quatre-vingts
1	un(e)	21	vingt et un(e)	81	quatre-vingt-un(e)
2	deux	22	vingt-deux	82	quatre-vingt-deux
3	trois	23	vingt-trois	90	quatre-vingt-dix
4	quatre	24	vingt-quatre	91	quatre-vingt-onze
5	cinq	25	vingt-cinq	92	quatre-vingt-douze
6	six	26	vingt-six	100	cent
7	sept	27	vingt-sept	101	cent un
8	huit	28	vingt-huit	200	deux cents
9	neuf	29	vingt-neuf	201	deux cent un
10	dix	30	trente	300	trois cents
11	onze	31	trente et un(e)	800	huit cents
12	douze	32	trente-deux	1.000	mille
13	treize	40	quarante	2.000	deux mille
14	quatorze	50	cinquante	3.000	trois mille
15	quinze	60	soixante	10.000	dix mille
16	seize	70	soixante-dix	19.000	dix-neuf mille
17	dix-sept	71	soixante et onze	40.000	quarante mille
18	dix-huit	72	soixante-douze	500.000	cinq cent mille
19	dix-neuf	73	soixante-treize	1.000.000	un million

- The word **et** is used only in 21, 31, 41, 51, 61, and 71.
- **Vingt (trente, quarante,** and so on) **et une** is used when the number refers to a feminine noun: **trente et une cassettes.**
- The **s** is dropped from **quatre-vingts** and is not added to multiples of **cent** when these numbers are followed by another number: **quatre-vingt-cinq; deux cents,** *but* **deux cent six.** The number **mille** never takes an **s** to agree with a noun: **deux mille insectes.**
- **Un million** is followed by **de** + a noun: **un million de francs.**
- In writing numbers, a period is used in French where a comma is used in English.

LES NOMBRES ORDINAUX

1er, 1ère	premier, première	9e	neuvième	17e	dix-septième
2e	deuxième	10e	dixième	18e	dix-huitième
3e	troisième	11e	onzième	19e	dix-neuvième
4e	quatrième	12e	douzième	20e	vingtième
5e	cinquième	13e	treizième	21e	vingt et unième
6e	sixième	14e	quatorzième	22e	vingt-deuxième
7e	septième	15e	quinzième	30e	trentième
8e	huitième	16e	seizième	40e	quarantième

French-English Vocabulary

English-French Vocabulary

French-English Vocabulary

This list includes both active and passive vocabulary in this textbook. Active words and phrases are those listed in the **Vocabulaire** section at the end of each chapter. You are expected to know and be able to use active vocabulary. All entries in heavy black type in this list are active. All other words are passive. Passive vocabulary is for recognition only.

The number after each entry refers to the chapter where the word or phrase is introduced. Nouns are always given with an article. If it is not clear whether the noun is masculine or feminine, *m.* (masculine) or *f.* (feminine) follows the noun. Some nouns that are generally seen only in the plural, as well as ones that have an irregular plural form, are also given with gender indications and the abbreviation *pl.* (plural) following them. An asterisk (*) before a word beginning with *h* indicates an aspirate *h*. Phrases are alphabetized by the key word(s) in the phrase.

The following abbreviations are also used in this vocabulary: *pp.* (past participle), *inv.* (invariable), and *adj.* (adjective).

à *to, in (a city or place)*, 11; **à côté de** *next to*, 12; **à la** *to, at*, 6; **A bientôt.** *See you soon.* 1; à carreaux *checked*, 10; **A demain.** *See you tomorrow.* 1; à fleurs *flowered*, 10; à la carte *pick and choose*, 3; à la française *French-style*, 1; **à la mode** *in style*, 10; à part ça *aside from that*, 11; à pois *polka dot*, 10; à propos de *in regard to, about*, 4; **A quelle heure?** *At what time?* 6; à rayures *striped*, 10; **A tout à l'heure!** *See you later!* 1; **A votre service.** *At your service; You're welcome.* 3; Et maintenant, à toi. *And now, it's your turn.* 1
l' abbaye (f.) *abbey*, 6
abîmer *to ruin*, 10
s' abonner *to subscribe*; abonnez-vous à... *subscribe to...* , 3
l' abricot (m.) *apricot*, 5
abriter *to house*, 11
absent(e) *absent*, 2
accepter *to accept*, 6
accompagner *to accompany*, 4
l' accord (m.) *agreement*; Fais l'accord... *Make the agreement...* , 7
l' accueil (m.) *reception, welcome*, 4
accueille (accueillir) *to welcome*
l' achat (m.) *purchase*, 3
acheter *to buy*, 9; **Achète (-moi)...** *Buy (me)...* , 8; Je n'achète pas... *I don't buy / I'm not buying...* , 3
l' acra de morue (m.) *cod fritter*

l' activité (f.) *activity*, 4
l' **addition** (f.) *check, bill*, 5; **L'addition, s'il vous plaît.** *The check, please.* 5
adhésif (-ive) *adhesive*, 3
admirer *to admire*, 7
adorable *adorable*, 7
adorer *to adore*, 1; **J'adore...** *I adore...* 1; J'adorerais... *I would adore...* , 1
l' **aérobic** (f.) *aerobics*, 4; **faire de l'aérobic** *to do aerobics*, 4
l' aéroport (m.) *airport*, 11
les affaires (f.) *business, business affairs*, 8
affectueux (-euse) *affectionate*, 7
afin de *in order to*, 7
l' Afrique (f.) *Africa*, 8
l' **âge** (m.) *age*, 1; **Tu as quel âge?** *How old are you?* 1
âgé(e) *older*, 7
l' agenda (m.) *planner*, 4
agit : il s'agit de *it's concerned with; it's about*, 6
agréable *pleasant*, 4
ai : J'ai... *I have...* , 2; **J'ai... ans.** *I am... years old.* 1; **J'ai besoin de...** *I need...* , 8; **J'ai faim.** *I'm hungry.* 5; **J'ai l'intention de...** *I intend to...* , 11; **J'ai soif.** *I'm thirsty.* 5; **Je n'ai pas de...** *I don't have...* , 3
l' aide-mémoire (m.) *memory aid*, 3
aider *to help*, 10; **(Est-ce que) je peux vous aider?** *May I help you?* 10
l' ail (m.) *garlic*, 8
les ailes (f.) *wings*, 12
aimé(e) (pp. of aimer) *loved*, 1

aimer *to like*, 1; **J'aime mieux...** *I prefer...* , 1; **J'aimerais... pour aller avec...** *I'd like... to go with...* , 10; **Je n'aime pas...** *I don't like...* , 1; **Moi, j'aime (bien)...** *I (really) like...* , 1; **Tu aimes...?** *Do you like...?* 1
l' aire de pique-nique aménagée (f.) *equipped picnic area*, 6
l' aise (f.) *ease*, 7
ajouter *to add*, 10
l' **algèbre** (f.) *algebra*, 2
l' Algérie (f.) *Algeria*, 0
l' alimentation (f.) *food*, 12
les aliments (m.) *nutrients*, 8
allé(e) (pp. of aller) *went*, 9; **Je suis allé(e)...** *I went...* , 9; **Tu es allé(e) où?** *Where did you go?* 9
l' allée (f.) *path, driveway*, 4
l' **allemand** (m.) *German (language)*, 2
aller *to go*, 6; **Ça va aller mieux!** *It's going to get better!* 9; **On peut y aller...** *We can go there...* , 12
allez : Allez au tableau! *Go to the blackboard!* 0; **Allez, viens!** *Come along!* 0
Allô? *Hello?* 9
l' allocation de naissance (f.) *money provided as a birth allowance by the French government*, 7; l'allocation familiale (f.) *money provided by the French government to large families*, 7
allons : Allons-y! *Let's go!* 4; **Allons...** *Let's go...* , 6
l' aloco (m.) *dish from West Africa made from fried plantain bananas and usually eaten as a snack*, 5
alors *well, then*, 3
l' alphabet (m.) *alphabet*, 0

l' ambiance (f.) *atmosphere,* 2
aménagé(e) *equipped,* 6
américain(e) *American (adj.),* 0
l' **ami(e)** *friend,* 1
amical(e) (pl. amicaux) *friendly,* 2
amicalement *sincerely (to close a letter),* 1
l' amitié (f.) *friendship,* 1
l' amour (m.) *love,* 1
l' amphithéâtre (m.) *amphitheater,* 9
amusant(e) *funny,* 7
s' amuser *to have fun,* 11; **Amuse-toi bien!** *Have fun!* 11; **Qu'est-ce que tu fais pour t'amuser?** *What do you do to have fun?* 4; **Tu t'es bien amusé(e)?** *Did you have fun?* 11
l' **an** (m.) *year,* 1; **J'ai... ans.** *I am . . . years old.* 1
l' **ananas** (m.) *pineapple,* 8
ancien(ne) *old; former,* 6; l'ancienne gare *the former train station,* 6
l' Andorre (article not commonly used) *Andorra,* 0
l' **anglais** (m.) *English (language),* 1
l' animal (m.) *animal,* 1; animal domestique *pet,* 7
l' animateur (m.) *camp counselor,* 11
les animations (f.) *activities,* 11
animé(e) *animated, lively,* 8
l' année (f.) *year,* 4
l' année scolaire (f.) *school year,* 2
l' anniversaire (m.) *anniversary; birthday,* 7
annoncer *to announce,* 7
les annonces (f.) *ads,* 1; les petites annonces *personal or business ads,* 1
anthracite *charcoal grey,* 10
antillais(e) (adj.) *Antillean, from the Antilles (islands in the Caribbean Sea),* 12
antique *ancient,* 9
les antiquités (f.) *antiquities, antiques,* 6
août *August,* 4; **en août** *in August,* 4
l' **appareil** (m.) *phone,* 9; **Qui est à l'appareil?** *Who's calling?* 9
l' **appareil-photo** (m.) *camera,* 11
appartient (appartenir) à *to belong to,* 9
s' **appeler** *to call oneself, to be called,* 1; **Il/Elle s'appelle comment?** *What's his/her name?* 1; **Il/Elle s'appelle...** *His/Her name is . . . ,* 1; **Je m'appelle...** *My name is . . . ,* 1; **Tu t'appelles comment?** *What's your name?* 1
apporter *to bring,* 9; **Apportez-moi..., s'il vous plaît.** *Please bring me . . . ,* 5
apprendre *to learn,* 0
approprié(e) *appropriate,* 7
l' **aprèm** (m.) *afternoon,* 2; cet aprèm *this afternoon,* 2

après *after, afterward,* 9; **Et après?** *And afterwards?* 9
l' après-guerre (m.) *post-war,* 11
l' **après-midi** (m.) *afternoon; in the afternoon,* 2; **l'après-midi libre** *afternoon off,* 2
l' arabe (m.) *Arabic (language),* 1
l' arbre (m.) *tree,* 12
l' archéologue (m.) *archaeologist,* 9
l' ardoise (f.) *writing slate,* 3
l' arène (f.) *amphitheater,* 9
l' **argent** (m.) *money,* 11
l' arôme (m.) *aroma, odor,* 8
l' arrivée (f.) *arrival,* 6
arroser *to sprinkle,* 8
l' art (m.) *art,* 1
l' article (m.) *article, item,* 8
l' artiste (m./f.) *artist,* 0
les **arts plastiques** (m. pl.) *art class,* 2
as : Tu as...? *Do you have . . . ?* 3; **Tu as quel âge?** *How old are you?* 1; **De quoi est-ce que tu as besoin?** *What do you need?* 8
l' ascenseur (m.) *elevator,* 6
l' ascension (f.) *ascent, climb,* 6; ascension en haut de la tour *ascent/climb to the top of the tower,* 6
l' **aspirateur** (m.) *vacuum cleaner,* 7; **passer l'aspirateur** *to vacuum,* 7
l' aspirine (f.) *aspirin,* 12
Asseyez : Asseyez-vous! *Sit down!* 0
assez *enough, fairly,* 2
assis(e) *seated, sitting,* 12
assidu(e) *regular (punctual),* 2
l' **assiette** (f.) *plate,* 5
assuré(e) (pp. of assurer) *assured,* 1
l' **athlétisme** (m.) *track and field,* 4; **faire de l'athlétisme** *to do track and field,* 4
attachant(e) *loving,* 7
attendre *to wait for,* 9
Attention! *Watch out!* 7
attentivement *attentively,* 9
l' attiéké (m.) *ground manioc root,* 8
attirer *to attract,* 9
au *to, at,* 6; *to, in (before a masculine noun),* 11; **au métro...** *at the . . . metro stop,* 6; au milieu *in the middle,* 7; **au revoir** *goodbye,* 1; Au secours! *Help!* 9
l' auberge de jeunesse (f.) *youth hostel,* 11
aucun(e) *none,* 7
aujourd'hui *today,* 2
aussi *also,* 1; **Moi aussi.** *Me too.* 2
l' **automne** (m.) *autumn, fall,* 4; **en automne** *in the fall,* 4
autour de *around,* 8
autre *other,* 4
aux *to, in (before a plural noun),* 6
Av. (abbrev. of avenue) (f.) *avenue,* 6
avant *before,* 1

avec *with,* 1; **avec moi** *with me,* 6; **Avec qui?** *With whom?* 6
l' aventure (f.) *adventure,* 11
avez : Qu'est-ce que vous avez comme...? *What kind of . . . do you have?* 5; **Vous avez...?** *Do you have . . . ?* 2
l' **avion** (m.) *plane,* 12; **en avion** *by plane,* 12, **un billet d'avion** *plane ticket,* 11
l' **avis** (m.) *opinion,* 9; **A ton avis, qu'est-ce que je fais?** *In your opinion, what do I do?* 9
l' avocat (m.) *avocado,* 8
avoir *to have,* 2; **avoir faim** *to be hungry,* 5; avoir hâte de *to be in a hurry (to do something),* 7; avoir la flemme *to be lazy,* 9; avoir lieu *to take place,* 7; avoir raison *to be right,* 2; **avoir soif** *to be thirsty,* 5
avons : Nous avons... *We have . . . ,* 2
avril April, 4; **en avril** *in April,* 4
ayant : ayant pu donner *having been able to give,* 2

B

le baby (foot) *table soccer game,* 5
le bac(calauréat) *secondary school exam for entering a university,* 2
le bachelier *someone who has passed the **bac,*** 2
le bagage *luggage,* 10
la **baguette** *long, thin loaf of bread,* 12
la baie *bay*
la balade à cheval *horseback ride,* 7
se balader *to stroll,* 6
le balcon *balcony,* 12
le ballon *ball,* 4
le bambou *bamboo,* 12
la **banane** *banana,* 8
le banc *(park) bench,* 12
les bandes dessinées (f.) *comic strips,* 2
la **banque** *bank,* 12
barbant(e) *boring,* 2
le **base-ball** *baseball,* 4; **jouer au base-ball** *to play baseball,* 4
le basilic *basil,* 5
le **basket(-ball)** *basketball,* 4; **jouer au basket(-ball)** *to play basketball,* 4
les **baskets** (f.) *sneakers,* 3
le **bateau** *boat,* 11; **en bateau** *by boat,* 12; **faire du bateau** *to go boating,* 11
le bateau-mouche *river boat,* 6
le bâtiment *building,* 12
bd (abbrev. of boulevard) (m.) *boulevard,* 6

beau (belle) *nice, pretty,* 4; **Il fait beau.** *It's nice weather.* 4

Beaucoup *A lot.* 4; **Oui, beaucoup.** *Yes, very much.* 2; **Pas beaucoup.** *Not very much.* 4

le **beau-père** *stepfather; father-in-law,* 7

le **bébé** *baby,* 7

belge *Belgian* (adj.), 1

la **Belgique** *Belgium,* 0

la **belle-mère** *stepmother; mother-in-law,* 7

le **besoin** *need,* 8; **De quoi est-ce que tu as besoin?** *What do you need?* 8; **J'ai besoin de...** *I need . . . ,* 8

la **bête** *animal,* 12

le **beurre** *butter,* 8

la **bibliothèque** *library,* 6

le **bic** *ballpoint pen,* 3

bien *well,* 1; **Je veux bien.** *Gladly.* 8; **Je veux bien.** *I'd really like to.* 6; **J'en veux bien.** *I'd like some.* 8; **Moi, j'aime (bien)...** *I (really) like . . . ,* 1; **Très bien.** *Very well.* 1

Bien sûr. *Of course.* 3; *certainly,* 9; **Oui, bien sûr.** *Yes, of course.* 7

bientôt *soon,* 1; **A bientôt.** *See you soon.* 1

Bienvenue! *Welcome!* 0

le **bien-vivre** *good living, the good life,* 6

le **bifteck** *steak,* 8

les **bijoux** (m.) *jewelry,* 10

le **billet** *ticket,* 11; **un billet d'avion** *plane ticket,* 11; **un billet de train** *train ticket,* 11

la **biologie** *biology,* 2

bizarre *strange,* 7

blanc(he) *white,* 3

le **blanc-manger** *coconut pudding*

bleu(e) *blue,* 3; **bleu clair** *light blue,* 10; **bleu foncé** *dark blue,* 10

blond(e) *blond,* 7

le **blouson** *jacket,* 10

le **bœuf** *beef,* 8

Bof! *(expression of indifference),* 1

boire *to drink,* 5; **Qu'est-ce qu'il y a à boire?** *What is there to drink?* 5

le **bois** *wood,* 12

la **boisson** *drink, beverage,* 5; **Qu'est-ce que vous avez comme boissons?** *What do you have to drink?* 5

la **boîte** *box, can,* 8; **une boîte de** *a can of,* 8

le **bon** *coupon,* 6

bon(ne) *good,* 5; **Bon courage!** *Good luck!* 2; **Bon voyage!** *Have a good trip!* 11; **Bon, d'accord.** *Well, OK.* 8; **de bons conseils** *good advice,* 1; **Oui, très bon.** *Yes, very good.* 9; **pas bon** *not good,* 5

Bonjour *Hello,* 1

bonne (f. of **bon**) *good,* 5; **Bonne chance!** *Good luck!* 11; **Bonne idée.** *Good idea.* 4; **Bonnes vacances!** *Have a good vacation!* 11

le **bord** *side, edge;* **au bord de la mer** *to/on the coast,* 11

les **bottes** (f.) *boots,* 10

les **boucles d'oreilles** (f.) *earrings,* 10

le **boudin créole** *spicy Creole sausage,* 12

bouger *to move,* 10

bouillant(e) *boiling,* 8

la **boulangerie** *bakery,* 12

la **boule** *ball,* 8

la **boum** *party,* 6; **aller à une boum** *to go to a party,* 6

le **bouquiniste** *bookseller who has a stand along the Seine River in Paris,* 5

la **bouteille** *bottle,* 8; **une bouteille de** *a bottle of,* 8

la **boutique** *store, shop,* 3; **une boutique de souvenirs** *souvenir shop,* 3

le **bracelet** *bracelet,* 3

la **Bretagne** *Brittany (region of northwest France),* 7

la **brioche** *brioche, light, slightly sweet bread made with a rich yeast dough,* 8

la **brochure** *brochure,* 4

la **broderie** *embroidery,* 10

brun(e) *brunette,* 7

le **bulletin trimestriel** *report card,* 2

le **bureau** *office, desk,* 8; **bureau de tabac** *newsstand,* 9

le **bus** *bus,* 12; **en bus** *by bus,* 12, **rater le bus** *to miss the bus,* 9

la **buvette** *refreshment stand,* 12

byzantin(e) *Byzantine; of the style of art and architecture developed in Eastern Europe between the 4th and 15th centuries (characterized by domes and elaborate mosaics),* 12

C'est... *It's . . . ,* 2; **C'est...** *This is . . . ,* 7; **C'est qui?** *Who is it?* 2; **C'est combien?** *How much is it?* 3; **C'est du gâteau.** *It's a piece of cake.* 8; **C'est pas de la tarte.** *It's not easy.* 8; **C'est tout.** *That's all.* 1; **Ça, c'est...** *This/That is . . . ,* 12; **Non, c'est impossible.** *No, that's impossible.* 7

C'était barbant! *It was boring!* 11

ça *that; it;* **Ça boume?** *How's it going?* 2; **Ça va.** *Fine.* 1; **Ça va?** *How are things going?* 1; **Ça, c'est...** *This/That is . . . ,* 12; **Ça m'est égal** *It doesn't matter; I don't care.* 10; **Ça ne me dit rien.** *That doesn't interest me.* 4; **I don't feel like it.** 6; **ça suffit** *that's enough,* 12; **Et après ça...** *And after that, . . . ,* 9; **Oui, ça a été.** *Yes, it was fine.* 9

ça fait : Ça fait combien, s'il vous plaît? *How much is it, please?* 5;

la **cabine téléphonique** *phone booth,* 9

le **cabinet de toilette** *small room with a sink and counter,* 11

caché(e) (pp. of **cacher**) *hidden,* 11

le **cadeau** *gift,* 11

le **café** *coffee, café,* 5; le café au lait *coffee with hot milk,* 8; le café crème *coffee with cream,* 5

le **cahier** *notebook,* 0

la **calculatrice** *calculator,* 3; une calculatrice-traductrice *translating calculator,* 3

le **caleçon** *leggings,* 4

le **calendrier** *calendar,* 6

la **Californie** *California,* 4

le **camarade** (la camarade) *friend;* camarade de classe *classmate,* 7

le **camembert** *Camembert cheese,* 5

le **caméscope** *camcorder,* 4

le **camp de sport** *sports camp,* 9

la **campagne** *countryside,* 11; **à la campagne** *to/in the countryside,* 11

le **camping** *camping,* 11; **faire du camping** *to go camping,* 11

le **Canada** *Canada,* 4

le **canal** *channel,* 3

le **canari** *canary,* 7

le **caniveau** *sidewalk gutter,* 7

la **cantine** *cafeteria,* 9; **à la cantine** *at the school cafeteria,* 9

la **capitale** *capital,* 5

car *because,* 4

la **caractéristique** *characteristic,* 8

la **carambole** *star fruit,* 12

la **carcasse** *body,* 12

le **cardigan** *sweater,* 10

le **carnaval** *carnival,* 11

la **carotte** *carrot,* 8

la **carrière** *quarry,* 11

la **carte** *map,* 0; *menu,* 12; à la carte *pick and choose,* 3; **La carte, s'il vous plaît.** *The menu, please.* 5

les **cartes** (f.) *cards,* 4; **jouer aux cartes** *to play cards,* 4

la **cartouche** *cartridge,* 3; cartouche d'encre *ink cartridge,* 3

le **carvi** *cumin (Afrique),* 8; graines de carvi *cumin seeds,* 8

la **casquette** *cap,* 10

la **cassette** *cassette tape,* 3

la **cassette vidéo** *videocassette,* 4

le **catalogue** *catalog,* 10

la **catégorie** *category,* 8

la **cathédrale** *cathedral,* 1

le **cauchemar** *nightmare,* 11; **C'était un véritable cauchemar!** *It was a real nightmare!* 11

ce *this; that,* 3; **Ce sont...** *These/Those are . . . ,* 7
la ceinture *belt,* 10
célèbre *famous, well-known,* 4
cent *one hundred,* 3; **deux cents** *two hundred,* 3
la centaine *a hundred or so;* des centaines d'années *hundreds of years,* 9
le centre *center,* 4
le centre commercial *mall,* 6
le centre-ville *city center,* 12
cependant *however,* 11
le cercle *circle, group,* 6; au cercle français *at French Club,* 4
certain(e) *certain, some,* 7
ces *these, those,* 3
cet *this, that,* 3
cette *this; that,* 3
chacun *each (person),* 5; Chacun ses goûts! *To each his own!* 1
la chaise *chair,* 0
chaleureux (-euse) *warm,* 9
la chambre *room,* 7; **ranger ta chambre** *to pick up your room,* 7
le champignon *mushroom,* 8
la chance *luck,* 11; **Bonne chance!** *Good luck!* 11
le changement *change,* 10
changer *to change,* 7
chanter *to sing,* 9
le chanteur *singer (male),* 9
la chanteuse *singer (female),* 9
Chantilly : la crème Chantilly *sweetened whipped cream,* 5
le chapeau *hat,* 10
le chapitre *chapter,* 9
chaque *each,* 4
chargé(e) *busy,* 2
le chariot *shopping cart,* 8
la chasse *hunting,* 7; une chasse au trésor *treasure hunt,* 3
le chat *cat,* 7
le chaton *kitten,* 7
chaud(e) *hot,* 4; **Il fait chaud.** *It's hot.* 4
chauffé(e) *heated,* 11
les chaussettes (f.) *socks,* 10
les chaussures (f.) *shoes,* 10; les chaussures à crampons *spikes,* 4
le chef-d'œuvre *masterpiece,* 6
la chemise *shirt (man's),* 10
la chemise *folder,* 3
le chemisier *shirt (woman's),* 10
le chèque *check,* 0
cher (chère) *dear,* 1; *expensive,* 3; **C'est trop cher.** *It's too expensive.* 10
chercher *to look for,* 9; **Je cherche quelque chose pour...** *I'm looking for something for . . . ,* 10
chéri(e) (noun) mon chéri/ma chérie *darling, sweetie,* 8
le cheval *horse,* 12; le cheval de bois *wooden horse, carousel horse,* 12

chez... *to/at . . . 's house,* 6; **chez le disquaire** *at the record store,* 12; **Je suis bien chez... ?** *Is this . . . 's house?* 9
chic *chic,* 10
le chien *dog,* 7; **promener le chien** *to walk the dog,* 7
le chiffre *number,* 0
la chimie *chemistry,* 2
chimique *chemical,* 9
le chocolat *chocolate,* 1; **un chocolat** *hot chocolate,* 5
la chocolaterie *chocolate shop,* 12
choisi (pp. of choisir) *decided, chosen;* **Vous avez choisi?** *Have you decided/chosen?* 5
choisir *to choose, to pick,* 10
le choix *choice,* 8
la chorale *choir,* 2
la chose *thing,* 5; **J'ai des tas de choses (trucs) à faire.** *I have lots of things to do.* 5
le chou *cabbage,* 1; mon chou *my darling, dear,* 1
chouette *cool,* 9; **Très chouette.** *Very cool.* 9
chrétien(ne) *Christian,* 9
la chute *waterfall,* 4
ci-dessous *below,* 8
le cimetière *cemetery,* 9
le cinéma *movie theater,* 6; *movies,* 1
cinq *five,* 9
cinquième *fifth,* 9
la Cité des Papes *monument in Avignon, France; a citadel of palaces where French popes lived and ruled in the 14th century,* 11
le citron *lemon,* 8
le citron pressé *lemonade,* 5
clair(e) *light (color),* 10
le classeur *loose-leaf binder,* 3
classique *classical,* 4
le client (la cliente) *customer,* 5
le climat *climate,* 11
climatisé(e) *air-conditioned,* 11
le clocher *steeple,* 12
le club *club,* 11
le coca *cola,* 5
le coco *coconut,* 8
le code de la route *rules of the road; test,* 12
le cœur *heart,* 9
le coin *corner,* 12; **au coin de** *on the corner of,* 12
le col *collar,* 10; au col montant *with turtleneck,* 10
le collant *hose,* 10
la colle *glue,* 3; un pot de colle *container of glue,* 3
la collection *collection,* 10
le collège *junior high school,* 2
la colonie de vacances *summer camp,* 11
coloré(e) *colorful,* 8
le coloris *color, shade,* 3

combien *how much, how many,* 3; **C'est combien,... ?** *How much is . . . ?* 5; **C'est combien?** *How much is it?* 3; **Ça fait combien, s'il vous plaît?** *How much is it, please?* 5
le combiné *(telephone) receiver,* 9
comique *comic, comical;* un film comique *comedy (movie),* 6
commander *to order,* 5
comme *like, as,* 4; **Comme ci comme ça.** *So-so.* 1; Qu'est-ce qu'ils aiment comme cours? *What subjects do they like?* 2; **Qu'est-ce que tu fais comme sport?** *What sports do you play?* 4; **Qu'est-ce que vous avez comme... ?** *What kind of . . . do you have?* 5
le commencement *beginning,* 9
commencer *to begin, to start,* 9
comment *what,* 0; *how,* 1; **(Comment) ça va?** *How's it going?* 1; Comment dit-on? *How do you say it?* 1; Comment le dire? *How should you say it?* 1; **Comment tu trouves... ?** *What do you think of . . . ?* 2; **Comment tu trouves ça?** *What do you think of that/it?* 2; Il/Elle est comment? *What is he/she like?* 7; **Ils/Elles sont comment?** *What are they like?* 7; **Tu t'appelles comment?** *What is your name?* 0
le commentaire *commentary,* 9
le commerçant *store owner,* 8
la Communauté financière africaine (CFA) *African Financial Community; the group of African countries that share a common currency (the CFA franc),* 3
la compagnie aérienne (f.) *airline company,* 10
le compagnon *companion,* 7
comparer *to compare,* 10
le compas *compass,* 3
compétent(e) *competent,* 2
compléter *to complete,* 4
le compliment *compliment,* 10
comprends : Tu comprends? *Do you understand?* 2
compris(e) *included,* 5
compris (pp. of comprendre): Tu as compris? *Did you understand?* 1
le concert *concert,* 1
le concombre *cucumber,* 8
conçu(e) (pp. of concevoir) *conceived,* 9
confier *to confide,* 9
la confiture *jam,* 8
connais : Tu les connais? *Do you know them?* 0; Tu connais ces nombres? *Do you recognize these numbers?* 2

la connaissance *acquaintance;*
   Faisons connaissance! *Let's get
   acquainted.* 1
connu(e) (pp. of connaître) *knew;
   known;* le plus connu *the best-
   known* (adj.), 6
le conseil *advice,* 1; de bons conseils
   good advice, 1; demander conseil
   to ask for advice, 11
conseiller *to advise, to counsel;*
   Qu'est-ce que tu me conseilles?
   What do you advise me to do? 9
le conseiller *adviser,* 12
la conseillère *adviser,* 12
   conservé (pp. of conserver) *kept,* 2;
   ce bulletin doit être conservé(e)
   this report card must be kept, 2;
   preserved (food); c'est plus sûr et
   bien conservé *it's safer and better
   preserved,* 8
   consoler *to console (someone), to
   make (someone) feel better, to
   comfort,* 9
   construit(e) (pp. of construire)
   constructed, built, 9
   contenir *to contain,* 9
   content(e) *happy, pleased,* 7
le contenu *contents,* 8
   continuer *to continue,* 12; **Vous
   continuez jusqu'au prochain feu
   rouge.** *You keep going until the
   next light.* 12
le contraste *contrast,* 8
   contraster *to contrast,* 8
   contre *against,* 2
la conversation *conversation,* 7
   cool *cool,* 2
le **copain** (la copine) *friend,* 1
le cordon *cord, string;* le cordon de
   serrage *drawstring,* 10
le cornichon *pickle,* 8
le corps *body,* 8
   correct(e) *correct, proper,* 9
le correspondant (la correspondante)
   pen pal, 1
   correspondre *to write; to
   correspond,* 1; Fais correspondre…
   Match …, 6
la corvée ménagère *household
   chore,* 7
le costume *costume, traditional
   dress,* 9
la côte *coast,* 11
le **côté** *side;* **à côté de** *next to,* 12;
   du côté de mon père *on my
   father's side (of the family),* 7
le **coton** *cotton,* 10; **en coton** *(made
   of) cotton,* 10
la **couleur** *color,* 3; **De quelle couleur
   est…?** *What color is …?* 3
le coup *hit, blow;* le coup de fil
   phone call, 9
la coupe *dish(ful),* 5
la coupe Melba *vanilla ice cream,
   peaches, whipped cream, and fruit
   sauce,* 5

courir *to run,* 7
le **cours** *course,* 2; **le cours de
   développement personnel et
   social (DPS)** *health,* 2; **Tu as
   quels cours…?** *What classes do
   you have …?* 2
les **courses** (f.) *shopping, errands,* 7;
   faire les courses *to do the
   shopping,* 7; **J'ai des courses à
   faire.** *I have errands to do.* 5
   court(e) *short (length),* 10
le **cousin** *male cousin,* 7
la **cousine** *female cousin,* 7
   coûteux (-euse) *expensive,* 8
le crabe *crab,* 5; les crabes farcis
   deviled land crabs, 9
la **cravate** *tie,* 10
le **crayon** *pencil,* 3; des crayons de
   couleur *colored pencils,* 3
   créer *to create,* 11
la crème fraîche *thick cream like
   sour cream but without the sour
   flavor; used to make sauces and
   toppings,* 5
le créole *creole language,* 12
la **crêpe** *very thin pancake,* 5
la crêperie *café or restaurant which
   specializes in crêpes,* 5
   crépiter *to crackle,* 12
le creuset *melting pot;* le creuset de
   l'Afrique *the melting pot of
   Africa,* 8
   croire *to believe;* Tu crois? *Do you
   think so?* 10
la croisière *cruise,* 11
le croissant *croissant; flaky, buttery
   roll eaten at breakfast,* 5
la croissanterie *croissant shop,* 12
le **croque-monsieur** *toasted ham and
   cheese sandwich,* 5
   cru(e) *uncooked,* 5
le **cuir** *leather,* 10; **en cuir** *(made
   of) leather,* 10
   cuire *to cook, to bake,* 8
la culture *culture,* 7
   culturel(le) *cultural,* 0

D'abord,… *First, …,* 9
D'accord. *O.K.* 4; **Bon, d'accord.**
   Well, O.K. 8; **D'accord, si tu…
   d'abord…** *O.K, if you …, first.* 7;
   Tu es d'accord? *Is that O.K. with
   you?* 7
d'après *according to,* 4
d'habitude *usually,* 4
dans *in,* 6
danser *to dance,* 1
   la danse *dance,* 2
le danseur (la danseuse) *dancer,* 9
   de *from,* 0; *of,* 0; **de l'** *some,* 8;

de la *some,* 8; **Je n'ai pas de…** *I
   don't have …,* 3; **Je ne fais pas
   de…** *I don't play/do …,* 4
   déambuler *to stroll,* 11
   débarrasser la table *to clear the
   table,* 7
le débutant (la débutante)
   beginner, 4
   décaféiné(e) *decaffeinated,* 5
   décédé(e) *deceased,* 7
   décembre *December,* 4; **en
   décembre** *in December,* 4
le décès *death,* 7
   déchiffrer *to decode,* 7
   décider *to decide,* 5; **Vous avez
   décidé de prendre…?** *Have you
   decided to take …?* 10
   décontracté(e) *relaxed,* 11
la découverte *discovery,* 3
   découvrir *to discover,* 8
   décrire *to describe,* 7
   décrocher *to take down; to unhook;
   quand l'interlocuteur décroche
   when the speaker picks up (the
   phone),* 9
   dedans *inside,* 3
   défavorable *unfavorable,
   disapproving,* 7
   dégoûtant(e) *gross,* 5
   dehors *outside,* 8
   déjà *already,* 9
   déjeuner *to have lunch,* 9; **le
   déjeuner** *lunch,* 2
   délicieux (-euse) *delicious,* 5
   délirer *to be delirious;* La techno
   me fait délirer. *I'm wild about
   techno music.* 1
   délivré(e) (pp. of delivrer) : il
   n'en sera pas délivré de
   duplicata *duplicates will not
   be issued,* 2
le deltaplane *hang-glider;* faire du
   deltaplane *to go hang-gliding,* 4
   demain *tomorrow,* 2; **À demain.**
   See you tomorrow. 1
   demander *to ask, to ask for,* 7;
   demander conseil *to ask for
   advice,* 11
   demi(e) *half;* **et demi** *half past
   (after* **midi** *and* **minuit**), 6; **et
   demie** *half past,* 6
le demi-frère *stepbrother,* 7; *half-
   brother,* 7
la demi-sœur *stepsister,* 7; *half-
   sister,* 7
   démodé(e) *out of style,* 10
   démonté(e) *dismantled,* 12
le dentiste (la dentiste) *dentist,* 1
le départ *departure,* 6
le département d'outre-mer *overseas
   department,* 12
   dépêchez : Dépêchez-vous de…
   hurry up and …, 1
   déplorable *deplorable,* 2
   déposer *to deposit,* 12
   déprimé(e) *depressed,* 9

depuis *for (a certain amount of time)*, 9; *since*, 12

le **dérivé** *derivative, by-product*; le sucre et ses dérivés *sugar and its by-products*, 8

dernier (-ière) *last*; la semaine dernière *last week*, 9

derrière *behind*, 12

des *some*, 3

les dés (m.) *dice*; découper en dés *to dice*, 8

dès que *as soon as*, 9

désagréable *unpleasant*, 4

la description *description*, 7

désirer *to desire, to want*; **Vous désirez?** *What would you like?* 10

désolé(e) : Désolé(e), je suis occupé(e). *Sorry, I'm busy.* 6; **Désolé(e), mais je ne peux pas.** *Sorry, but I can't.* 4

le dessert *dessert*, 0

le dessin *drawing*, 3

le détail *detail*, 9

détailler *to slice*, 8

détester *to hate, to detest*, 6

deux *two*, 0; les deux *both*, 7

la deuxième étape *second step*, 1

devant *in front of*, 6

devenir *to become*, 9

devez : vous devez *you must*, 11

deviennent : Que deviennent...? *What happened to . . . ?* 7

deviner *to guess*, 7; Devine! *Guess!* 0

devoir *to have to, must*, 7

les **devoirs** (m.) *homework*, 2; **J'ai des devoirs à faire.** *I've got homework to do.* 5

le dévouement *devotion*, 7

devrais : Tu devrais... *You should . . .* , 9

la diapo(sitive) *photographic slide*, 11

la dictée *dictation*, 0

le **dictionnaire** *dictionary*, 3

la différence *difference*, 2

différent(e) *different*, 7

difficile *difficult*, 2

dimanche *Sunday*, 2; **le dimanche** *on Sundays*, 2

dîner *to have dinner*, 9; **le dîner** *dinner*, 8

dingue *crazy*, 1; Je suis dingue de... *I'm crazy about . . .* , 1

dire *to say*; 1; *to tell*, 9; Comment le dire? *How should you say it?* 1; Dis,... *Say, . . .* , 2; **Ça ne me dit rien.** *That doesn't interest me.* 4; Comment dit-on...? *How do you say . . . ?* 1; Jacques a dit... *Simon says . . .* , 0; Qu'est-ce qu'on se dit? *What are they saying to themselves?* 2; **Vous pouvez lui dire que j'ai téléphoné?** *Can you tell her/him that I called?* 9

direct(e) *direct*; en direct *live*, 7

la direction *direction*, 12

la discothèque *dance club*, 6

discuter *to discuss*, 7; Ne discute pas! *Don't argue!* 3

disponible *available*, 8

le **disquaire** *record store*, 12; **chez le disquaire** *at the record store*, 12

le **disque compact/CD** *compact disc/CD*, 3

distant(e) *distant*, 2

la distribution *cast (of a movie, play, etc.)*, 1; une distribution étincelante *a brilliant cast*, 1

divers(e) *various*, 3

le document *document*, 7

dois : Non, tu dois... *No, you've got to . . .* , 7

le dolmen *dolmen*, 1

le dom-tom *abbreviation of départements et territoires d'outre-mer; overseas departments and territories of France such as Martinique and Réunion*, 3

domestique : animal domestique *pet*, 7

le domicile *place of residence*, 4

la domination *domination*, 9

dominer *to tower over*, 12

dommage *too bad*, 10

donc *so, therefore*, 11

donner *to give*, 5; **Donnez-moi... , s'il vous plaît.** *Please give me . . .* , 5

donner sur *to overlook*, 11

dont *of which*, 7

dormir *to sleep*, 1

le dos *back*, 12; **un sac à dos** *backpack*, 3

doucement *gently*, 12

la douche *shower*, 11; avec douche ou bains *with shower or bath*, 11

doué(e) *gifted, talented*, 2

la douzaine *dozen*, 8; **une douzaine de** *a dozen*, 8

les draps (m.) *linens, sheets*, 11

dressé(e) *pointed*, 7

droit(e) *straight*, 10

la droite *right (direction)*; **à droite (de)** *to the right*, 12

du *some*, 8

le duplicata (inv.) *duplicate*; il n'en sera pas délivré de duplicata *duplicates will not be issued*, 2

durable *long-lasting*, 11

durcir *to harden*, 8

la durée *duration*, 7

durer *to last*, 11

l' **eau** (f.) *water*, 5; **l'eau minérale** *mineral water*, 5; le

sirop de fraise (à l'eau) *water with strawberry syrup*, 5

s' **ébattre** *to frolic*, 7

l' **échange** (m.) *exchange*, 7; en échange de *in exchange for*, 7

l' **échantillon** (m.) *sample*, 2

l' **écharpe** (f.) *scarf*, 10

l' **échelle** (f.) *scale*, 6

s' **éclater** *to have fun, to have a ball*, 4

l' **école** (f.) *school*, 1; A l'école *At school*, 0

l' écolier (m.), l'écolière (f.) *schoolboy/schoolgirl*, 3

l' économie (f.) *economics*, 2

écouter *to listen*, 1; Ecoute! *Listen!* 0; **écouter de la musique** *to listen to music*, 1; **Ecoutez!** *Listen!* 0; **Je t'écoute.** *I'm listening.* 9

l' écran (m.) *screen*, 11

l' écrin (m.) *case*, 6

écrire *to write*, 2; Ecris-moi. *Write me.* 1

écris : Ecris cinq phrases... *Write five sentences . . .* , 12

l' édifice (m.) *edifice, building*, 6

l' **éducation physique et sportive (EPS)** (f.) *physical education*, 2; l'éducation civique et morale (f.) *civics class*, 2

efficace *efficient*, 9

égrener *to shell*, 8

égyptien(ne) *Egyptian* (adj.), 6

Eh bien... *Umm . . . (expression of hesitation)*, 5

élastique *elastic* (adj.), 3

élémentaire *elementary; basic*, 8

l' éléphant (m.) *elephant*, 0

l' **élève** (m./f.) *student*, 2

l' emballage (m.) *packaging*, 9

embêtant(e) *annoying*, 7

émincer *to slice thinly*, 8

l' émission (f.) *TV program*, 4

empêche (empêcher) *to prevent, to keep from doing*, 2

l' emploi *use, job*; un emploi du temps *schedule*, 2

emprunter *to borrow*, 12

en *in*, 1; **en** *some, of it, of them, any, none*, 8; **en** *to, in (before a feminine country)*, 11; **en coton** *(made of) cotton*, 10; **en cuir** *(made of) leather*, 10; en français *in French*, 1; **en jean** *(made of) denim*, 10; en retard *late*, 2; en solde *on sale*, 10; **en vacances** *on vacation*, 4; **Je n'en veux plus.** *I don't want anymore.* 8; **Oui, j'en veux bien.** *Yes, I'd like some.* 8; Qu'en penses-tu? *What do you think (about it)?* 1; **Vous avez ça en...?** *Do you have that in . . . ? (size, fabric, color)*, 10

encore *again, more*; **Encore de...?** *More. . . ?* 8; *still*, 9

encourager *to encourage*, 8
l' **endroit** (m.) *place*, 12
énerver *to annoy*, 2
l' **enfant** (m./f.) *child*, 7; l'enfant unique *only child*, 7
enfin *finally*, 9
enjoué(e) *playful*, 7
ennuyer *to bore*, 2
ennuyeux (-euse) *boring*, 11; **C'était ennuyeux.** *It was boring*, 11
l' **enquête** (f.) *survey*, 1
l' **enseignement** (m.) *teaching*, 2
ensemble *together*, 4
l' **ensemble** (m.) *collection, ensemble*, 3
ensuite : Ensuite, ... *Next,/Then,* ..., 9
entendre *to hear;* s'entendre avec *to get along with,* 7
Entendu. *Agreed.* 6
entendu dire que : Il a entendu dire que... *He heard that* ..., 12
l' **enthousiasme** (m.) *enthusiasm*, 2
entier (-ière) *whole, entire;* le monde entier *all over the world*, 1
entrant *entering*, 2
entre *between*, 12
l' **entrée** (f.) *entry, entrance;* Entrée libre *"Browsers welcomed,"* 3
l' **enveloppe** (f.) *envelope*, 12
l' **envie** (f.) *desire; need;* **J'ai envie de...** *I feel like* ..., 11
les **environs** (m. pl.) *surroundings*, 9
s' **envoler** *to fly away*, 12
envoyer *to send*, 12; **envoyer des lettres** *to send letters*, 12
l' **épi** (m.) *ear (of a plant)*, 8; l'épi de maïs *ear of corn*, 8
l' **épicerie** (f.) *grocery store*, 12
éplucher *to clean, to peel*, 8
l' **éponge** (f.) *sponge*, 3
épouvantable *terrible, horrible*, 9; **C'était épouvantable.** *It was horrible.* 9
l' **EPS** (l'éducation physique et sportive) *gym class*, 3
l' **équipe interscolaire** (f.) *school team*, 4
l' **équitation** (f.) *horseback riding*, 1; **faire de l'équitation** *to go horseback riding*, 1
es : Tu es d'accord? *Is that OK with you?* 7
l' **escale** (f.) *docking (of a boat)*, 11
l' **escalier** (m.) *staircase*, 6
les **escargots** (m.) *snails*, 1
l' **espace** (m.) *space, area*, 7
l' **espagnol** (m.) *Spanish (language)*, 2
espère : J'espère que oui. *I hope so.* 1
l' **espoir** (m.) *hope*, 7
essayer *to try; to try on*, 10; **Je peux essayer...?** *Can I try on* ...? 10;

Je peux l'/les essayer? *Can I try it/them on?* 10
est : Il/Elle est... *He/She is* ..., 7; **Quelle heure est-il?** *What time is it?* 6; **Qui est à l'appareil?** *Who's calling?* 9
Est-ce que *(Introduces a yes-or-no question)*, 4; **(Est-ce que) je peux...?** *May I* ...? 7
et *and*, 1; **Et après ça...** *And after that,* ..., 9; **Et toi?** *And you?* 1
l' **étage** (m.) *floor, story (of a building)*, 6
était : C'était épouvantable. *It was horrible.* 9
étaler *to spread*, 8
l' **étape** (f.) *part*, 1; première étape *first part*, 1; deuxième étape *second part*, 1; troisième étape *third part*, 1
l' **état** (m.) *state*, 0
les **Etats-Unis** (m. pl.) *United States*, 0
l' **été** (m.) *summer*, 4; **en été** *in the summer*, 4
été (pp. of être) *was*, 9
étincelant(e) *brilliant*, 1
étoilé(e) *starry*, 12
étonné(e) (pp. of étonner) *surprised*, 7
étranger (-ère) *foreign*, 11
l' **étranger** (m.) *foreign countries;* à l'étranger *abroad*, 11
être *to be*, 7; **C'est...** *This is* ..., 7; **Ce sont...** *These (those) are* ..., 7; **Elle est...** *She is* ..., 7; **Il est...** *He is* ..., 7; **Il est...** *It is* ... *(time)*, 6; **Ils/Elles sont...** *They're* ..., 7; **Oui, ça a été.** *Yes, it was fine.* 9
l' **étude** (f.) *study hall*, 2
l' **étudiant(e)** (m./f.) *student*, 0
étudier *to study*, 1
eu (pp. of avoir) *had, got*, 9
l' **euro** *European Community monetary unit*, 3; Ça fait... euros./C'est... euros. *It's* ... *euros.* 5
l' **Europe** (f.) *Europe*, 0
l' **événement** (m.) *event*, 9
évident(e) *evident, obvious*, 12
évider *to scoop out*, 8
éviter *to avoid*, 9
exactement *exactly*, 9
l' **examen** (m.) *exam*, 1; **passer un examen** *to take a test*, 9
excellent(e) *excellent*, 5; **Oui, excellent.** *Yes, excellent.* 9
excusez : Excusez-moi. *Excuse me.* 3
exemplaire *exemplary*, 7
l' **explication** (f.) *explanation*, 12
expliquer *to explain*, 7
l' **exposition** (f.) *exhibit*, 12
l' **expression** (f.) *expression*, 1

la **face** *face, side;* **en face de** *across from*, 12
facile *easy*, 2
la **façon** *way, manner*, 10
la **faim** *hunger;* **avoir faim** *to be hungry*, 5; **Non, merci. Je n'ai plus faim.** *No thanks. I'm not hungry anymore.* 8
faire *to do, to make, to play*, 4; **Désolé(e), j'ai des devoirs à faire.** *Sorry, I have homework to do.* 5; **J'ai des courses à faire.** *I have errands to do.* 5; **Qu'est-ce que tu vas faire...?** *What are you going to do* ...? 6; **Tu vas faire quoi...?** *What are you going to do* ...? 6; **faire de l'équitation** *to go horseback riding*, 1; faire de la course *to race (running)*, 4; faire de la gymnastique *to do gymnastics*, 4; faire des haltères *to lift weights*, 4; **faire du bateau** *to go sailing,* **faire du sport** *to play sports*, 1; faire du surf *to surf*, 4; **faire la cuisine** *to cook, do the cooking*, 8; **faire la vaisselle** *to do the dishes*, 7; **faire le ménage** *to do housework*, 1; faire les boutiques *to go shopping*, 1; **faire les courses** *to do the shopping*, 7; **faire les magasins** *to go shopping*, 1; **faire les vitrines** *to window-shop*, 6; **faire un pique-nique** *to have a picnic*, 6; **faire une promenade** *to go for a walk*, 6
fais : A ton avis, qu'est-ce que je fais? *In your opinion, what do I do?* 9; Fais-moi... *Make me* ..., 3; **Je fais...** *I play/do* ..., 4; Ne t'en fais pas! *Don't worry!* 9; **Qu'est-ce que tu fais comme sport?** *What sports do you play?* 4; **Qu'est-ce que tu fais pour t'amuser?** *What do you do to have fun?* 4; **Qu'est-ce que tu fais...?** *What do you do* ...? 4
faisons : Faisons connaissance! *Let's get acquainted.* 1
fait : Quel temps fait-il? *What's the weather like?* 4; **Il fait beau.** *It's nice weather.* 4; **Il fait chaud.** *It's hot.* 4; **Il fait frais.** *It's cool.* 4; **Il fait froid.** *It's cold.* 4
fait (pp. of faire) *done, made*, 9; **J'ai fait...** *I did/made* ..., 9; **Qu'est-ce que tu as fait?** *What did you do?* 9
la **famille** *family*, 7
la **fantaisie** *fancy*, 10
le **fantôme** *ghost*, 0

la **farine** *flour*, 8
le **fast-food** *fast-food restaurant*, 6
favorable *favorable, approving*, 7
favori(te) *favorite*, 12
faut : Il me faut... *I need . . .* , 3;
   Qu'est-ce qu'il te faut pour... ?
   What do you need for . . . ?
   (informal), 3; **Qu'est-ce qu'il te
   faut?** *What do you need?* 8;
   Qu'est-ce qu'il vous faut pour... ?
   What do you need for . . . ?
   (formal), 3
le **fauve** *wildcat*, 6
faux (fausse) *false*, 2
les **féculents** (m.) *starches*, 8
la **féerie** *extravaganza*, 11
la **femme** *wife*, 7
la **fenêtre** *window*, 0
le **fer forgé** *wrought iron*, 12
ferai : je me ferai une joie de... *I'll
   gladly . . .* , 1
fermez : Fermez la porte. *Close the
   door.* 0
le **festival** *festival*, 9
la **fête** *party*, 1; **faire la fête** *to live it
   up*, 1
fêter *to celebrate*, 7
le **feu** *fire*, 12
le **feu rouge** *traffic light*, 12; **Vous
   continuez jusqu'au prochain feu
   rouge.** *You keep going until the
   next light.* 12
la **feuille** *sheet; leaf;* **une feuille de
   papier** *sheet of paper*, 0
le **feutre** *marker*, 3
février *February*, 4; **en février** *in
   February*, 4
la **fidélité** *loyalty*, 7
le **fil** *cord, thread;* **sans fil** *cordless*, 9
le **filet** *a type of net or mesh bag*, 3
la **fille** *girl*, 0; **la fille** *daughter*, 7
le **film** *movie*, 6; **voir un film** *to see
   a movie*, 6; **un film d'aventures**
   adventure film, 1
le **fils** *son*, 7; **fils-à-papa** *daddy's
   boy*, 10
la **fin** *end*, 4
finalement *finally*, 9
fistuleux (-euse) *hollow*, 11
le **flamant** *flamingo;* **flamant rose**
   pink flamingo, 9
la **flamme** *flame*, 12
le **flanc** *side, flank*, 12
la **fleur** *flower*, 1
le **fleuve** *river*, 9
le **flipper** *pinball*, 5
la **flûte** *flute*, 0
la **fois** *time;* **une fois par semaine**
   once a week, 4
folklorique *folkloric, traditional*,
   11
follement *madly*, 1
foncé(e) *dark (color)*, 10
fonder *to found*, 9
la **fontaine** *fountain*, 12
le **foot** *soccer*, 4

le **football** *soccer*, 1; **le football
   américain** *football*, 4; **jouer au
   foot(ball)** *to play soccer*, 4; **jouer
   au football américain** *to play
   football*, 4
la **forêt** *forest*, 0; **en forêt** *to/in the
   forest*, 11
la **forme** *form, structure*, 7
formidable : C'était formidable!
   It was great! 11
le **fort** *fort*, 12
fort(e) *strong*, 7
fou (folle) *crazy*, 9
le **foulard** *scarf*, 10
le **four** *oven*, 8
le **fournisseur** *supplier*, 8
les **fournitures** (f. pl.) **scolaires** *school
   supplies*, 3
la **fourrure** *fur*, 7
le **foutou** *a paste made from
   boiled plantains, manioc, or
   yams; it is common in Côte
   d'Ivoire.* 8
le **foyer** *home*, 7
fraîche *cool, cold*, 5
le **frais** *cool place*, 8; **au frais** *in a
   cool place*, 8
les **frais** (m. pl.) *cost, expenses*, 11
frais *cool (temperature)*, 4; **Il
   fait frais.** *It's cool.* 4 ; *fresh*,
   12; **des fruits et des légumes
   frais** *fresh fruits and vegetables*, 12
la **fraise** *strawberry*, 8; **un sirop de
   fraises (à l'eau)** *water with
   strawberry syrup*, 5
le **franc** *(former monetary unit of
   France) franc*, 3
le **franc de la Communauté financière
   africaine (CFA)** *the currency of
   francophone Africa*, 8
le **français** *French (language)*, 1;
   français(e) *French (adj.)*, 0; *A la
   française* **French-style**, 2
francophone *French-speaking*, 0
la **fréquence** *frequency*, 4
le **frère** *brother*, 7
les **friandises** (f.) *sweets*, 6
les **frites** (f. pl.) *French fries*, 1
froid(e) *cold*, 4; **Il fait froid.** *It's
   cold.* 4
le **fromage** *cheese*, 5
la **fromagerie** *cheese shop*, 12
les **fruits** (m.) *fruit*, 8
fui (pp. of fuir) *fled*, 1
le **fun** *fun*, 4; **C'est l' fun!** *(in Canada)*
   It's fun! 4

gagner *to win, to earn*, 9
la **garantie** *guarantee*, 3

le **garçon** *boy*, 9
garder *to look after*, 7
la **gare** *train station*, 6 ; **la gare
   routière** *bus station*, 12
le **garrot** *withers, shoulder height of
   an animal such as a horse*, 7
le **gâteau** *cake*, 8
la **gâterie** *little treat*, 9
la **gauche** *left (direction);* **à gauche**
   to the left, 12
la **Gaule** *Gaul; the division of the
   ancient Roman Empire (in
   Western Europe) occupied by the
   Gauls*, 9
le **gazon** *lawn*, 7; **tondre le
   gazon** *to mow the lawn*, 7
généralement *in general,
   usually*, 11
génial(e) *great*, 2
le **génie** *genius*, 6
les **genoux** (m.) *knees*, 7; **une paire de
   genoux** *pair of knees, lap*, 7
les **gens** (m. pl.) *people*, 9
gentil(le) *nice*, 7
la **géographie** *geography*, 2
la **géométrie** *geometry*, 2
la **glace** *ice cream*, 1
la **glace** *ice;* **faire du patin à glace**
   to ice-skate, 4
le **golf** *golf*, 4; **jouer au golf** *to play
   golf*, 4
les **gombos** (m.) *okra*, 8
la **gomme** *eraser*, 3
les **gorges** (f.) *canyons*, 11
la/le **gosse** *kid*, 2; **être traité comme
   un gosse** *to be treated like
   a kid*, 2
la **gouache** *paint*, 3
le **goût** *taste*, 4
le **goûter** *afternoon snack*, 8
goûter *to taste*, 8
le **gouvernement** *government*, 8
la **goyave** *guava*, 8
grâce à *thanks to*, 11
gradué(e) *graduated*, 3; **une règle
   graduée** *graduated ruler*, 3
la **graine** *seed*, 8
la **grammaire** *grammar*, 1; **grammaire
   en contexte** *grammar in context*, 1
le **gramme** *gram (unit of
   measurement)*, 8
grand(e) *tall*, 7; *big*, 10
grand-chose : Pas grand-chose.
   Not much. 6
grandir *to grow*, 10
la **grand-mère** *grandmother*, 7
le **grand-père** *grandfather*, 7
gratuit(e) *free*, 6
grec(que) *Greek (adj.)*, 6
gris(e) *grey*, 3
gros(se) *fat*, 7
grossir *to gain weight*, 10
la **grotte** *cave*, 11
le **groupe** *musical group*, 2; **le groupe**
   group, 7
le **gruyère** *Gruyère cheese*, 5

la Guadeloupe *Guadeloupe*, 0
le guichet *ticket window*, 6
la Guyane française *French Guiana*, 0

habitant : habitant le monde entier
living all over the world, 1
habite : J'habite à... *I live in . . .* , 1
l' habitude (f.) *habit*, 4; **d'habitude**
usually, 4
habituellement *usually*, 2
* haché(e) (pp. of hacher)
minced, 8
Haïti (no article) *Haiti*, 0
*le **hamburger** *hamburger*, 1
*les **haricots** (m.) *beans*, 8; **les haricots
verts** (m. pl.) *green beans*, 8
l' harmonie (f.) *harmony*, 10
*la **harpe** *harp*, 11
*la **hâte** *hurry, haste*; Elle a hâte de...
She can't wait to . . . , 7
* haut(e) *tall, high*, 6
*le **haut-parleur** *loudspeaker*, 11
*le **havre** *haven*, 7
l' hébergement (m.) *lodging*, 6
l' hélicoptère (m.) *helicopter*, 0
*le **héros** *hero*, 11
hésite : Euh... J'hésite. *Well, I'm
not sure.* 10
hésiter *to hesitate*, 10
l' **heure** (f.) *hour; time*, 1; **à l'heure
de** *at the time of*, 1; **A quelle
heure?** *At what time?* 6; **A
tout à l'heure!** *See you later!* 1;
l'heure officielle *official time
(24-hour system)*, 2; **Quelle
heure est-il?** *What time is it?* 6;
Tu as... à quelle heure? *At what
time do you have . . . ?* 2
heures *o'clock*, 2; **à... heures**
at . . . o'clock, 2; **à... heures
quarante-cinq** *at . . . forty-five*,
2; **à... heures quinze** *at . . .
fifteen*, 2; **à... heures trente**
at . . . thirty, 2
heureusement *luckily, fortunately*, 4
heureux (-euse) *happy*; **Très
heureux(-euse).** *Pleased to meet
you.* 7
hier *yesterday*, 9
l' **histoire** (f.) *history*, 2
l' historien (m.) *historian*, 9
l' **hiver** (m.) *winter*, 4; **en hiver** *in
the winter*, 4
*le **hockey** *hockey*, 4; **jouer au hockey**
to play hockey, 4
l' hôpital (pl. -aux) *hospital*, 0
l' horreur (f.) *horror*; un film
d'horreur *horror movie*, 6
horrible *terrible*, 10
*le **hot-dog** *hot dog*, 5

l' hôtel (m.) *hotel*, 0; l'hôtel de ville
(m.) *town hall*, 1
*le houx *holly*, 11
l' huile d'olive (f.) *olive oil*, 5
* hurler *to shriek, to cry out*, 12
l' hypermarché (m.) *hypermarket*, 8

l' **idée** (f.) *idea*, 4; **Bonne idée.**
Good idea. 4
identifier *to identify, to point
out*, 7
l' identité (f.) *identity*; une photo
d'identité *photo ID*, 1
l' igloo (m.) *igloo*, 0
l' igname (f.) *yam*, 8
il y a *there is, there are*, 5; il y a du
soleil/du vent *it's sunny/windy*, 4;
Qu'est-ce qu'il y a à boire? *What
is there to drink?* 5
l' île (f.) *island*, 0
illogique *illogical*, 3
l' image (f.) *image*, 7
imagines : Tu imagines? *Can you
imagine?* 4
l' impératif (m.) *command (verb
form), imperative*, 10
important(e) *important*, 8
imprimé(e) *printed*, 10
inaperçu(e) *unnoticed*, 11
inclus(e) *included*, 6
incompétent(e) *incompetent*, 2
incroyable *unbelievable*, 9
l' industrie (f.) *industry*, 4
l' influence (f.) *influence*, 12
l' **informatique** (f.) *computer
science*, 2
l' instrument de géométrie (m.)
*instrument for geometry (compass,
etc.)*, 3
intelligent(e) *smart*, 7
l' **intention** (f.) *intention*; **J'ai
l'intention de...** *I intend to . . .* , 11
l' interclasse (m.) *break (between
classes)*, 2
intéressant(e) *interesting*, 2
international(e) *international*, 5
l' interphone (m.) *intercom*, 9
l' **interro(gation)** (f.) *quiz*, 9; **rater
une interro** *to fail a quiz*, 9
intervenu(e) (pp. of intervenir)
intervened, 9
l' interviewé(e) (m./f.) *interviewee*, 2
intime *personal*, 1
l' intonation (f.) *intonation*, 1
inventer *to invent*, 7
l' invitation (f.) *invitation*, 6
l' invité(e) (m./f.) *guest*, 8
inviter *to invite*, 7
ivoirien(ne) *from the Republic of
Côte d'Ivoire*, 1

J

jamais : ne... jamais *never*, 4
le jambon *ham*, 5
janvier *January*, 4; **en janvier** *in
January*, 4
le jardin *garden*, 0
jaune *yellow*, 3
le jazz *jazz*, 4
je *I*, 0
le jean *(pair of) jeans*, 3; **en jean**
made of denim, 10
le jeu *game*; un jeu de rôle *role-
playing exercise*, 1; **jouer à des jeux
vidéo** *to play video games*, 4
jeudi *Thursday*, 2; **le jeudi** *on
Thursdays*, 2
jeune *young*, 7; les jeunes *youths*, 4
le jogging *jogging*, 4; **faire du
jogging** *to jog*, 4
la joie *joy*, 1
joignant (joindre) *attached*, 1
joli(e) *pretty*, 4
jouer *to play*, 4; **Je joue...**
I play . . . , 4; **Je ne joue pas...**
I don't play . . . , 4; **jouer à...**
to play (a game) . . . , 4
joueur (-euse) *playful*, 7
le jour *day*, 2; le jour férié (m.)
holiday, 6
le journal *journal*, 1; *newspaper*, 12
la journée *day*, 2
juillet *July*, 4; **en juillet** *in July*, 4
juin *June*, 4; **en juin** *in June*, 4
la jupe *skirt*, 10
le jus d'orange *orange juice*, 5
le jus de fruit *fruit juice*, 5
le jus de pomme *apple juice*, 5
jusqu'à *up to, until*, 12; **Vous allez
tout droit jusqu'à...** *You go
straight ahead until you get to . . .* , 12
juste *just*, 4

K

le kangourou *kangaroo*, 0
le kilo(gramme) *kilogram*, 8; **un kilo
de** *a kilogram of*, 8
le kilomètre *kilometer*, 12

L

la *the*, 1; *her, it* (f.), 9
là *there*, 12; **-là** *there (noun
suffix)*, 3; **(Est-ce que)... est là, s'il**

vous plaît? *Is . . . , there, please?* 9;
là-bas *there; over there*, 8
là-bas *there, over there*, 9
laid(e) *ugly*, 9
la laine *wool*, 10
laisser *to leave*, 9; **Je peux laisser un message?** *Can I leave a message?* 9
le lait *milk*, 8
laitier (-ière) *dairy*, 8; **les produits laitiers (m.)** *dairy products*, 8
la langue *language*, 1
large *baggy*, 10; *large wide*; 107 mètres de large *107 meters wide*, 9
le latin *Latin (language)*, 2
laver *to wash*, 7; **laver la voiture** *to wash the car*, 7
le *the*, 1; *him, it*, 9
la légende *map key*, 12
la légèreté *lightness*, 6
les légumes (m.) *vegetables*, 8
les *the*, 1; *them*, 9
la lettre *letter*, 12; **envoyer des lettres** *to send letters*, 12
leur *to them*, 9
leur/leurs *their*, 7
levez : Levez la main! *Raise your hand!* 0; **Levez-vous!** *Stand up!* 0
la levure *yeast*, 8
la liaison *liaison; pronunciation of a normally silent consonant at the end of a word as if it were the first letter of the word that follows*, 2
la librairie *bookstore*, 12
la librairie-papeterie *bookstore and stationery store*, 3
libre *free*, 2
liégeois : café ou chocolat liégeois *coffee or chocolate ice cream with whipped cream*, 5
le lieu *place*; avoir lieu *to take place*, 7; ... aura lieu... *... will take place . . .* , 7
la limonade *lemon soda*, 5
le lin *linen*, 10
le lion *lion*, 0
le liquide correcteur *correction fluid*, 3
lire *to read*, 1
lisant : en lisant *while reading*, 11
lisons : Lisons! *Let's read!* 1
la liste *list*, 8
la litote *understatement*, 5
le litre *liter*, 8; **un litre de** *a liter of*, 8
la livraison *delivery*, 12
la livre *pound*, 8; **une livre de** *a pound of*, 8
le livre *book*, 0
le livret scolaire *a student's personal gradebook*, 3
la location *rental*, 4
logique *logical*, 3
loin *far*, 12; **loin de** *far from*, 12
long(ue) *long*, 10
longtemps (adv.) *a long time*, 9

la longueur *length*, 10
louer *to rent*, 12
la Louisiane *Louisiana*, 0
lu (pp. of lire) *read*, 9
lui *to him, to her*, 9
lumineux (-euse) *luminous, lit up*, 3
lundi *Monday*, 2; **le lundi** *on Mondays*, 2
les lunettes de soleil (f. pl.) *sunglasses*, 10
le Luxembourg *Luxembourg*, 0
le lycée *high school*, 2
le lycéen *high school student*, 2

ma *my*, 7
madame (Mme) *ma'am, Mrs.*, 1; **Madame!** *Waitress!* 5
mademoiselle (Mlle) *miss, Miss*, 1; **Mademoiselle!** *Waitress!* 5
le madras *madras (fabric or pattern)*, 10
le magasin *store*, 1; **faire les magasins** *to go shopping*, 1; grand magasin *department store*, 10
le magazine *magazine*, 3
le magnétoscope *videocassette recorder, VCR*, 0
magnifique *magnificent, splendid*, 9
mai *May*, 4; **en mai** *in May*, 4
maigrir *to lose weight*, 10
le maillot de bain *bathing suit*, 10
la main *hand*, 0
maintenant *now*, 2; **Je ne peux pas maintenant.** *I can't right now.* 8
le maire *mayor*, 12
la mairie *city hall*, 4
mais *but*, 1
le maïs *corn*, 8
la Maison des jeunes et de la culture (MJC) *recreation center*, 6
le maître *master, owner*, 7
maîtriser *to master*, 4
la majorité *majority*, 2
mal *bad*, 1; **Pas mal.** *Not bad.* 1
la malchance *misfortune*, 7
le mâle *male (refers to animals)*, 7
malheureusement *unfortunately*, 7
le Mali *Mali*, 0
la manche *sleeve*, 10
le manchot *penguin*, 6
le manège *carousel*, 12
manger *to eat*, 6
la mangue *mango*, 8
manque : Qu'est-ce qui manque? *What's missing?* 2
manqué(e) (pp. of manquer) *missed*; garçon manqué *tomboy*, 10

le manteau *coat*, 10
le maquis *maquis; kind of outdoor restaurant in Côte d'Ivoire*, 5
le marchand (la marchande) *merchant, shopkeeper*, 8
le marché *market*, 8
mardi *Tuesday*, 2; **le mardi** *on Tuesdays*, 2
le mari *husband*, 7
le mariage *marriage*, 7
le Maroc *Morocco*, 0
marocain(e) *Moroccan (adj.)*, 1
marron (inv.) *brown*, 3
mars *March*, 4; **en mars** *in March*, 4
martiniquais(e) *from Martinique*, 1
la Martinique *Martinique*, 0
le masque *mask*, 8
le match *game*, 6; **regarder un match** *to watch a game (on TV)*, 6; **aller voir un match** *to go see a game (in person)*, 6
les maths (les mathématiques) (f. pl.) *math*, 1
la matière *school subject*, 2; *fabric*, 10
les matières grasses (f.) *fat*, 8
le matin *morning, in the morning*, 2
mauvais(e) *bad*, 5; **C'est pas mauvais!** *It's pretty good!* 5; **Oh, pas mauvais.** *Oh, not bad.* 9; **Très mauvais.** *Very bad.* 9
méchant(e) *mean*, 7
mécontent(e) *unhappy*, 2
les médicaments (m.) *medicine*, 12
meilleur(e) *best*, 7; les meilleurs amis *best friends*, 7
le mélange *mixture*, 12
mélanger *to mix*, 8
méli-mélo *mishmash*, 1
le membre *member*; le membre de la famille *family member*, 7
même *same*, 4
la mémé *granny, grandma*, 9
le ménage *housework*, 1; **faire le ménage** *to do housework*, 1
le mensuel *monthly publication*, 9
la menthe à l'eau *beverage made with mint syrup and water*, 5
le menu *meal, menu*, 8
méprisant(e) *contemptuous*, 2
la mer *sea*; **au bord de la mer** *to/on the coast*, 11
Merci. *Thank you*, 3; **Non, merci.** *No, thank you.* 8
mercredi *Wednesday*, 2; **le mercredi** *on Wednesdays*, 2
la mère *mother*, 7
mes *my*, 7
le message *message*, 9; **Je peux laisser un message?** *May I leave a message?*, 9
mesurer *to measure*, 9
le mètre *meter*, 9
le métro *subway*, 12; **au métro...** *at the . . . metro stop*, 6; **en métro** *by subway*, 12

métropolitain(e) *metropolitan,* 2

mets : mets en ordre *put into order,* 6

mettre *to put, to put on, to wear,* 10; **Je ne sais pas quoi mettre pour...** *I don't know what to wear for (to) . . . ,* 10; **Mets... Wear . . . ,** 10; **Qu'est-ce que je mets?** *What shall I wear?* 10

meublé(e) *furnished,* 11

mexicain(e) (adj.) *Mexican,* 5

miam-miam *yum-yum,* 5

midi *noon,* 6; **Il est midi.** *It's noon.* 6; **Il est midi et demi.** *It's half past noon.* 6

mieux *better,* 9; **Ça va aller mieux!** *It's going to get better!* 9; **J'aime mieux...** *I prefer . . . ,* 1

mignon(ne) *cute,* 7

le milieu *middle;* au milieu *in the middle,* 7

millier (m.) *a thousand or so;* des milliers d'autres visiteurs *thousands of other tourists,* 9

mince *slender,* 7

minuit *midnight,* 6; **Il est minuit.** *It's midnight.* 6; **Il est minuit et demi.** *It's half past midnight.* 6

la minute *minute,* 9; **Tu as une minute?** *Do you have a minute?* 9

mis (pp. of mettre) *put, placed,* 10

la mise *putting, setting;* mise en pratique *putting into practice,* 1; mise en train *getting started,* 1

la mise en scène *production,* 1

mixte *mixed,* 5

le mobilier *furniture,* 6

la mobylette *motor scooter,* 11

moche *tacky,* 10

la mode *style,* 10; **à la mode** *in style,* 10; **à la dernière mode** *in the latest fashion,* 10

le mode d'emploi *instructions,* 9

modéré(e) *moderate,* 11

moderne *modern,* 8

moi *me,* 2; **Moi aussi.** *Me too.* 2; **Moi, non.** *I don't.* 2; **Moi non plus.** *Neither do I.* 2; **Moi, si.** *I do.* 2; **Pas moi.** *Not me.*

moins (with numbers) *minus, lower,* 0; **moins cinq** *five to,* 6; **moins le quart** *quarter to,* 6

le mois *month,* 4

le moment *moment,* 5; **Un moment, s'il vous plaît.** *One moment, please.* 5

mon *my,* 7

Monaco *Monaco,* 0

le monde *world,* 0

le moniteur *monitor,* 12

monsieur (M.) *sir, Mr.,* 1; **Monsieur!** *Waiter!* 5

le monstre *monster,* 0

la montagne *mountain,* 4; **à la montagne** *to/in the mountains,* 11

la montée *ascent,* 6

monter *to climb, to rise,* 6

la montre *watch,* 3

montrer *to show,* 9

le monument *monument,* 6

se moquer de *to make fun of,* 9

le moral *morale,* 2

le morceau *piece,* 8; **un morceau de** *a piece of,* 8

le mot *word,* 11; un petit mot *a little note,* 5

le motif *reason, pattern,* 9

la moto(cyclette) *motorcycle,* 12

le moulin *windmill,* 9

la mousseline *chiffon,* 8

la moutarde *mustard,* 8

moyen(ne) *average,* 2; travail moyen *average work,* 2

le Moyen Age *Middle Ages,* 9

la moyenne *average,* 2

le musée *museum,* 6

la musique *music,* 2; **écouter de la musique** *to listen to music,* 1; la musique classique *classical music,* 4

le mystère *mystery,* 5

nager *to swim,* 1

le nain *dwarf,* 6

la naissance *birth,* 7

la natation *swimming,* 4; **faire de la natation** *to swim,* 4

national(e) *national,* 8

naturel(le) *natural,* 3

nautique *nautical;* **faire du ski nautique** *to water-ski,* 4

ne : ne... pas *not,* 1; **ne... pas encore** *not yet,* 9; **ne... jamais** *never,* 4; **ne... ni grand(e) ni petit(e)** *neither tall nor short,* 7; n'est-ce pas? *isn't that so? (tag question added to the end of a declarative phrase to make it a question)*

né(e) (pp. of naître) *born,* 9

la Négritude *movement which asserts the values and spirit of black African civilizations,* 0

la neige *snow,* 4

neige : Il neige. *It's snowing.* 4

le neveu *nephew,* 7

niçois(e) (adj.) *from Nice, France,* 5

la nièce *niece,* 7

le Niger *Niger,* 0

le niveau *level,* 6

le nocturne *late-night opening,* 6

le Noël *Christmas,* 0

noir(e) *black,* 3

la noisette *hazelnut,* 5

la noix *nut,* 5

la noix de coco *coconut,* 8

le nom *name,* 1; nom de famille *last name*

le nombre *number,* 2

nombreux(-euse) *numerous, many,* 9

non *no,* 1; **Moi non plus.** *Neither do I.* 2; **Moi, non.** *I don't.* 2; **Non, c'est...** *No, it's . . . ,* 4; **Non, merci.** *No, thank you.* 8; **Non, pas trop.** *No, not too much.* 2

nos *our,* 7

la note *note;* la note culturelle *culture note,* 1

notre *our,* 7

nouveau (nouvelle) *new,* 7

la Nouvelle-Angleterre *New England,* 0

les nouvelles (f.) *news,* 9

novembre *November,* 4; **en novembre** *in November,* 4

le nuage *cloud,* 12

nul(le) *useless,* 2

le numéro *number,* 0; un numéro de téléphone *telephone number,* 3; les numéros *issues (for magazines, etc.),* 3

nutritionnel(le) *nutritive, having to do with nutrition,* 8

l' objet (m.) *object,* 6; objets trouvés *lost and found,* 3

l' observation (f.) *observation,* 2

l' occasion (f.) *occasion,* 10

occupé(e) : C'est occupé. *It's busy.* 9; **Désolé(e), je suis occupé(e).** *Sorry, I'm busy.* 6

s'occuper de *to take care of,* 7

octobre *October,* 4; **en octobre** *in October,* 4

l' odeur (f.) *aroma, smell,* 8

l' œil (m.) *eye,* 12

l' œuf (m.) *egg,* 8

offre (offrir) *to offer;* Le plus grand centre du sport au Canada offre... *The largest sports center in Canada offers . . . ,* 4

l' oignon (m.) *onion,* 8

l' oiseau (m.) *bird,* 12

ombragé(e) (pp. of ombrager) *shaded,* 11

l' omelette (f.) *omelette,* 5

on *one, we, you, they,* 1; Comment dit-on...? *How do you say . . . ?* 1; On est dans la purée. *We're in trouble.* 8; **On fait du ski?** *How about skiing?* 5; **On joue au base-ball?** *How about playing baseball?* 5; **On peut...** *We can . . . ,*

6; **On va au café?** *Shall we go to the café?* 5; **On...?** *How about . . . ?* 4

l' **oncle** (m.) *uncle*, 7
l' **opéra** (m.) *opera house*, 10
l' **opinion** (f.) *opinion*, 7
opposé(e) *opposite*, 12
opulent(e) *rich*, 7
l' **or** (m.) *gold*, 12
orange (inv.) *orange (color)*, 3
l' **orange** (f.) *orange*, 8; **le jus d'orange** *orange juice*
l' **ordinateur** (m.) *computer*, 3
l' **ordre** (m.) *order*, 9; l'ordre chronologique (m.) *chronological order*, 3
l' **organisation** (f.) *organization*, 1
original(e) *original*, 10
l' **otarie** (f.) *sea lion*, 6
ôter *to cut out*, 8
ou *or*, 1
où *where*, 6; **Où (ça)?** *Where?* 6; **Où est-ce que tu vas aller... ?** *Where are you going to go . . . ?* 11; **Tu es allé(e) où?** *Where did you go?* 9
oublier *to forget*, 9; **Je n'ai rien oublié.** *I didn't forget anything.* 11; **Oublie-le/-la/-les!** *Forget him/her/them!* 9; **J'ai oublié.** *I forgot.* 3; **N'oublie pas de...** *Don't forget . . .* , 8; **Tu n'as pas oublié... ?** *You didn't forget . . . ?* 11
l' **ouest** *West*, 8
oui *yes*, 1; **Oui, c'est...** *Yes it's . . .* , 4; **Oui, s'il te/vous plaît.** *Yes, please.* 8
ouvert(e) *open*, 6
l' **ouverture** (f.) *opening*, 6
ouvrez : Ouvrez vos livres à la page... *Open your books to page . . .* , 0

la page *page*, 0
le **pagne** *a piece of dyed African cloth*, 10
le **pain** *bread*, 8
la **paire** *pair*, 5; une paire de genoux *pair of knees, lap*, 7
le **palais** *palace*, 1; le palais de justice *court, courthouse*, 1
le **pamplemousse** *grapefruit*, 5
le **panier** *basket*, 3
le **pantalon** *pair of pants*, 10
la **papaye** *papaya*, 8
la **papeterie** *stationery store*, 12; librairie-papeterie *bookstore/ stationery store*, 3
le **papier** *paper*, 0; **des feuilles** (f.) **de papier** *sheets of paper*, 3

le **paquet** *package, box*, 8; **un paquet de** *a package/box of*, 8
par *by*, 12; *per*, 6; par hasard *by chance*, 12; prix par personne *price per person*, 6
le **parachute** *parachute*, 0
le **paragraphe** *paragraph*, 7
paraître *to appear; seem*, 12
le **parapluie** *umbrella*, 11
le **parc** *park*, 6
parce que *because*, 5; **Je ne peux pas parce que...** *I can't because . . .* , 5
Pardon. *Pardon me.* 3; **Pardon, madame... , s'il vous plaît?** *Excuse me, ma'am . . . , please?* 12; **Pardon, monsieur. Je cherche... , s'il vous plaît.** *Excuse me, sir. I'm looking for . . . , please.* 12
le **parent** *parent, relative*, 7
paresseux (-euse) *lazy*, 2
parfait(e) *perfect*, 3; **C'est parfait.** *It's perfect.* 10
parfois *sometimes*, 4
parfumer *to flavor*, 8
la **parfumerie** *perfumery, perfume shop*, 11
parisien(ne) (adj.) *Parisian*, 5
parlé (pp. of parler) *talked, spoke*, 9; **Nous avons parlé.** *We talked.* 9
parler *to talk*, 1; *to speak*, 9; **(Est-ce que) je peux parler à... ?** *Could I speak to. . . ?* 9; **Je peux te parler?** *Can I talk to you?* 9; **parler au téléphone** *to talk on the phone*, 1; Parlons! *Let's talk!* 2
parmi *among*, 9
partagé(e) *split, shared*, 6
le **partenaire** (la partenaire) *partner*, 7
partir *to leave*, 11; **Tu ne peux pas partir sans...** *You can't leave without . . .* , 11
pas *not*, 1: **pas bon** *not good*, 5; **Pas ce soir.** *Not tonight.* 7; pas content du tout *not happy at all*, 2; **Il/Elle ne va pas du tout avec...** *It doesn't go at all with . . .* , 10; **Pas grand-chose.** *Not much.* 6; **Pas mal.** *Not bad.* 10; **pas mauvais** *not bad*, 9; **Pas question!** *Out of the question!* 7; **pas super** *not so hot*, 2; **Pas terrible.** *Not so great.* 1; pas du tout *not at all*, 4
le **passeport** *passport*, 1
les **passe-temps** (m. pl.) *pastimes*, 4
passé (pp. of passer) : **Ça s'est bien passé?** *Did it go well?* 11; **Qu'est-ce qui s'est passé?** *What happened?* 9; **Tu as passé un bon week-end?** *Did you have a good weekend?* 9
passer *to pass*, 12; *to go by*, 12; **Tu pourrais passer à... ?** *Could you go by . . . ?* 12; **Vous passez...** *You'll pass . . .* ,

12; **passer l'aspirateur** *to vacuum*, 7; **passer un examen** *to take a test*, 9
passerais : je passerais le bac... *I would take the bac . . .* , 2
passionnant(e) *fascinating*, 2
la **pastille** *tablet*, 3
la **pâte** *dough*, 8; la pâte d'arachide *peanut butter*, 8; la pâte de tomates *tomato paste*, 8
le **pâté** *pâté*, 0
les **pâtes** (f. pl.) *pasta*, 11
le **patin** *skating*, 1; **faire du patin à glace** *to ice-skate*, 4
le **patin à roulettes** *rollerskating*, 4
le **patinage** *skating*, 4
patiner *to skate*, 4
la **patinoire** *skating rink*, 6
la pâtisserie *pastry shop, pastry*, 12
le **patrimoine** *heritage*, 6
patronal(e) *having to do with saints*; la fête patronale *patron saint's holiday*, 12
les **pattes d'eph** (f. pl.) *bell-bottoms*, 10
pauvre *poor*, 7
le **pays** *country*, 6
le **paysage** *landscape*, 11
la pêche *peach*, 8
peindre *to paint*, 9
la **peinture** *painting*, 6
pendant *during*, 1
pénible *annoying*, 7
penser *to think*; **J'ai pensé à tout.** *I've thought of everything.* 11; Qu'en penses-tu? *What do you think (about it)?* 1
perdre *to lose*, 9
perdu(e) (pp. of perdre) *lost*, 1
le **père** *father*, 7
permettre *to allow*, 9
le **permis de conduire** *driver's license*, 12; le permis accompagné *learner's permit (driving)*, 12; le permis probatoire *learner's permit (driving)*, 12
la **permission** *permission*, 7
le **personnage** *individual, character*, 9
la **personnalité** *personality*, 7
la **personne** *person*, 7; personnel(le) *personal*, 4
petit(e) *short (height)*, 7; *small (size)*, 10; petites annonces *classified ads*, 1
le **petit copain** *boyfriend*, 2
le petit déjeuner *breakfast*, 8
le **petit-fils** *grandson*, 7
la **petite copine** *girlfriend*, 2
la **petite-fille** *granddaughter*, 7
les **petits-enfants** (m.) *grandchildren*, 7
les petits pois (m.) *peas*, 8
peu *not very*, 2; à peu près *about, approximately*, 9; peu content *not very happy*, 2; un peu *a little*, 6
peut : On peut... *We can . . .* , 6
peut-être *maybe, perhaps*, 11

peux : Désolé(e), mais je ne peux pas. *Sorry, but I can't.* 4; **Tu peux...?** *Can you...?* 8
la pharmacie *drugstore*, 12
la philosophie *philosophy*, 2
le phoque *seal*, 6
la photo *picture, photo*, 4; **faire de la photo** *to do photography*, 4; **faire des photos** *to take pictures*, 4
la photographie *photography*, 1
les photographies (f. pl.) *photographs*, 6
la phrase *sentence*, 4
la physique *physics*, 2
physiquement *physically*, 7
la pièce *play*, 6; **voir une pièce** *to see a play*, 6
le pied *foot*, 12; **à pied** *on foot*, 12
la Pierre Levée *name of a megalith in Poitiers, France*, 1
la pince : des pantalons à pinces *pleated pants*, 10
le pinceau *paintbrush*, 3
le pingouin *penguin*, 0
le pique-nique *picnic*, 6; **faire un pique-nique** *to have a picnic*, 6
la piscine *swimming pool*, 6
pittoresque *picturesque*, 8
la pizza *pizza*, 1
la place *place*; Services... de location sur place *On-site rentals*, 4
la plage *beach*, 1
la plaine *plain*, 4
le plaisir *pleasure, enjoyment*, 4; **Oui, avec plaisir.** *Yes, with pleasure.* 8
plaît : Il/Elle me plaît, mais il/elle est cher/chère. *I like it, but it's expensive.* 10; **Il/Elle te/vous plaît?** *Do you like it?* 10; Ça te plaît? *Do you like it?* 2; **s'il vous/te plaît** *please*, 3
la planche *board*; **faire de la planche à voile** *to go windsurfing*, 11
la plaque *plate (of metal or glass)*; la plaque d'immatriculation *license plate*, 0
le plat *dish (food)*, 5; les plats à emporter (m.) *food to go*, 11
plein(e) de *a lot of*, 8; une ville pleine d'animation *a city full of life*, 8
pleut : Il pleut. *It's raining.* 4
la plongée *diving*; **faire de la plongée** *to go scuba diving*, 11
plus *plus (math)*, 2; *(with numbers)* *higher*, 0; **Je n'en veux plus.** *I don't want any more*, 8; **Moi non plus.** *Neither do I.* 2; **Non, merci. Je n'ai plus faim.** *No thanks. I'm not hungry anymore.* 8
plusieurs (inv.) *several*, 7
la poche *pocket*, 10
le poème *poem*, 0
le point *point*, 10; le point d'intérêt *tourist attraction*, 4

la poire *pear*, 8
le poisson *fish*, 7
la poissonnerie *fish shop*, 12
la poitrine *chest*, 10
le poivre *pepper*, 8
le poivron *green or red pepper*, 5
poliment *politely*, 8
la pollution *pollution*, 1
la pomme *apple*, 8; **jus de pom**me *apple juice*, 5
la pomme de terre *potato*, 8
le pompiste *gas pump attendant*, 11
la population *population*, 4
le porc *pork*, 8
le port *port*, 8
la porte *door*, 0
le portefeuille *wallet*, 3
le porte-monnaie *change purse*, 5
porter *to wear*, 10
le portugais *Portuguese (language)*, 2
poser des questions *to ask questions*, 7
possible *possible*, 3
la poste *post office*, 12
le poster *poster*, 0
le pot de colle *container of glue*, 3
la poubelle *trashcan*, 7; **sortir la poubelle** *to take out the trash*, 7
la poudre *powder*, 8
la poule *(animal) chicken*, 8
le poulet *chicken (meat)*, 8
pour *for*, 2; **Qu'est-ce qu'il te faut pour...** *What do you need for...?* *(informal)*, 3; **Qu'est-ce que tu fais pour t'amuser?** *What do you do to have fun?* 4
pourquoi *why*, 0; **Pourquoi est-ce que tu ne mets pas...?** *Why don't you wear...?* 10; **Pourquoi pas?** *Why not?* 6; **Pourquoi tu ne... pas?** *Why don't you...?* 9
pourrais : Tu pourrais passer à ...? *Could you go by...?* 12
pourtant *yet, nevertheless*, 9
pouvoir *to be able to, can*, 8; **(Est-ce que) je peux...?** *May I...?* 7; **Tu peux...?** *Can you...?* 8; **Je ne peux pas maintenant.** *I can't right now.* 8; **Je peux te parler?** *Can I talk to you?*, 9; **Non, je ne peux pas.** *No, I can't.* 12; **On peut...** *We can...*, 6; **Qu'est-ce que je peux faire?** *What can I do?* 9; **(Est-ce que) tu pourrais me rendre un petit service?** *Could you do me a favor?* 12; **Tu pourrais passer à...?** *Could you go by...?*, 12
pratique *practical*, 3
précieusement *carefully*, 2
précisant : en précisant *specifying*, 1
préféré(e) *favorite*, 4
la préfecture (de police) *police station*, 12
la préférence *preference*, 3
préférer *to prefer*, 1; **Je préfère...**

I prefer..., 1
premier (-ière) *first*, 1; la première étape *first step*, 1
prendre *to take or to have (food or drink)*, 5; **Je vais prendre..., s'il vous plaît.** *I'm going to have...*, *please.* 5; **On peut prendre...** *We can take...*, 12; **Prends...** *Get...*, 8; *Have...*, 5; **Je le/la/les prends.** *I'll take it/them.* 10; **Tu prends...?** *Will you have...?*, 8; *Are you taking...?*, 11; **Prenez une feuille de papier.** *Take out a sheet of paper.* 0; **Vous prenez...?** *What are you having?* 5; *Will you have...?*, 8; **Prenez la rue... puis traversez la rue...** *You take... Street, then cross... Street*, 12; **Vous avez décidé de prendre...?** *Have you decided to take...?* 10; **Vous le/la/les prenez?** *Are you going to take it/them?* 10
le prénom *first name*, 1
préparer *to prepare (something)*, 8; **se préparer** *to prepare (oneself), to get ready*, 10
près *close*, 12; **près de** *close to*, 12
la présentation *presentation, introduction*, 7
présenter *to introduce*; **Je te (vous) présente...** *I'd like you to meet...*, 7; Présente-toi! *Introduce yourself!* 0
presque *almost*, 12
la presqu'île *peninsula*, 12
prévoir *to anticipate*, 4
prévu(e) (pp. of prévoir) *planned*; **Je n'ai rien de prévu.** *I don't have any plans.* 11
principal(e) *main*; la ville principale *main city*, 12
le printemps *spring*, 4; **au printemps** *in the spring*, 4
pris (pp. of prendre) *took, taken*, 9
le prisonnier *prisoner*, 4
le prix *price*, 6
le problème *problem*, 9; **J'ai un petit problème.** *I've got a little problem.* 9
prochain(e) *next*, 12; **Vous continuez jusqu'au prochain feu rouge.** *You keep going until the next light.* 12
les produits laitiers (m.) *dairy products*, 8
le prof(esseur) *teacher*, 0
les progrès (m.) *progress*, 11
le projet *project*, 6
la promenade *walk*, 6; **faire une promenade** *to go for a walk*, 6
promener *to walk*, 6; **promener le chien** *to walk the dog*, 7; **se promener** *to take a walk*, 12
promets (promettre) *to promise*, 1
le pronom *pronoun*, 8
prononcer *to pronounce*, 1; ne se

prononcent pas   *no response,* 2
la prononciation   *pronunciation,* 2
proposé(e) (pp. of proposer)   *given, suggested,* 5
proposer   *to propose, to suggest,* 5
prospérer   *to prosper, to do well,* 9
protéger   *to protect,* 9
la protéine   *protein,* 8
provençal(e)   *Provençal; from the Provence region of France,* 9
la Provence   *Provence; region in southeast France on the Mediterranean Sea,* 9
la publicité   *advertisment,* 10
le publiphone à cartes   *card-operated telephone,* 9
puis   *then,* 12; **Prenez la rue... puis traversez la rue...**   *Take . . . Street, then cross . . . Street,* 12
le pull(-over)   *pullover sweater,* 3
la punition   *punishment,* 9
purement   *purely,* 12
la pyramide   *pyramid,* 11

Q

qu'est-ce que   *what,* 1; **Qu'est-ce qu'il te faut pour...?**   *What do you need for . . . ? (informal),* 3; **Qu'est-ce qu'il vous faut pour...?**   *What do you need for . . . ? (formal),* 3; Qu'est-ce qu'il y a dans...?   *What's in the . . . ?* 3; Qu'est-ce qu'il y a?   *What's wrong?* 2; Qu'est-ce qu'on fait?   *What are we/they doing?* 4; **Qu'est-ce que je peux faire?**   *What can I do?* 9; **Qu'est-ce que tu as fait...?**   *What did you do . . . ?* 9; **Qu'est-ce que tu fais...?**   *What do you do . . . ?* 4; **Qu'est-ce que tu vas faire...?**   *What are you going to do . . . ?* 6; **Qu'est-ce que vous avez comme boissons?**   *What do you have to drink?* 5; **Qu'est-ce qu'il y a à boire?**   *What is there to drink?* 5; Qu'est-ce qui manque?   *What's missing?* 2
qu'est-ce qui   *what (subj.),* 9; Qu'est-ce qui s'est passé?   *What happened?* 9
quand   *when,* 6; **Quand (ça)?**   *When?* 6
la quantité   *quantity,* 8
quarantième   *fortieth,* 7
le quart   *quarter,* 6; **et quart**   *quarter past,* 6; **moins le quart**   *quarter to,* 6
que   *that; what,* 1; Que sais-je?   *self-check (What do I know?),* 1
le quartier   *neighborhood,* 4
le Québec   *Quebec,* 0
québécois(e)   *from Quebec,* 1

quel(le)   *what, which,* 1; Ils ont quels cours?   *What classes do they have?* 2; **Tu as quel âge?**   *How old are you?* 1; **Tu as quels cours...?**   *What classes do you have . . . ?* 2; **Tu as... à quelle heure?**   *At what time do you have . . . ?* 2; **Quelle heure est-il?**   *What time is it?* 6; **Quel temps fait-il?**   *What's the weather like?* 4
quelque   *some,* 10
quelqu'un   *someone,* 1
quelque chose   *something,* 6; **Je cherche quelque chose pour...**   *I'm looking for something for . . . ,* 10
quelquefois   *sometimes,* 4
la question   *question,* 0
le questionnaire   *questionnaire, survey,* 4
qui   *who,* 0; **Avec qui?**   *With whom?* 6; C'est qui?   *Who is it?* 2; Qui suis-je?   *Who am I?* 0
la quiche   *quiche: a type of custard pie with a filling, such as ham, bacon, cheese, or spinach,* 5
quittez : Ne quittez pas. (telephone)   *Hold on.* 9
quoi   *what,* 10; **De quoi est-ce que tu as besoin?**   *What do you need?* 5; **Je ne sais pas quoi mettre pour...**   *I don't know what to wear for/to . . . ,* 10; **Tu as quoi...?**   *What do you have . . . ?* 2 **Tu vas faire quoi?**   *What are you going to do?* 6
quotidien(ne)   *everyday,* 6

R

le rabat   *flap,* 3
le raccourci   *shortcut,* 2
raconter   *to tell,* 9
la radio   *radio,* 3
le radis   *radish,* 8
le raisin   *grapes,* 8
la randonnée   *hike,* 11; **faire de la randonnée**   *to go hiking,* 11
ranger   *to arrange, straighten;* **ranger ta chambre**   *to pick up your room,* 7
le rap   *rap music,* 1
râpé(e) (pp. of râper)   *grated,* 8
rapidement   *rapidly, quickly,* 7
rappeler   *to call back,* 9; **Vous pouvez rappeler plus tard?**   *Can you call back later?* 9; Tu te rappelles?   *Do you remember?* 3; *to remind,* 12
le rapport   *relationship,* 7
rapporter   *to bring back,* 8; **Rapporte-moi...**   *Bring me*

back . . . , 8; **Tu me rapportes...?**   *Will you bring me . . . ?* 8
rarement   *rarely,* 4
rater   *to fail,* 9; *to miss,* 9; **rater le bus**   *to miss the bus,* 9; **rater une interro**   *to fail a quiz,* 9
le rayon   *department,* 3; au rayon de musique   *in the music department,* 3
la rayonne   *rayon,* 10
la réalité   *reality,* 11
la recette   *recipe,* 8
recevoir   *to receive,* 1
reconstruit(e) (pp. of reconstruire)   *reconstructed,* 12
la récré(ation)   *break,* 2
recueilli (pp. of recueillir)   *to take in,* 7
refaire   *to redo, remake,* 8
réfléchir   *to think about,* 2; *to reflect;* Réfléchissez.   *Think about it.* 2
le reflet   *reflection,* 10
le refuge   *animal shelter,* 7
le réfugié   *refugee,* 1
le refus   *refusal,* 6
refuser   *to refuse,* 7
le regard   *look,* 7
regarder   *to look,* 10; *to watch,* 1; **Non, merci, je regarde.**   *No, thanks, I'm just looking.* 10; **Regarde, voilà...**   *Look, here's/there's/it's . . . ,* 12; **regarder la télé**   *to watch TV,* 1; **regarder un match**   *to watch a game (on TV),* 6; **Regardez la carte!**   *Look at the map!* 0
la règle   *ruler,* 3
regrette : Je regrette.   *Sorry.* 3; **Je regrette, mais je n'ai pas le temps.**   *I'm sorry, but I don't have time.* 8
regroupé(e)   *rearranged,* 6
rejoint (pp. of rejoindre)   *rejoined,* 7
la relation   *relation,* 7
relier   *to connect,* 9
religieux(-euse)   *religious,* 9
relire   *to re-read, to read again,* 7
remarquable   *remarkable, exceptional,* 3
le remboursement   *repayment,* 9
la rencontre   *encounter,* 1
rencontrer   *to meet,* 9
le rendez-vous   *rendez-vous, date, appointment,* 12
rendre   *to return something,* 12; rendre un service   *to do (someone) a favor,* 12; **Rendez-vous...**   *We'll meet . . . ,* 6; pour les rendre plus originales   *to make them more original,* 10
le renfort   *reinforcement; renforts aux épaules   reinforced shoulder seams,* 10
les renseignements (m.)   *information,* 9
la rentrée   *back to school,* 2
rentrer   *to go home,* 8
le repas   *meal,* 8

le répertoire *index,* 9
répéter *to rehearse, practice,* 9; **Répétez!** *Repeat!* 0
le répondant *respondent,* 4
le répondeur *answering machine,* 9
répondre *to answer,* 9; **Ça ne répond pas.** *There's no answer.* 9
la réponse *response, answer,* 2
reposer *to rest, to relax;* laisser reposer *to let stand,* 8; se reposer *to relax,* 11
représenté(e) (pp. of représenter) *represented,* 7
représenter *to represent,* 8
la république de Côte d'Ivoire *the Republic of Côte d'Ivoire,* 0
la réserve *reserve,* 8
respectueux (-euse) *respectful,* 2
ressemblez : si vous me ressemblez *if you're like me,* 1
la ressource *resource,* 4
le restaurant *restaurant,* 6
la restauration *dining,* 6
rester *to stay, to remain,* 11
le resto *restaurant,* 11
le résultat *result,* 10
retard : en retard *late,* 2
retirer *to take out, to remove;* **retirer de l'argent** *to withdraw money,* 12
le retour *return,* 6
rétro (inv.) *retro,* 10
retrouve : Bon, on se retrouve... *OK, we'll meet . . . ,* 6
retrouver *to find again,* 6
la Réunion *the island of Réunion,* 0
rêvait (imp. of rêver) *to dream,* 7
le rêve *dream,* 11
revenir *to come back,* 5
riche *rich,* 8
ridicule *ridiculous,* 10
rien *nothing,* 6; *anything,* 11; **Ça ne me dit rien.** *I don't feel like it.* 4; **Je n'ai rien oublié.** *I didn't forget anything.* 11; **Rien de spécial.** *Nothing special.* 6
rigoler *to laugh,* 10
le riz *rice,* 8
la robe *dress,* 10
le rocher *rock,* 11
rocheux (-euse) *rocky,* 12
le rock *rock (music),* 4
le rôle *role,* 7
le roller *skating;* **faire du roller en ligne** *to in-line skate,* 4
romain(e) *Roman* (adj.), 9
le roman *novel,* 3
roman(e) *Romanesque; of the style of architecture developed in Europe in the 11th and 12th centuries (characterized by heavy, massive walls and arches, etc.),* 12
rond(e) *round,* 12
le rond-point *traffic circle,* 12
ronronner *to purr,* 7
le rosbif *roast beef,* 5

rose *pink,* 3
la rose *rose,* 0
le rôti *roast,* 5
rouge *red,* 3
le rouleau *roll,* 3; un rouleau protège-livres *a roll of plastic material to protect books,* 3
rouspètent (rouspéter) *to complain,* 9
la routine quotidienne *daily routine,* 11
roux (rousse) *redheaded,* 7
le ruban *ribbon, tape;* ruban adhésif transparent *transparent adhesive tape,* 3
la rue *street,* 12
la ruine *ruin,* 9
le rythme *rhythm,* 4

s'il te plaît *(informal) please,* 3; **Oui, s'il te plaît.** *Yes, please. (informal),* 8
s'il vous plaît *please,* 3 *(formal);* **Oui, s'il vous plaît.** *Yes, please. (formal),* 8
sa *his, her,* 7
le sac *bag;* **le sac à dos** *backpack,* 3
le sachet *bag, packet,* 3
sage *wise,* 12
sais : Je n'en sais rien. *I have no idea.* 11; **Je ne sais pas.** *I don't know.* 10; **Que sais-je?** *self-check (What do I know?),* 1
la saison *season,* 4; la basse saison *off season,* 12; la haute saison *tourist season,* 12
la salade *salad,* 8
les salades (f.) *heads of lettuce,* 8
salé(e) *salty, salted,* 5
saler *to salt,* 8
la salle *room,* 2; la salle de classe *classroom,* 2
Salut *Hi! or Goodbye!* 1
samedi *Saturday,* 2; **le samedi** *on Saturdays,* 2
les sandales (f.) *sandals,* 10
le sandwich *sandwich,* 5; **un sandwich au fromage** *cheese sandwich,* 5; **un sandwich au jambon** *ham sandwich,* 5; **un sandwich au saucisson** *salami sandwich,* 5
sans *without,* 3; sans doute *probably,* 10
la sauce *sauce,* 5
la sauce arachide *sauce made of peanut butter with beef, chicken, or fish, hot peppers, peanut oil, garlic, onions, tomato paste, tomatoes, and other vegetables,* 8

la sauce pimentée *spicy sauce,* 8
le saucisson *salami,* 5
le saumon *salmon,* 5
sauvage (adj.) *savage,* 9
savais : Savais-tu que... ? *Did you know . . . ?,* 2
savoir *to know,* 1
scellé(e) (pp. of sceller) *sealed,* 9
la science-fiction *science fiction,* 1
les sciences naturelles (f. pl.) *natural science,* 2
scolaire *having to do with school,* 2; la vie scolaire *school life,* 2
la séance *showing (at the movies),* 6
la seconde *second,* 9; **Une seconde, s'il vous plaît.** *One second, please.* 9
le secours *aid, help;* le poste de secours *first-aid station,* 6
secret (secrète) *secret,* 8
le séjour *stay, residence,* 7
le sel *salt,* 8
selon *according to,* 8
la semaine *week,* 4; **une fois par semaine** *once a week,* 4
semblable *similar, the same,* 7
le semestre *semester,* 12
le Sénégal *Senegal,* 0
le sens *sense,* 8; le sens de l'orientation *sense of direction,* 12
sensass (sensationnel) *fantastic,* 10
sept *seven,* 0
septembre *September,* 4; **en septembre** *in September,* 4
sera : ce sera *it will be,* 6
le serpent *snake,* 0
serré(e) *tight,* 10
le serveur (la serveuse) *waiter/waitress,* 5
le service *service,* 3; rendre un service *to do (someone) a favor,* 12; **A votre service.** *At your service; You're welcome,* 3
service compris *tip included,* 5
ses *his, her,* 7
le sésame *sesame,* 8
sévère *severe, harsh,* 0
le short *(pair of) shorts,* 3
si *yes (to contradict a negative question),* 2; **Moi, si.** *I do.* 2; **Oui, si tu veux.** *Yes, if you want to.* 7
sicilien(ne) (adj.) *Sicilian,* 5
le siècle *century,* 6
le signe *sign,* 12
la similarité *similarity,* 2
simple *simple,* 10
simplement *simply,* 6
sinon *otherwise; other than that,* 9
le sirop de fraise (à l'eau) *water with strawberry syrup,* 5
la situation *situation,* 7
situé(e) *situated, located,* 8

le ski *skiing*, 1; **faire du ski** *to ski*, 4; **faire du ski nautique** *to water-ski*, 4

la sœur *sister*, 7

la soie *silk*, 10

la soif *thirst*; **avoir soif** *to be thirsty*, 5

soigné(e) *with attention to detail*, 10

soigneusement *carefully*, 11

le soir *evening; in the evening*, 4; **Pas ce soir.** *Not tonight.* 7

sois (command form of être) : Ne sois pas découragée! *Don't be discouraged!* 9

soit *either;* soit chez moi, ou bien chez eux *whether at my house or at theirs*, 5

les **soldes** (m.) *sales*, 6

le **soleil** *sun, sunshine*, 4

le **solfège** *music theory*, 4

la **solution** *solution*, 9

le **sommet** *top, summit*, 6

le **son** *sound*, 8

son *his, her*, 7

le **sondage** *poll*, 1

la **sonnerie** *ringing (of the telephone)*, 9

sont : Ce sont... *These/Those are ...*, 7; **Ils/Elles sont...** *They are ...*, 7; **Ils/Elles sont comment?** *What are they like?* 7

la **sorte** *kind;* toutes sortes de *all kinds of*, 8

sorti(e) (pp. of sortir) *went out*, 9; **Après, je suis sorti(e).** *Afterwards, I went out.* 9

la **sortie** *dismissal (when school gets out)*, 2

sortir *to go out*, 1; *to take out*, 7; **sortir avec les copains** *to go out with friends*, 1; **sortir la poubelle** *to take out the trash*, 7

souterrain(e) *underground*, 11

le **souvenir** *souvenir*, 11

souvent *often*, 4

spécial(e) *special*, 6; **Rien de spécial.** *Nothing special.* 6

la **spécialité** *specialty dish*, 4

le **spectacle** *show*, 11

le **spectateur** *spectator, audience member*, 9

le **sport** *gym*, 2; *sports*, 1; **faire du sport** *to play sports*, 1; **Qu'est-ce que tu fais comme sport?** *What sports do you play?* 4

le **sportif** (la **sportive**) *sportsman (sportswoman)*, 4

le **stade** *stadium*, 6

la **stalactite** *stalactite*, 11

la **station-service** *service station, gas station*, 11

la **statue** *statue*, 12

le **steak-frites** *steak and French fries*, 5

la **stratégie** *strategy*, 1

le **style** *style;* **C'est tout à fait ton style.** *It looks great on you!* 10

le **stylo** *pen*, 0; un stylo plume *fountain pen*, 3

la **subvention** *subsidy*, 7

le **sucre** *sugar*, 8

sucré(e) *sweet*, 8

le **sud** *South*, 9

suggérer *to suggest*, 11

suis : Qui suis-je? *Who am I?* 0; **Désolé(e), je suis occupé(e).** *Sorry, I'm busy.* 6; **Je suis bien chez...?** *Is this .... 's house?* 9

suisse *Swiss* (adj.), 1; la Suisse *Switzerland*, 0

suivant(e) *following*, 2

suivre *to follow*, 9

le **sujet** *subject*, 10

super *super*, 2; **Super!** *Great!* 1; **pas super** *not so hot*, 2

le **supermarché** *supermarket*, 8

supplémentaire *supplementary, additional*, 1

supportez (supporter) *to put up with*, 2

sur *on;* sur place *on-site*, 4; sur un total de *out of a total of*, 4

le **surligneur** *highlighting marker*, 3

surtout *especially*, 1

le **sweat-shirt** *sweatshirt*, 3

sympa (abbrev. of **sympathique**) *nice*, 7

ta *your*, 7

la **table** *table*, 7; la table de comparaison de tailles *size conversion chart*, 10

le **tableau** *blackboard*, 0; *painting*, 8

la **tache** *spot*, 7

la **tâche domestique** *household chore*, 9

la **taille** *size*, 10; taille unique *one size fits all*, 10; **en taille...** *in size...*, 10

la **taille élastiquée** *elastic waist*, 10

le **taille-crayon** *pencil sharpener*, 3

tant : tant privée que professionelle *private as well as professional*, 9

la **tante** *aunt*, 7

tard *late;* plus tard *later*, 8

le **tarif** : tarif réduit *reduced fee*, 6

la **tarte** *pie*, 8

le **tas** *pile, heap;* **J'ai des tas de choses à faire.** *I have lots of things to do.* 5

le **taux de réussite** *rate of success*, 2

le **taxi** *taxi*, 12; **en taxi** *by taxi*, 12

le **Tchad** *Chad*, 0

Tchao! *Bye!* 1

la **techno** *techno music*, 1; La techno me fait délirer. *I'm wild about techno (music)*, 1

le **tee-shirt** *T-shirt*, 3

la **télécarte** *phone card*, 9

le **télécopieur** *fax machine*, 9

le **téléphone** *telephone*, 0; **parler au téléphone** *to talk on the phone*, 1; le téléphone à pièces *coin-operated telephone*, 9; le téléphone sans fil *cordless telephone*, 9

téléphoné (pp. of téléphoner) *called, phoned*, 9; **Vous pouvez lui dire que j'ai téléphoné?** *Can you tell him/her that I called?* 9

téléphoner *to call, to phone*, 9; **Téléphone-lui/-leur!** *Call him/her/them!* 9

téléphonique : la cabine téléphonique *phone booth*, 9

la **télévision** *television*, 0; **regarder la télé(vision)** *to watch TV*, 1

tellement *so; so much;* **Pas tellement.** *Not too much.* 4

le **temps** *time*, 4; *weather*, 4; **de temps en temps** *from time to time*, 4; **Je regrette, mais je n'ai pas le temps.** *I'm sorry, but I don't have time.* 8; Quel temps est-ce qu'il fait à...? *How's the weather in...?* 4; **Quel temps fait-il?** *What's the weather like?* 4

Tenez. *Here you are. (formal, plural)*, 10

le **tennis** *tennis*, 4; **jouer au tennis** *to play tennis*, 4

la **tenue** *outfit;* une tenue de gymnastique *gym uniform*, 3

la **terminale** *final year of French high school, usually spent preparing for the* **bac**, 2

termine (terminer) *to finish*, 2

la **terrasse** *terrace*, 4

terrible *terrible, awful;* **Pas terrible.** *Not so great.* 1

le **territoire d'outre-mer** *overseas territory*, 12

tes *your*, 7

le **test** *test*, 10

le **théâtre** *theater*, 6; **faire du théâtre** *to do drama*, 4

théorique *theoretical*, 12

les **thermes** (m. pl.) *thermal baths*, 9

le **thon** *tuna*, 5

Tiens! *Hey!* 3

tient (tenir) *to hold*, 12

le **tiers** *one third;* un tiers de la population *one third of the population*, 12

le **tilleul** *lime green*, 10

le **timbre** *stamp*, 12

timide *shy*, 7

le **tissu** *cloth, fabric*, 10

toi *you*, 1; **Et toi?** *And you?* 1

le **tollé** *outcry*, 12

la **tomate** *tomato*, 8

tomber *to fall*, 10

ton *your*, 7

tondre *to mow*, 7; **tondre le gazon** *to mow the lawn*, 7

le top : le top des radios *the top radio stations*, 3
le total *total*, 10
toujours *still, always*, 9
la tour *tower*, 5
le tour *measurement*; tour de poitrine *chest size*, 10; le tour *turn*; à ton tour *Now it's your turn.* 7
tournez : Vous tournez... *You turn . . .*, 12
le tournoi *tournament*, 4
tous *all*, 2
tout(e) *all*, 2; **A tout à l'heure!** *See you later!* 1; **J'ai pensé à tout.** *I've thought of everything.* 11; pas du tout *not at all*, 2; **Il/Elle ne va pas du tout avec...** *It doesn't go at all with . . .*, 10; **C'est tout à fait ton style.** *It looks great on you!* 10; **tout de suite** *right away*, 6; **C'est tout de suite à...** *It's right there on the . . .*, 12; **J'y vais tout de suite.** *I'll go right away.* 8; **Vous allez tout droit jusqu'à...** *You go straight ahead until you get to . . .*, 12; **tout(e) seul(e)** *all alone*, 12
tout le monde (m.s.) *everyone*, 7
la tradition *tradition*, 8
traditionnel(le) *traditional*, 8
le train *train*, 12; **en train** *by train*, 12; **un billet de train** *train ticket*, 11
traité : être traité comme un gosse *to be treated like a kid*, 2
le trajet *route*, 12
la tranche *slice*, 8; **une tranche de** *a slice of*, 8
transparent(e) *transparent*, 3
le travail *work*, 3
le travail scolaire *school work*, 2
travailler *to work*, 9; travailler la pâte *to knead the dough*, 8
les travaux pratiques (m. pl.) *lab*, 2
traverser *to cross*, 12
très *very*, 1; **Très bien.** *Very well.* 1; **Très heureux (heureuse).** *Pleased to meet you.* 7
le trésor *treasure*, 3; chasse au trésor *treasure hunt*, 3
trois *three*, 0
troisième *third*, 9; la troisième étape *third step*, 1
la trompette *trumpet*, 0
trop *too (much)*, 10; **Il/Elle est trop cher/chère.** *It's too expensive.* 10; **Non, pas trop.** *No, not too much.* 2
tropical(e) *tropical*, 8
la trousse *pencil case*, 3
trouver *to find*, 9; **Comment tu trouves ça?** *What do you think of that/it?* 2; **Comment tu trouves...?** *What do you think of . . .?* 2; **Je le/la/les trouve...** *I think it's/they're . . .*, 10; **Tu trouves?** *Do you think so?* 10

le truc *thing*, 5; **J'ai des trucs à faire.** *I have some things to do.* 5
tu *you*, 0; **Tu te rappelles?** *Do you remember?*, 7
la Tunisie *Tunisia*, 0
typique *typical, characteristic*, 8
typiquement *typically, characteristically*, 8

un (m.) *a, an*, 3
une (f.) *a, an*, 3
l' **uniforme** (m.) *uniform*, 0
universel(le) *universal*, 12
utiliser *to use*, 10

va : Ça va. *Fine.* 1; (Comment) ça va? *How's it going?* 1; **Comment est-ce qu'on y va?** *How can we get there?* 12; **Il/Elle me va?** *Does it suit me?* 10; **Il/Elle ne te/vous va pas du tout.** *It doesn't look good on you at all.* 10; **Il/Elle ne va pas du tout avec...** *It doesn't go at all with . . .*, 10
les vacances (f. pl.) *vacation*, 1; **Bonnes vacances!** *Have a good vacation!* 11; **en colonie de vacances** *to/at a summer camp*, 11; **en vacances** *on vacation*, 4
vais : Je vais... *I'm going . . .*, 6; *I'm going (to) . . .*, 11; **J'y vais tout de suite.** *I'll go right away.* 8
la vaisselle *dishes*, 7; **faire la vaisselle** *to do the dishes*, 7
valable *valid*, 6
la valise *suitcase*, 11
la vanille *vanilla*, 8
vas : Qu'est-ce que tu vas faire? *What are you going to do?* 6
la vedette *celebrity*, 1
végétarien(ne) *vegetarian*, 5
le vélo *biking*, 1; **à vélo** *by bike*, 12; **faire du vélo** *to bike*, 4
le vendeur *salesperson*, 3
la vendeuse *salesperson*, 3
vendre *to sell*, 9
vendredi *Friday*, 2; **le vendredi** *on Fridays*, 2
la vente *sales*, 6
le verbe *verb*, 7
la verdure *vegetation*, 11
véritable *real*, 11; **C'était un véritable cauchemar!** *It was a real nightmare!* 11

le verre *glass*, 6
vers *about*, 6
vert(e) *green*, 3
la veste *suit jacket, blazer*, 10
le vêtement *clothing item*, 10
veux : Je veux bien. *I'd really like to.* 6; **Tu veux... avec moi?** *Do you want to . . . with me?* 6
la viande *meat*, 8
vide *empty*, 12
la vidéo *video*, 4; **faire de la vidéo** *to make videos*, 4; **des jeux vidéo** *video games*, 4
la vidéocassette *videotape*, 3
la vie scolaire *school life*, 2
viennois(e) *Viennese (adj.)*, 5
viens : Tu viens? *Will you come?* 6
vietnamien(ne) *Vietnamese (adj.)*, 1
vieux (vieille) *old*, 4
le village *town*, 4
la ville *city*, 12
le vinaigre *vinegar*, 8
la violence *violence*, 1
violet(te) *purple*, 3
la virgule *comma*, 3
la visite *visit, tour*, 12
visiter *to visit (a place)*, 9
le visiteur *visitor*, 9
vite *fast, quickly*, 2
la vitrine *window (of a shop)*; **faire les vitrines** *to window-shop*, 6
vivant(e) *lively, living*, 7
Vive...! *Hurray for . . .!* 3
vivre *to live*, 2; l'art de vivre *the art of living*, 12
le vocabulaire *vocabulary*, 1
Voici... *Here's . . .*, 7
Voilà. *Here.* 3; Voilà... *There's . . .*, 7
la voile *sailing*, 11; **faire de la planche à voile** *to go windsurfing*, 11; **faire de la voile** *to go sailing*, 11
voir *to see*, 6; **voir un film** *to see a movie*, 6; **aller voir un match** *to go see a game*, 6; **voir une pièce** *to see a play*, 6
le voisin (la voisine) *neighbor*, 1
la voiture *car*, 7; **en voiture** *by car*, 12; **laver la voiture** *to wash the car*, 7
la voix *voice*, 3
le volley(-ball) *volleyball*, 4; **jouer au volley(-ball)** *to play volleyball*, 4
volontiers *with pleasure, gladly*, 8
vos *your*, 7
votre *your*, 7
voudrais : Je voudrais... *I'd like . . .* 3
vouloir *to want*, 6; **Je n'en veux plus.** *I don't want anymore.* 8; **Je veux bien.** *I'd really like to.* 6; *Gladly.* 8; **Oui, j'en veux bien.** *Yes, I'd like some.* 8; **Oui, si tu veux.** *Yes, if you want to.* 7; **Tu veux...?** *Do you want . . .?*

6; **voulez : Vous voulez...?** *Do you want ...? 8*
vous *you*, 1
le voyage *voyage, trip*, 0
voyager *to travel*, 1; **Bon voyage!** *Have a good trip!* 11
vrai(e) *true*, 2
vraiment *really*, 11; **Non, pas vraiment.** *No, not really.* 11
vu (pp. of voir) *seen, saw*, 9
la vue *view*, 6

le **week-end** *on weekends*, 4; *weekend*, 6
le western *western (movie)*, 0

le xylophone *xylophone*, 0

y *there*, 12; **Allons-y!** *Let's go!* 4; **Comment est-ce qu'on y va?** *How can we get there?* 12; **J'y vais tout de suite.** *I'll go right away.* 8; **On peut y aller...** *We can go there ...* , 12

les yaourts (m.) *yogurt*, 8
les yeux (m. pl.) *eyes*, 8
la yole *skiff (a type of boat)*, 12
le yo-yo *yo-yo*, 0

le zèbre *zebra*, 0
zéro *a waste of time*, 2; *zero*, 0
le zoo *zoo*, 6
zoologique *zoological, having to do with animals*, 6
le zouk *zouk (style of music and dance)*, 12
Zut! *Darn!* 3

In this vocabulary, the English definitions of all active French words in the book have been listed, followed by their French equivalent. The number after each entry refers to the chapter in which the entry is introduced. It is important to use a French word in its correct context. The use of a word can be checked easily by referring to the chapter where it appears. French words and phrases are presented in the same way as in the French-English vocabulary.

a *un, une*, 3
able: to be able to *pouvoir*, 8
about *vers*, 6
across from *en face de*, 12
adore *adorer*, 1; **I adore...** *J'adore...*, 1
advise *conseiller*; **What do you advise me to do?** *Qu'est-ce que tu me conseilles?* 9
aerobics *l'aérobic* (f.), 4; **to do aerobics** *faire de l'aérobic*, 4
after *après*, 9; **And after that,...** *Et après ça...*, 9
afternoon *l'après-midi* (m.), 2; **afternoon off** *l'après-midi libre*, 2; **in the afternoon** *l'après-midi*, 2
afterwards *après*, 9; **Afterwards, I went out.** *Après, je suis sorti(e).* 9; **And afterwards?** *Et après?* 9
Agreed. *Entendu.* 6
algebra *l'algèbre* (f.), 2
all *tout(e):* **Not at all.** *Pas du tout.* 4
already *déjà*, 9
also *aussi*, 1
am: I am ... years old. *J'ai... ans.* 1
an *un, une*, 3
and *et*, 1
annoying *embêtant(e)*, 7; *pénible*, 7
answer *répondre*, 9; **There's no answer.** *Ça ne répond pas.* 9
any (of it) *en*, 8; **any more: I don't want any more.** *Je n'en veux plus.* 8
anything: I didn't forget anything. *Je n'ai rien oublié.* 11
apple *la pomme*, 8
apple juice *le jus de pomme*, 5
April *avril*, 4
are: These/those are ... *Ce sont...*, 7; **They're...** *Ils/Elles sont...*, 7
art class *les arts plastiques* (m. pl.), 2
at *à la, au, à l', aux*, 6; **at ... fifteen** *à... heure(s) quinze*, 2; **at ... forty-five** *à... heure(s) quarante-cinq*, 2; **at ... thirty** *à... heure(s) trente*, 2; **at ... ('s) house** *chez...*,

6; **at the record store** *chez le disquaire*, 12; **At what time?** *A quelle heure?* 6
August *août*, 4
autumn *l'automne* (m.), 4
aunt *la tante*, 7
avocado *l'avocat* (m.), 8

backpack *le sac à dos*, 3
bad *mauvais(e)*, 5; **Not bad.** *Pas mal.* 1; **Oh, pas mauvais.** *Oh, not bad.* 9; **Very bad.** *Très mauvais.* 9
bag *le sac*, 3
baggy *large*, 10
bakery *la boulangerie*, 12
banana *la banane*, 8
bank *la banque*, 12
baseball *le base-ball*, 4; **to play baseball** *jouer au base-ball*, 4
basketball *le basket(-ball)*, 4; **to play basketball** *jouer au basket (-ball)*, 4
bathing suit *le maillot de bain*, 10
be *être*, 7
be able to, can *pouvoir*, 8; **Can you ...?** *Tu peux... ?* 12
beach *la plage*, 1
beans *les haricots* (m.), 8; **green beans** *les haricots verts* (m.), 8
because *parce que*, 5
beef *le bœuf*, 8
begin *commencer*, 9
behind *derrière*, 12
belt *la ceinture*, 10
better *mieux*, 9; **It's going to get better!** *Ça va aller mieux!* 9
between *entre*, 12
big *grand(e)*, 10
bike *le vélo; faire du vélo*, 4; **by bike** *à vélo*, 12

biking *le vélo*, 1
binder: loose-leaf binder *le classeur*, 3
biology *la biologie*, 2
black *noir(e)*, 3
blackboard *le tableau*, 0; **Go to the blackboard!** *Allez au tableau!* 0
blazer *la veste*, 10
blond *blond(e)*, 7
blue *bleu(e)*, 3
boat *le bateau*, 11; **by boat** *en bateau*, 12; **to go boating** *faire du bateau*, 11
book *le livre*, 0
bookstore *la librairie*, 12
boots *les bottes* (f.), 10
boring *barbant(e)*, 2; **It was boring.** *C'était ennuyeux.* 11; *C'était barbant!* 11
borrow *emprunter*, 12
bottle *la bouteille*, 8; **a bottle of** *une bouteille de*, 8
box *le paquet*, 8; **a package/box of** *un paquet de*, 8
boy *le garçon*, 8
bracelet *le bracelet*, 3
bread *le pain*, 8; **long, thin loaf of bread** *la baguette*, 12
break *la récréation*, 2
breakfast *le petit déjeuner*, 8
bring *apporter*, 9; **Bring me back ...** *Rapporte-moi...*, 8; **Please bring me ...** *Apportez-moi...*, *s'il vous plaît.* 5; **Will you bring me ...?** *Tu me rapportes... ?* 8
brother *le frère*, 7
brown *marron* (inv.), 3
brunette *brun(e)*, 7
bus *le bus*, 12; **by bus** *en bus*, 12; **to miss the bus** *rater le bus*, 9
busy *occupé(e)*, 6; **It's busy.** *C'est occupé.* 9; **Sorry, I'm busy.** *Désolé(e), je suis occupé(e).* 6
but *mais*, 1
butter *le beurre*, 8
buy *acheter*, 9; **Buy (me) ...** *Achète(-moi)...*, 8
Bye! *Tchao!* 1

C

cafeteria *la cantine*, 9; **at the school cafeteria** *à la cantine*, 9

cake *le gâteau*, 8

calculator *la calculatrice*, 3

call *téléphoner*, 9; **Call him/her/them!** *Téléphone-lui/-leur!* 9; **Can you call back later?** *Vous pouvez rappeler plus tard?* 9; **Who's calling?** *Qui est à l'appareil?* 9

camera *l'appareil-photo* (m.), 11

camp *la colonie de vacances*, 11; **to/at a summer camp** *en colonie de vacances*, 11

camping *le camping*, 11; **to go camping** *faire du camping*, 11

can: to be able to, can *pouvoir*, 8; **Can I talk to you?** *Je peux te parler?* 9; **Can you...?** *Est-ce que tu peux...?* 12; **Can you...?** *Tu peux...?* 8; **Can I try on...?** *Je peux essayer...?* 10; **We can...** *On peut...*, 6; **What can I do?** *Qu'est-ce que je peux faire?* 9

can *la boîte*, 8; **a can of** *une boîte de*, 8

can't: I can't right now. *Je ne peux pas maintenant.* 8; **No, I can't.** *Non, je ne peux pas.* 12

canary *le canari*, 7

cap *la casquette*, 10

car *la voiture*, 7; **by car** *en voiture*, 12; **to wash the car** *laver la voiture*, 7

cards *les cartes* (f.), 4; **to play cards** *jouer aux cartes*, 4

carrot *la carotte*, 8

cassette tape *la cassette*, 3

cat *le chat*, 7

CD/compact disc *le disque compact/le CD*, 3

Certainly. *Bien sûr.* 9

chair *la chaise*, 0

check *l'addition* (f.), 5; **The check, please.** *L'addition, s'il vous plaît.* 5

cheese *le fromage*, 5; **toasted ham and cheese sandwich** *le croque-monsieur*, 5

chemistry *la chimie*, 2

chic *chic* (inv.), 10

chicken (animal) *la poule*, 8; **chicken meat** *le poulet*, 8

child *l'enfant* (m./f.), 7; **children** *les enfants*, 7

chocolate *le chocolat*, 1; **hot chocolate** *un chocolat*, 5

choir *la chorale*, 2

choose *choisir*, 10; **Have you chosen?** *Vous avez choisi?* 5

class *le cours*, 2; **What classes do you have...?** *Tu as quels cours...?* 2

clean: to clean the house *faire le ménage*, 7

clear: to clear the table *débarrasser la table*, 7

close: Close the door! *Fermez la porte!* 0

close to *près de*, 12

clothing *les vêtements*, 10

coast *le bord*, 11; **to/on the coast** *au bord de la mer*, 11

coat *le manteau*, 10

coconut *la noix de coco*, 8

coffee *le café*, 5

cola *le coca*, 5

cold *froid(e)* 4; **It's cold.** *Il fait froid.* 4

color *la couleur*, 3; **What color is...?** *De quelle couleur est...?* 3

come: Will you come? *Tu viens?* 6

compact disc/CD *le disque compact/le CD*, 3

computer *l'ordinateur* (m.), 3

computer science *l'informatique* (f.), 2

concert *le concert*, 1

continue *continuer*, 12

cool *cool*, 2; **It's cool out.** *Il fait frais.* 4; **Very cool (great).** *Très chouette.* 9

corn *le maïs*, 8

corner *le coin*, 12; **on the corner of** *au coin de*, 12

cotton (adj.) *en coton*, 10

could: Could you do me a favor? *(Est-ce que) tu peux me rendre un petit service?* 12; **Could you go by...?** *Tu pourrais passer à...?* 12

countryside *la campagne*, 11; **to/in the countryside** *à la campagne*, 11

course *le cours*, 2

course: Of course. *Bien sûr.* 3

cousin *le cousin (la cousine)*, 7

cross *traverser*, 12

cute *mignon(ne)*, 7

D

dairy products *les produits* (m.) *laitiers*, 8

dance *danser*, 1

dance *la danse*, 2

Darn! *Zut!* 3

daughter *la fille*, 7

day *le jour*, 2

December *décembre*, 4; **in December** *en décembre*, 4

decided: Have you decided? *Vous avez choisi?* 5; **Have you decided to take...?** *Vous avez décidé de prendre...?* 10

delicious *délicieux(-euse)*, 5

denim *le jean*, 10; **in denim** *en jean*, 10

deposit *déposer*, 12; **to deposit money** *déposer de l'argent*, 12

dictionary *le dictionnaire*, 3

difficult *difficile*, 2

dinner *le dîner*, 8; **to have dinner** *dîner*, 9

dishes *la vaisselle*, 7; **to do the dishes** *faire la vaisselle*, 7

dismissal (when school gets out) *la sortie*, 2

do *faire*, 4; **Do you play/do...?** *Est-ce que tu fais...?* 4; **I do.** *Moi, si.* 2; **to do homework** *faire les devoirs*, 7; **to do the dishes** *faire la vaisselle*, 7; **I don't play/do...** *Je ne fais pas de...*, 4; **I have errands to do.** *J'ai des courses à faire.* 5; **I play/do...** *Je fais...*, 4; **In your opinion, what do I do?** *A ton avis, qu'est-ce que je fais?* 9; **Sorry. I have homework to do.** *Désolé(e). J'ai des devoirs à faire.* 5; **What are you going to do...?** *Qu'est-ce que tu vas faire...?* 6; *Tu vas faire quoi...?* 6; **What can I do?** *Qu'est-ce que je peux faire?* 9; **What did you do...?** *Qu'est-ce que tu as fait...?* 9; **What do you advise me to do?** *Qu'est-ce que tu me conseilles?* 9; **What do you do...?** *Qu'est-ce que tu fais...?* 4; **What do you do when...?** *Qu'est-ce que tu fais quand...?* 4

dog *le chien*, 7; **to walk the dog** *promener le chien*, 7

done, made *fait* (pp. of faire), 9

door *la porte*, 0

down: You go down this street to the next light. *Vous continuez jusqu'au prochain feu rouge.* 12

dozen *la douzaine*, 8; **a dozen** *une douzaine de*, 8

drama *le théâtre*, 4; **to do drama** *faire du théâtre*, 4

dress *la robe*, 10

drink *la boisson*, 5; **What do you have to drink?** *Qu'est-ce que vous avez comme boissons?* 5; **What is there to drink?** *Qu'est-ce qu'il y a à boire?* 5

drugstore *la pharmacie*, 12

E

earn *gagner*, 9

earrings *les boucles d'oreilles* (f.), 10

easy *facile*, 2

eat *manger*, 6

egg *l'œuf* (m.), 8

English (language) *l'anglais* (m.), 1

envelope *l'enveloppe* (f.), 12

eraser   *la gomme*, 3
errands   *les courses* (f.), 7; **I have errands to do.**   *J'ai des courses à faire.* 5
especially   *surtout*, 1
euro   (European Community monetary unit) *l'euro* (m.); *Ça fait... euros./ C'est... euros.*   **It's . . . euros.** 5
evening   *le soir*, 4; **in the evening**   *le soir*, 4
everything   *tout*, 11; **I've thought of everything.**   *J'ai pensé à tout.* 11
exam   *l'examen* (m.), 1
excellent   *excellent(e)*, 5; **Yes, excellent.**   *Oui, excellent.* 9
excuse: Excuse me.   *Excusez-moi.* 3; **Excuse me, . . . , please?**   *Pardon, ... , s'il vous plaît?* 12; **Excuse me. Where is . . . , please?**   *Pardon. Où est... , s'il vous plaît?* 12; **Excuse me. I'm looking for . . . , please.**   *Pardon. Je cherche... , s'il vous plaît.* 12
expensive   *cher (chère)*, 10; **It's too expensive.**   *C'est trop cher.* 10

fail   *rater*, 9; **to fail a test**   *rater un examen*, 9; **to fail a quiz**   *rater une interro*, 9
fall   *l'automne* (m.), 4; **in the fall**   *en automne*, 4
fantastic   *sensass (sensationnel)*, 10
far from   *loin de*, 12
fascinating   *passionnant(e)*, 2
fat   *gros (se)*, 7
father   *le père*, 7
February   *février*, 4; **in February**   *en février*, 4
feel: I feel like . . .   *J'ai envie de...* , 11; **I don't feel like it.**   *Ça ne me dit rien.* 6
finally   *enfin*, 9; *finalement*, 9
find   *trouver*, 9
Fine.   *Ça va.* 1; **Yes, it was fine.**   *Oui, ça a été.* 9
first   *d'abord*, 7; **OK, if you . . . first.**   *D'accord, si tu... d'abord.* 7
fish   *le poisson*, 7
flour   *la farine*, 8
foot   *le pied*, 12; **on foot**   *à pied*, 12
football   *le football américain*, 4; **to play football**   *jouer au football américain*, 4
for   *pour*, 3; **What do you need for . . . ?** (informal)   *Qu'est qu'il te faut pour... ?* 3
forest   *la forêt*, 11; **to/in the forest**   *en forêt*, 11
forget   *oublier*, 9; **Don't forget . . .**   *N'oublie pas de...* , 8; **Forget him/**

her/them!   *Oublie-le/-la/-les!* 9; **I didn't forget anything.**   *Je n'ai rien oublié.* 11; **You didn't forget . . . ?**   *Tu n'as pas oublié... ?* 11
franc   (former monetary unit of France) *le franc*, 3
French   (language) *le français*, 1; **French fries**   *les frites* (f.), 1
Friday   *vendredi*, 2; **on Fridays**   *le vendredi*, 2
friend   *l'ami(e)* (m./f.), 1; **to go out with friends**   *sortir avec les copains*, 1
from   *de*, 0
front: in front of   *devant*, 6
fruit   *le fruit*, 8
fun: Did you have fun?   *Tu t'es bien amusé(e)?* 11; **Have fun!**   *Amuse-toi bien!* 11; **What do you do to have fun?**   *Qu'est-ce que tu fais pour t'amuser?* 4
funny   *amusant(e)*, 7

gain: to gain weight   *grossir*, 10
game   *le match*, 6; *to play video games*   *jouer à des jeux vidéo*, 4; **to watch a game (on TV)**   *regarder un match*, 6; **to go see a game**   *aller voir un match*, 6
geography   *la géographie*, 2
geometry   *la géométrie*, 2
German   (language) *l'allemand* (m.), 2
get: Get . . .   *Prends...* , 8; **How can we get there?**   *Comment est-ce qu'on y va?* 12
gift   *le cadeau*, 11
girl   *la fille*, 0
give   *donner*, 5; **Please give me . . .**   *Donnez-moi...* , *s'il vous plaît.* 5
Gladly.   *Je veux bien.* 8
go   *aller*, 6; **Go to the blackboard!**   *Allez au tableau!* 0; **I'm going . . .**   *Je vais...* , 6; **What are you going to do . . . ?**   *Tu vas faire quoi... ?* 6; **It doesn't go at all with . . .**   *Il/Elle ne va pas du tout avec...* , 10; **It goes very well with . . .**   *Il/Elle va très bien avec...* , 10; **to go out with friends**   *sortir avec les copains*, 1; **I'd like . . . to go with . . .**   *J'aimerais... pour aller avec...* , 10; **Afterwards, I went out.**   *Après, je suis sorti(e).* 9; **Could you go by . . . ?**   *Tu pourrais passer à... ?* 12; **Did it go well?**   *Ça s'est bien passé?* 11; **I'm going to have . . . , please.**   *Je vais prendre... , s'il vous plaît.* 5; **What are you going to do . . . ?**   *Qu'est-ce que tu vas faire... ?* 6; **I went . . .**   *Je suis*

allé(e)... , 9; **I'm going to . . .**   *Je vais...* , 11; **Let's go . . .**   *Allons...* , 6; **to go for a walk**   *faire une promenade*, 6; **We can go there . . .**   *On peut y aller...* , 12; **Where are you going to go . . . ?**   *Où est-ce que tu vas aller... ?* 11; **Where did you go?**   *Tu es allé(e) où?* 9; **You keep going until the next light.**   *Vous continuez jusqu'au prochain feu rouge.* 12; **How's it going?**   *(Comment) ça va?* 1
golf   *le golf*, 4; **to play golf**   *jouer au golf*, 4
good   *bon(ne)*, 5; **Have a good trip!**   *Bon voyage!* 11; **Did you have a good . . . ?**   *Tu as passé un bon... ?* 11; **It doesn't look good on you at all.**   *Il/Elle ne te/vous va pas du tout.* 10; **It's pretty good!**   *C'est pas mauvais!* 5; **not good**   *pas bon*, 5; **Yes, very good.**   *Oui, très bon.* 9
Goodbye!   *Au revoir!* 1; *Salut!* 1
got: No, you've got to . . .   *Non, tu dois...* , 7
grammar   *la grammaire*, 1
grandfather   *le grand-père*, 7
grandmother   *la grand-mère*, 7
grapes   *le raisin*, 8
great   *génial(e)*, 2; **Great!**   *Super!* 1; **It looks great on you!**   *C'est tout à fait ton style!* 10; **It was great!**   *C'était formidable!* 11; **Not so great.**   *Pas terrible*, 1
green   *vert(e)*, 3
green beans   *les *haricots verts* (m.), 8
grey   *gris(e)*, 3
grocery store (small)   *l'épicerie* (f.), 12
gross   *dégoûtant(e)*, 5
grow   *grandir*, 10
guava   *la goyave*, 8
gym   *le sport*, 2

half   *demi(e)*, 6; **half past**   *et demie*, 6; **half past** (after *midi* and *minuit*)   *et demi*, 6
ham   *le jambon*, 5; **toasted ham and cheese sandwich**   *le croque-monsieur*, 5
hamburger   *le hamburger*, 1
hand   *la main*, 0
happened: What happened?   *Qu'est-ce qui s'est passé?* 9
happy   *content(e)*, 7
hard   *difficile*, 2
hat   *le chapeau*, 10
have   *avoir*, 2; **At what time do you have . . . ?**   *Tu as... à quelle heure?* 2; **Did you have a good**

weekend? *Tu as passé un bon week-end?* 9; **Do you have ...?** *Vous avez... ?* 2; *Tu as... ?* 3; **Do you have that in ...?** (size, fabric, color) *Vous avez ça en... ?* 10; **Have ...** *Prends/Prenez... ,* 5; **What are you having?** *Vous prenez?* 5; **I don't have ...** *Je n'ai pas de... ,* 3; **I have some things to do.** *J'ai des trucs à faire.* 5; **I have ...** *J'ai... ,* 2; **I'll have ... , please.** *Je vais prendre... , s'il vous plaît.* 5; **to take or to have** (food or drink) *prendre,* 5; **We have ...** *Nous avons... ,* 2; **What classes do you have ...?** *Tu as quels cours... ?* 2; **What do you have ...?** *Tu as quoi... ?* 2; **What kind of ... do you have?** *Qu'est-ce que vous avez comme... ?* 5; **Will you have ...?** *Tu prends/Vous prenez... ?* 8

health *le cours de développement personnel et social (DPS),* 2

Hello. *Bonjour.* 1; **Hello?** (on the phone) *Allô?* 9

help: **May I help you?** *(Est-ce que) je peux vous aider?* 10

her *la,* 9; *son/sa/ses,* 7; **to her** *lui,* 9

Here. *Voilà.* 3; **Here's ...** *Voici... ,* 7

Hi! *Salut!* 1

hiking *la randonnée,* 11; **to go hiking** *faire de la randonnée,* 11

him *le,* 9; **to him** *lui,* 9

his *son/sa/ses,* 7

history *l'histoire* (f.), 2

hockey *le *hockey,* 4; **to play hockey** *jouer au hockey,* 4

Hold on. *Ne quittez pas.* 9

homework *les devoirs* (m.), 2; **I've got homework to do.** *J'ai des devoirs à faire.* 5; **to do homework** *faire les devoirs,* 7

horrible *épouvantable,* 9; **It was horrible.** *C'était épouvantable.* 9

horseback riding *l'équitation* (f.), 1; **to go horseback riding** *faire de l'équitation,* 1

hose (clothing) *le collant,* 10

hot *chaud,* 4; **It's hot.** *Il fait chaud.* 4; **not so hot** *pas super,* 2

hot chocolate *le chocolat,* 5

hot dog *le *hot-dog,* 5

house: **at my house** *chez moi,* 6; **Is this ...'s house?** *Je suis bien chez ?* 9; **to/at ...'s house** *chez... ,* 6

housework *le ménage,* 1; **to do housework** *faire le ménage,* 1

how: **How old are you?** *Tu as quel âge?* 1; **How about ...?** *On... ?* 4; **How do you like it?** *Comment tu trouves ça?* 5; **How much is ...?** *C'est combien... ?*

5; **How much is it?** *C'est combien?* 3; **How much is it, please?** (total) *Ça fait combien, s'il vous plaît?* 5; **How's it going?** *(Comment) ça va?* 1

how much *combien,* 3; **How much is ...?** *C'est combien,... ?* 3; **How much is it?** (total) *Ça fait combien, s'il vous plaît?* 5

hundred *cent,* 3; **two hundred** *deux cents,* 3

hungry: **to be hungry** *avoir faim,* 5; **No thanks. I'm not hungry anymore.** *Non, merci. Je n'ai plus faim.* 8

husband *le mari,* 7

I *je,* 1; **I do.** *Moi, si.* 2; **I don't.** *Moi, non.* 2

ice cream *la glace,* 1

ice-skate *faire du patin à glace,* 4

idea *l'idée* (f.), 4; **Good idea.** *Bonne idée.* 4; **I have no idea.** *Je n'en sais rien.* 11

if *si,* 7; **OK, if you ... first.** *D'accord, si tu... d'abord.* 7

impossible *impossible,* 7; **No, that's impossible.** *Non, c'est impossible.* 7

in *dans,* 6; **in** (a city or place) *à,* 11; **in** (before a feminine country) *en,* 11; **in** (before a masculine noun) *au,* 11; **in** (before a plural country) *aux,* 11; **in front of** *devant,* 6; **in the afternoon** *l'après-midi,* 2; **in the evening** *le soir,* 4; **in the morning** *le matin,* 2

in-line skate *le roller en ligne,* 4; **to in-line skate** *faire du roller en ligne,* 4

indifference: (expression of indifference) *Bof!* 1

intend: **I intend to ...** *J'ai l'intention de... ,* 11

interest: **That doesn't interest me.** *Ça ne me dit rien.* 4

interesting *intéressant(e),* 2

is: **He is ...** *Il est... ,* 7; **It's ...** *C'est... ,* 2; **She is ...** *Elle est... ,* 7; **There's ...** *Voilà... ,* 7; **This is ...** *C'est... ; Voici... ,* 7

it *le, la,* 9

It's ... *C'est... ,* 2; **It's ...** *Il est...* (time), 6; **It's ... euros.** *C'est... euros.* 5; *Ça fait... euros.* 5; **No, it's ...** *Non, c'est... ,* 4; **Yes, it's ...** *Oui, c'est... ,* 4

jacket *le blouson,* 10; **suit jacket** *la veste,* 10

jam *la confiture,* 8

January *janvier,* 4; **in January** *en janvier,* 4

jeans *le jean,* 3

jog *faire du jogging,* 4

jogging *le jogging,* 4

juice *le jus,* 5; **orange juice** *le jus d'orange,* 5; **apple juice** *le jus de pomme,* 5

July *juillet,* 4; **in July** *en juillet,* 4

June *juin,* 4; **in june** *en juin,* 4

kilogram *le kilo(kilogramme),* 8; **a kilogram of** *un kilo de,* 8

kind: **What kind of ... do you have?** *Qu'est-ce que vous avez comme... ?* 5

know: **I don't know.** *Je ne sais pas.* 10

lab *les travaux pratiques* (m. pl.), 2

later: **Can you call back later?** *Vous pouvez rappeler plus tard?* 9; **See you later!** *A tout à l'heure!* 1

Latin (language) *le latin,* 2

lawn *le gazon,* 7; **to mow the lawn** *tondre le gazon,* 7

learn *apprendre,* 0

leather *le cuir,* 10; **in leather** *en cuir,* 10

leave *partir,* 11; **Can I leave a message?** *Je peux laisser un message?* 9; **You can't leave without ...** *Tu ne peux pas partir sans... ,* 11

left *la gauche,* 12; **to the left** *à gauche (de),* 12

lemon *le citron,* 8

lemon soda *la limonade,* 5

lemonade *le citron pressé,* 5

let's: **Let's go ...** *Allons... ,* 6; **Let's go!** *Allons-y!* 4

letter *la lettre,* 12; **to send letters** *envoyer des lettres,* 12

lettuce *la salade* (f.), 8

library *la bibliothèque,* 6

like *aimer,* 1; **I'd really like ...** *Je voudrais bien... ,* 11; **Do you**

like...? *Tu aimes... ?* 1; **Do you like it?** *Il/Elle te (vous) plaît?* 10; **How do you like...?** *Comment tu trouves... ?* 10; **How do you like it?** *Comment tu trouves ça?* 5; **I (really) like...** *Moi, j'aime (bien)...,* 1; **I don't like...** *Je n'aime pas...,* 1; **I like it, but it's expensive.** *Il/Elle me plaît, mais il/elle est cher (chère).* 10; **I'd like...** *Je voudrais...,* 3; **I'd like...to go with...** *J'aimerais... pour aller avec...,* 10; **I'd really like to.** *Je veux bien.* 6; **I'd like to buy...** *Je voudrais acheter...,* 3; **What would you like?** *Vous désirez?* 10

like: What are they like? *Ils/Elles sont comment?* 7; **What is he like?** *Il est comment?* 7; **What is she like?** *Elle est comment?* 7

listen *écouter,* 1; **Listen!** *Ecoutez!* 0; **I'm listening.** *Je t'écoute.* 9; **to listen to music** *écouter de la musique,* 1

liter *le litre,* 8; **a liter of** *un litre de,* 8

long *long (ue),* 10

look: Look at the map! *Regardez la carte!* 0; **It doesn't look good on you at all.** *Il/Elle ne te/vous va pas du tout.* 10; **I'm looking for something for...** *Je cherche quelque chose pour...,* 10; **It looks great on you!** *C'est tout à fait ton style!* 10; **Look, here's/there's/ it's...** *Regarde, voilà...,* 12; **No, thanks, I'm just looking.** *Non, merci, je regarde.* 10; **to look for** *chercher,* 9

look after: to look after... *garder...,* 7

looks: It looks great on you! *C'est tout à fait ton style!* 10

loose-leaf binder *le classeur,* 3

lose *perdre,* 9; **to lose weight** *maigrir,* 10

lot: A lot. *Beaucoup.* 4

lots: I have lots of things to do. *J'ai des tas de choses à faire.* 5

lower (number) *moins,* 0

luck *la chance,* 11; **Good luck!** *Bon courage!* 2; **Bonne chance!** 11

lunch *le déjeuner,* 2; **to have lunch** *déjeuner,* 9

ma'am *madame (Mme),* 1

made *fait (pp of faire),* 9

magazine *le magazine,* 3

make *faire,* 4

mall *le centre commercial,* 6

mango *la mangue,* 8

map *la carte,* 0

March *mars,* 4; **in March** *en mars,* 4

market *le marché,* 8

math *les maths (f. pl.), les mathématiques,* 1

May *mai,* 4; **in May** *en mai,* 4

may: May I...? *(Est-ce que) je peux...?* 7; **May I help you?** *(Est-ce que) je peux vous aider?* 10

me *moi,* 2; **Me, too.** *Moi aussi.* 2; **Not me.** *Pas moi.* 2

mean *méchant(e),* 7

meat *la viande,* 8

medicine *les médicaments (m.),* 12

meet *retrouver,* 6; *rencontrer,* 9; **I'd like you to meet...** *Je te (vous) présente...,* 7; **Pleased to meet you.** *Très heureux (heureuse).* 7; **O.K., we'll meet...** *Bon, on se retrouve...,* 6; **We'll meet...** *Rendez-vous...,* 6

menu *la carte,* 5; **The menu, please.** *La carte, s'il vous plaît.* 5

message *le message,* 9; **Can I leave a message?** *Je peux laisser un message?* 9

metro *le métro,* 12; **at the...metro stop** *au métro...,* 6

midnight *minuit,* 6; **It's midnight.** *Il est minuit.* 6; **It's half past midnight.** *Il est minuit et demi.* 6

milk *le lait,* 8

mineral water *l'eau minérale (f.),* 5

minute *la minute,* 9; **Do you have a minute?** *Tu as une minute?* 9

miss, Miss *mademoiselle (Mlle),* 1

miss *rater,* 9; **to miss the bus** *rater le bus,* 9

moment *le moment,* 5; **One moment, please.** *Un moment, s'il vous plaît.* 5

Monday *lundi,* 2; **on Mondays** *le lundi,* 2

money *l'argent (m.),* 11

More...? *Encore de...?* 8; **I don't want any more.** *Je n'en veux plus.* 8

morning *le matin,* 2; **in the morning** *le matin,* 2

mother *la mère,* 7

mountain *la montagne,* 11; **to/in the mountains** *à la montagne,* 11

movie *le film,* 6; **to see a movie** *voir un film,* 6

movie theater *le cinéma,* 6; **the movies** *le cinéma,* 1

mow: to mow the lawn *tondre le gazon,* 7

Mr. *monsieur (M.),* 1

Mrs. *madame (Mme),* 1

much: How much is...? *C'est combien,...?* 5; **How much is it, please?** *Ça fait combien, s'il vous plaît?* 5; **How much is it?** *C'est combien?* 3; **No, not too much.** *Non, pas trop.* 2; **Not much.** *Pas*

grand-chose. 6; **Not too much.** *Pas tellement.* 4; **Not very much.** *Pas beaucoup.* 4; **Yes, very much.** *Oui, beaucoup.* 2

museum *le musée,* 6

mushroom *le champignon,* 8

music *la musique,* 2

my *mon/ma/mes,* 7

name: His/Her name is... *Il/Elle s'appelle...,* 1; **My name is...** *Je m'appelle...,* 0; **What is your name?** *Tu t'appelles comment?* 0

natural science *les sciences naturelles (f.),* 2

need: I need... *Il me faut...,* 3; **I need...** *J'ai besoin de...,* 8; **What do you need for...?** (formal) *Qu'est-ce qu'il vous faut pour...?* 3; **What do you need for...?** (informal) *Qu'est-ce qu'il te faut pour...?* 3; **What do you need?** *De quoi est-ce que tu as besoin?* 8

neither: Neither do I. *Moi non plus.* 2; **neither tall nor short** *ne... ni grand(e) ni petit(e),* 7

never *ne... jamais,* 4

next *prochain(e),* 12; **You go down this street to the next light.** *Vous continuez jusqu'au prochain feu.* 12

next to *à côté de,* 12

nice *gentil (gentille),* 7; *sympa (sympathique),* 7; **It's nice weather.** *Il fait beau.* 4

nightmare *le cauchemar,* 11; **It was a real nightmare!** *C'était un véritable cauchemar!* 11

no *non,* 1

noon *midi,* 6; **It's noon.** *Il est midi.* 6; **It's half past noon.** *Il est midi et demi.* 6

not: Oh, not bad. *Oh, pas mal/ mauvais.* 9; **not yet** *ne... pas encore,* 9; **Not at all.** *Pas du tout.* 4; **Not me.** *Pas moi.* 2; **Not so great.** *Pas terrible.* 1; **not very good** *pas bon,* 5; **No, not really.** *Non, pas vraiment.* 11; **No, not too much.** *Non, pas trop.* 2

notebook *le cahier,* 0, 3

nothing *rien,* 6; **Nothing special.** *Rien de spécial.* 6

novel *le roman,* 3

November *novembre,* 4; **in November** *en novembre,* 4

now *maintenant,* 2; **I can't right now.** *Je ne peux pas maintenant.* 8

o'clock *...heures*, 2; **at ... o'clock** *à... heure(s)*, 2

October *octobre*, 4; **in October** *en octobre*, 4

of *de*, 0; **of course** *bien sûr*, 3; **of it** *en*, 8; **of them** *en*, 8

often *souvent*, 4

O.K. *D'accord.* 4; **Is that O.K. with you?** *Tu es d'accord?* 7; **Well, O.K.** *Bon, d'accord.* 8; **Yes, it was O.K.** *Oui, ça a été.*

okra *les gombos* (m.), 8

old: How old are you? *Tu as quel âge?* 1; **I am ... years old.** *J'ai... ans.* 1; **older** *âgé(e)*, 7

omelet *l'omelette* (f.), 5

on: Can I try on ...? *Je peux essayer le/la/les... ?* 10; **on foot** *à pied*, 12; **on Fridays** *le vendredi*, 2; **on Mondays** *le lundi*, 2; **on Saturdays** *le samedi*, 2; **on Sundays** *le dimanche*, 2; **on Thursdays** *le jeudi*, 2; **on Tuesdays** *le mardi*, 2; **on Wednesdays** *le mercredi*, 2

once: once a week *une fois par semaine*, 4

onion *l'oignon* (m.), 8

open: Open your books to page ... *Ouvrez vos livres à la page... ,* 0

opinion *l'avis* (m.), 9; **In your opinion, what do I do?** *A ton avis, qu'est-ce que je fais?* 9

or *ou*, 1

orange (color) *orange* (inv.), 3

orange *l'orange* (f.), 8

orange juice *le jus d'orange*, 5;

our *notre/nos*, 7

out: Out of the question! *Pas question!* 7; **out of style**, *démodé(e),* 10

package *le paquet*, 8; **a package/box of** *un paquet de*, 8

page *la page*, 0

pancake: a very thin pancake *la crêpe*, 5

pants *le pantalon*, 10

papaya *la papaye*, 8

paper *le papier*, 0; **sheets of paper** *les feuilles de papier* (f.), 3

pardon: Pardon me. *Pardon.* 3

parent *le parent*, 7

park *le parc*, 6

party *la boum*, 6; **to go to a party** *aller à une boum*, 6

pass: You'll pass ... *Vous passez...,* 12

passport *le passeport*, 11

pastry *la pâtisserie*, 12; **pastry shop** *la pâtisserie*, 12

peach *la pêche*, 8

pear *la poire*, 8

peas *les petits pois* (m.), 8

pen *le stylo*, 0

pencil *le crayon*, 3; **pencil case** *la trousse*, 3; **pencil sharpener** *le taille-crayon*, 3

perfect *parfait(e)*, 10; **It's perfect.** *C'est parfait.* 10

phone *le téléphone*, 1; **to talk on the phone** *parler au téléphone*, 1

photography: to do photography *faire de la photo*, 4

physical education *l'éducation physique et sportive (EPS)* (f.), 2

physics *la physique*, 2

pick *choisir*, 10; **to pick up your room** *ranger ta chambre*, 7

picnic *le pique-nique*, 6; **to have a picnic** *faire un pique-nique*, 6

picture *la photo*, 4; **to take pictures** *faire des photos*, 4

pie *la tarte*, 8

piece *le morceau*, 8; **a piece of** *un morceau de*, 8

pineapple *l'ananas* (m.), 8

pink *rose*, 3

pizza *la pizza*, 1

place *l'endroit* (m.), 12

plane *l'avion* (m.), 12; **by plane** *en avion*, 12

plane ticket *le billet d'avion*, 11

plans: I don't have any plans. *Je n'ai rien de prévu.* 11

plate *l'assiette* (f.), 5

play *la pièce*, 6; **to see a play** *voir une pièce*, 6

play *jouer*, 4; *faire*, 4; **I don't play/ do ...** *Je ne fais pas de... ,* 4; **I play ...** *Je joue... ,* 4; **I play/ do ...** *Je fais... ,* 4; **to play baseball** *jouer au base-ball*, 4; **to play basketball** *jouer au basket (-ball)*, 4; **to play football** *jouer au football américain*, 4; **to play golf** *jouer au golf*, 4; **to play hockey** *jouer au hockey*, 4; **to play soccer** *jouer au foot(ball)*, 4; **to play sports** *faire du sport*, 1; **to play tennis** *jouer au tennis*, 4; **to play video games** *jouer à des jeux vidéo*, 4; **to play volleyball** *jouer au volley(-ball)*, 4; **What sports do you play?** *Qu'est-ce que tu fais comme sport?* 4

please *s'il te/vous plaît*, 3; **Yes, please.** *Oui, s'il te/vous plaît.* 8

pleased: Pleased to meet you. *Très heureux (-euse).* 7

pleasure *le plaisir*, 8; **Yes, with pleasure.** *Oui, avec plaisir.* 8

pork *le porc*, 8

post office *la poste*, 12

poster *le poster*, 0

potato *la pomme de terre*, 8

pound *la livre*, 8; **a pound of** *une livre de*, 8

practice *répéter*, 9

prefer *préférer*, 1; **I prefer ...** *Je préfère... ,* 1; *J'aime mieux... ,* 1

problem *le problème*, 9; **I've got a little problem.** *J'ai un petit problème.* 9

pullover (sweater) *le pull-over*, 3

purple *violet(te)*, 3

put *mettre*, 10; **to put on** *mettre,* 10

quarter *le quart*, 6; **quarter past** *et quart*, 6; **quarter to** *moins le quart*, 6

question: Out of the question! *Pas question!* 7

quiche *la quiche*, 5

quiz *l'interro(gation)* (f.), 9

R

radio *la radio*, 3

rain: It's raining. *Il pleut.* 4

raise: Raise your hand! *Levez la main!* 0

rarely *rarement*, 4

read *lire*, 1; **read** *lu* (pp. of *lire*), 9

really *vraiment*, 11; **I (really) like ...** *Moi, j'aime (bien)... ,* 1; **I'd really like ...** *Je voudrais bien... ,* 11; **I'd really like to.** *Je veux bien.* 6; **No, not really.** *Non, pas vraiment.* 11

record store *le disquaire*, 12; **at the record store** *chez le disquaire*, 12

recreation center *la Maison des jeunes et de la culture (MJC)*, 6

red *rouge*, 3; **redheaded** *roux (rousse)*, 7

rehearse *répéter*, 9

relative *le parent*, 7

Repeat! *Répétez!* 0

restaurant *le restaurant*, 6

retro (style) *rétro* (inv.), 10

return: to return something *rendre*, 12

rice *le riz*, 8

ride: to go horseback riding *faire de l'équitation*, 1

right   *la droite,* 12; **to the right**   *à droite (de),* 12

right away   *tout de suite,* 6; **Yes, right away.**   *Oui, tout de suite.* 5; **I'll go right away.**   *J'y vais tout de suite.* 8

right now   *maintenant,* 8; **I can't right now.**   *Je ne peux pas maintenant.* 8

right there: It's right there on the . . .   *C'est tout de suite à... ,* 12

room   *la chambre,* 7; **to pick up your room**   *ranger ta chambre,* 7

ruler   *la règle,* 3

S

sailing   *la voile,* 11; **to go sailing**   *faire de la voile,* 11; *faire du bateau,* 11

salad   *la salade,* 8

salami   *le saucisson,* 5

sandals   *les sandales (f.),* 10

sandwich   *un sandwich,* 5; **cheese sandwich**   *un sandwich au fromage,* 5; **ham sandwich**   *un sandwich au jambon,* 5; **salami sandwich**   *un sandwich au saucisson,* 5; **toasted ham and cheese sandwich**   *le croque-monsieur,* 5

Saturday   *samedi,* 2; **on Saturdays**   *le samedi,* 2

saw   *vu* (pp. of *voir*), 9

scarf   *l'écharpe (f.),* 10

school   *l'école (f.),* 1

science class   *les sciences naturelles,* 2

scuba diving   *la plongée,* 11; **to go scuba diving**   *faire de la plongée,* 11

sea   *la mer,* 11

second   *la seconde,* 9; **One second, please.**   *Une seconde, s'il vous plaît.* 9

see   *voir,* 6; **See you later!**   *A tout à l'heure!* 1; **See you soon.**   *A bientôt.* 1; **See you tomorrow.**   *A demain.* 1; **to go see a game**   *aller voir un match,* 6; **to see a movie**   *voir un film,* 6; **to see a play**   *voir une pièce,* 6

seen   *vu* (pp. of *voir*), 9

sell   *vendre,* 9

send   *envoyer,* 12; **to send letters**   *envoyer des lettres,* 12

sensational   *sensass,* 10

September   *septembre,* 4; **in September**   *en septembre,* 4

service: At your service; You're welcome.   *A votre service.* 3

shall: Shall we go to the café?   *On va au café?* 5

sheet   *la feuille,* 0; **a sheet of paper**   *une feuille de papier,* 0

shirt (man's)   *la chemise,* 10; **(woman's)**   *le chemisier,* 10

shoes   *les chaussures (f.),* 10

shop: to go shopping   *faire les magasins,* 1; **to window-shop**   *faire les vitrines,* 6; **Can you do the shopping?**   *Tu peux aller faire les courses?* 8

shopping   *les courses (f.),* 7; **to do the shopping**   *faire les courses,* 7

short (height)   *petit(e),* 7; (length)   *court(e),* 10

shorts: (pair of) shorts   *le short,* 3

should: You should . . .   *Tu devrais... ,* 9; **You should talk to him/her/them.**   *Tu devrais lui/leur parler.* 9

show   *montrer,* 9

shy   *timide,* 7

sing   *chanter,* 9

sir   *monsieur (M.),* 1

sister   *la sœur,* 7

Sit down!   *Asseyez-vous!* 0

size   *la taille,* 10

skate: to ice-skate   *faire du patin à glace,* 4; **to in-line skate**   *faire du roller en ligne,* 4

ski   *faire du ski,* 4; **How about skiing?**   *On fait du ski?* 5; **to water-ski**   *faire du ski nautique,* 4; **skiing**   *le ski,* 1

skirt   *la jupe,* 10

sleep   *dormir,* 1

slender   *mince,* 7

slice   *la tranche,* 8; **a slice of**   *une tranche de,* 8

small   *petit(e),* 10

smart   *intelligent(e),* 7

snack: afternoon snack   *le goûter,* 8

snails   *les escargots (m.),* 1

sneakers   *les baskets (f. pl.),* 3

snow: It's snowing.   *Il neige.* 4

so: not so great   *pas terrible,* 5

So-so.   *Comme ci comme ça.* 1

soccer   *le football,* 1; *le foot,* 4; **to play soccer**   *jouer au foot(ball),* 4

socks   *les chaussettes (f.),* 10

soda: lemon soda   *la limonade,* 5

some   *des,* 3; **some**   *du, de la, de l', des,* 8; **some (of it)**   *en,* 8; **Yes, I'd like some.**   *Oui, j'en veux bien.* 8

something   *quelque chose,* 6; **I'm looking for something for . . . ,**   *Je cherche quelque chose pour... ,* 10

sometimes   *quelquefois,* 4

son   *le fils,* 7

soon: See you soon.   *A bientôt.* 1

Sorry.   *Je regrette.* 3; *Désolé(e).* 5; **Sorry, but I can't.**   *Désolé(e), mais je ne peux pas.* 4; **I'm sorry, but I don't have time.**   *Je regrette, mais je n'ai pas le temps.* 8; **Sorry, I'm busy.**   *Désolé(e), je suis occupé(e).* 6

Spanish (language)   *l'espagnol (m.),* 2

speak   *parler,* 9; **Could I speak to . . . ?**   *(Est-ce que) je peux parler à... ?* 9

special   *spécial(e),* 6; **Nothing special.**   *Rien de spécial.* 6

sports   *le sport,* 1; **to play sports**   *faire du sport,* 1; **What sports do you play?**   *Qu'est-ce que tu fais comme sport?* 4

spring   *le printemps,* 4; **in the spring**   *au printemps,* 4

stadium   *le stade,* 6

stamp   *le timbre,* 12

stand: Stand up!   *Levez-vous!* 0

start   *commencer,* 9

stationery store   *la papeterie,* 12

steak   *le bifteck,* 8; **steak and French fries**   *le steak-frites,* 5

stop: at the . . . metro stop   *au métro... ,* 6

store   *le magasin,* 1

straight ahead   *tout droit,* 12; **You go straight ahead until you get to . . .**   *Vous allez tout droit jusqu'à... ,* 12

strawberry   *la fraise,* 8; **water with strawberry syrup**   *le sirop de fraise (à l'eau),* 5

street   *la rue,* 12; **Take . . . Street, then cross . . . Street.**   *Prenez la rue... , puis traversez la rue... ,* 12

strong   *fort(e),* 7

student   *l'élève* (m./f.), 2

study   *étudier,* 1

study hall   *l'étude (f.),* 2

style   *la mode,* 10; **in style**   *à la mode,* 10; **out of style**   *démodé(e),* 10

subway   *le métro,* 12; **by subway**   *en métro,* 12

sugar   *le sucre,* 7

suit: Does it suit me?   *Il/Elle me va?* 10; **It suits you really well.**   *Il/Elle te/vous va très bien.* 10

suit jacket   *la veste,* 10

suitcase   *la valise,* 11

summer   *l'été* (m.), 4; **in the summer**   *en été,* 4

summer camp   *la colonie de vacances,* 11; **to/at a summer camp**   *en colonie de vacances,* 11

Sunday   *dimanche,* 2; **on Sundays**   *le dimanche,* 2

sunglasses   *les lunettes de soleil (f. pl.),* 10

super   *super,* 2

supermarket   *le supermarché,* 8

sure: I'm not sure.   *J'hésite.* 10

sweater   *le cardigan,* 10

sweatshirt   *le sweat-shirt,* 3

swim   *nager,* 1; *faire de la natation,* 4

swimming   *la natation,* 4

swimming pool   *la piscine,* 6

syrup: water with strawberry syrup   *le sirop de fraise (à l'eau),* 5

T-shirt *le tee-shirt*, 3
table *la table*, 7; **to clear the table** *débarrasser la table*, 7
tacky *moche*, 10; **I think it's (they're) really tacky.** *Je le/la/les trouve moche(s).* 10
take or have (food or drink) *prendre*, 5; **Are you taking it/them?** *Vous le/la/les prenez?* 10; **Are you taking…?** *Tu prends…?* 11; **Have you decided to take…?** *Vous avez décidé de prendre…?* 10; **I'll take it/them.** *Je le/la/les prends.* 10; **to take a test** *passer un examen*, 9; **to take pictures** *faire des photos*, 4; **We can take…** *On peut prendre…*, 12; **Take… Street, then … Street.** *Prenez la rue…, puis la rue…*, 12
take out: Take out a sheet of paper. *Prenez une feuille de papier.* 0; **to take out the trash** *sortir la poubelle*, 7
taken *pris (pp. of prendre)*, 9
talk *parler*, 1; **Can I talk to you?** *Je peux te parler?* 9; **to talk on the phone** *parler au téléphone*, 1; **We talked.** *Nous avons parlé.* 9
tall *grand(e)*, 7
taxi *le taxi*, 12; **by taxi** *en taxi*, 12
teacher *le professeur*, 0
telephone *le téléphone*, 0
television *la télévision*, 0
tell *dire*, 9; **Can you tell her/him that I called?** *Vous pouvez lui dire que j'ai téléphoné?* 9
tennis *le tennis*, 4; **to play tennis** *jouer au tennis*, 4
terrible *horrible*, 10
test *l'examen (m.)*, 1
Thank you. *Merci.* 3; **No thanks. I'm not hungry anymore.** *Non, merci. Je n'ai plus faim.* 8
that *ce, cet, cette*, 3; **This/That is …** *Ça, c'est…*, 12
theater *le théâtre*, 6
their *leur/leurs*, 7
them *les*, 9; **to them** *leur*, 9
then *ensuite*, 9
there *-là (noun suffix)*, 3; **there** *il y a*, 5; **there** *y, là*, 12; **Is … there, please?** *(Est-ce que)… est là, s'il vous plaît?* 9; **There's …** *Voilà…*, 7; **There is/There are …** *Il y a…*, 5; **What is there to drink?** *Qu'est-ce qu'il y a à boire?* 5
these *ces*, 3; **These/those are …** *Ce sont…*, 7
thing *la chose*, 5; *le truc*, 5; **I have lots of things to do.** *J'ai des tas de*

choses à faire. 5; **I have some things to do.** *J'ai des trucs à faire.* 5
think *penser*, 11; **I think it's/they're …** *Je le/la/les trouve…*, 10; **I've thought of everything.** *J'ai pensé à tout.* 11; **What do you think of …?** *Comment tu trouves…?* 2; **What do you think of that/it?** *Comment tu trouves ça?* 2
thirsty: to be thirsty *avoir soif*, 5
this *ce, cet, cette*, 3; **This is …** *C'est…*, 7; **This is …** *Voilà/Voici…*, 7; **This/That is …** *Ça, c'est…*, 12
those *ces*, 3; **These/Those are …** *Ce sont…*, 7
Thursday *jeudi*, 4; **on Thursdays** *le jeudi*, 2
ticket *le billet*, 11; **plane ticket** *le billet d'avion*, 11; **train ticket** *le billet de train*, 11
tie *la cravate*, 10
tight *serré(e)*, 10
time *le temps*, 8; **a waste of time** *zéro*, 2; **at the time of** *à l'heure de*, 1; **At what time do you have …?** *Tu as… à quelle heure?* 2; **At what time?** *A quelle heure?* 6; **from time to time** *de temps en temps*, 4; **I'm sorry, but I don't have time.** *Je regrette, mais je n'ai pas le temps.* 8; *Je suis désolé(e), mais je n'ai pas le temps.* 12; **What time is it?** *Quelle heure est-il?* 6
to *à la, au, à l', aux*, 6; **to (a city or place)** *à*, 11; **to (before a feminine country)** *en*, 11; **to (before a masculine noun)** *au*, 11; **to (before a plural noun)** *aux*, 11; **to her** *lui*, 9; **to him** *lui*, 9; **to them** *leur*, 9; **five to …** *moins cinq*, 6
today *aujourd'hui*, 2
tomato *la tomate*, 8
tomorrow *demain*, 2; **See you tomorrow.** *A demain.* 1
tonight *ce soir*, 7; **Not tonight.** *Pas ce soir.* 7
too (much) *trop*, 10; **It's/They're too …** *Il/Elle est (Ils/Elles sont) trop…*, 10; **Me too.** *Moi aussi.* 2; **No, it's too expensive.** *Non, c'est trop cher.* 10; **No, not too much.** *Non, pas trop.* 2; **Not too much.** *Pas tellement.* 4
track *l'athlétisme (m.)*, 4; **to do track and field** *faire de l'athlétisme*, 4
train *le train*, 12; **by train** *en train*, 12; **train ticket** *le billet de train*, 11
trash(can) *la poubelle*, 7; **to take out the trash** *sortir la poubelle*, 7
travel *voyager*, 1

trip *le voyage*, 11; **Have a good trip!** *Bon voyage!* 11
true *vrai*, 2
try: Can I try on …? *Je peux essayer…?* 10; **Can I try it (them) on?** *Je peux l'/les essayer?* 10
Tuesday *mardi*, 2; **on Tuesdays** *le mardi*, 2
turn *tourner*, 12; **You turn …** *Vous tournez…*, 12
TV *la télé(vision)*, 1; **to watch TV** *regarder la télé(vision)*, 1

umbrella *le parapluie*, 11
uncle *l'oncle (m.)*, 7
uncooked *cru(e)*, 5
until *jusqu'à*, 12; **You go straight ahead until you get to …** *Vous allez tout droit jusqu'à…*, 12
useless *nul(le)*, 2
usually *d'habitude*, 4

vacation *les vacances (f. pl.)*, 1; **Have a good vacation!** *Bonnes vacances!* 11; **on vacation** *en vacances*, 4
vacuum (verb) *passer l'aspirateur*, 7
VCR (videocassette recorder) *le magnétoscope*, 0
vegetables *les légumes (m.)*, 8
very *très*, 1; **Very well.** *Très bien.* 1; **Yes, very much.** *Oui, beaucoup.* 2
video *la vidéo*, 4; **to make videos** *faire de la vidéo*, 4; **video games** *des jeux vidéo*, 4
videocassette recorder (VCR) *le magnétoscope*, 0
videotape *la vidéocassette*, 3
visit (a place) *visiter*, 9
volleyball *le volley(-ball)*, 4; **to play volleyball** *jouer au volley(-ball)*, 4

W

wait for *attendre*, 9
Waiter! *Monsieur!* 5
Waitress! *Madame!* 5; *Mademoiselle!* 5

walk: to go for a walk *faire une promenade,* 6; **to walk the dog** *promener le chien,* 7
wallet *le portefeuille,* 3
want *vouloir,* 6; **Do you want...?** *Tu veux...?* 6; **Do you want...?** *Vous voulez...?* 8; **I don't want any more.** *Je n'en veux plus.* 8; **Yes, if you want to.** *Oui, si tu veux.* 7
wash *laver,* 7; **to wash the car** *laver la voiture,* 7
waste: a waste of time *zéro,* 2
watch *la montre,* 3
watch *regarder,* 1; **to watch a game (on TV)** *regarder un match,* 6; **to watch TV** *regarder la télé(vision),* 1
water *l'eau* (f.), 5; **mineral water** *l'eau minérale,* 5; **water with strawberry syrup** *le sirop de fraise (à l'eau),* 5
water ski *le ski nautique,* 4; **to water-ski** *faire du ski nautique,* 4
wear *mettre, porter,* 10; **I don't know what to wear for...** *Je ne sais pas quoi mettre pour...,* 10; **Wear...** *Mets...,* 10; **What shall I wear?** *Qu'est-ce que je mets?* 10; **Why don't you wear...?** *Pourquoi est-ce que tu ne mets pas...?* 10
weather *le temps,* 4; **What's the weather like?** *Quel temps fait-il?* 4
Wednesday *mercredi,* 2; **on Wednesdays** *le mercredi,* 2
week *la semaine,* 4; **once a week** *une fois par semaine,* 4
weekend *le week-end,* 6; **Did you have a good weekend?** *Tu as passé un bon week-end?* 9; **on weekends** *le week-end,* 4; **this weekend** *ce week-end,* 6
welcome: At your service; You're welcome. *A votre service.* 3
well *bien,* 1; **Did it go well?** *Ça s'est bien passé?* 11; **Very well.** *Très bien.* 1

went: Afterwards, I went out. *Après, je suis sorti(e).* 9; **I went...** *Je suis allé(e)...,* 9
what *comment,* 0; **What is your name?** *Tu t'appelles comment?* 0; **What do you think of...?** *Comment tu trouves...?* 2; **What do you think of that/it?** *Comment tu trouves ça?* 2; **What's his/her name?** *Il/Elle s'appelle comment?* 1
what *qu'est-ce que,* 1; **What are you going to do...?** *Qu'est-ce que tu vas faire...?* 6; **What do you do to have fun?** *Qu'est-ce que tu fais pour t'amuser?* 4; **What do you have to drink?** *Qu'est-ce que vous avez comme boissons?* 5; **What do you need for...?** (formal) *Qu'est-ce qu'il vous faut pour...?* 3; **What happened?** *Qu'est-ce qui s'est passé?* 9; **What kind of...do you have?** *Qu'est-ce que vous avez comme...?* 5
what *quoi,* 2; **I don't know what to wear for...** *Je ne sais pas quoi mettre pour...,* 10; **What are you going to do...?** *Tu vas faire quoi...?* 6; **What do you have...?** *Tu as quoi...?* 2; **What do you need?** *De quoi est-ce que tu as besoin?* 5
When? *Quand (ça)?* 6
where *où,* 6; **Where?** *Où (ça)?* 6; **Where are you going to go...?** *Où est-ce que tu vas aller...?* 11; **Where did you go?** *Tu es allé(e) où?* 9
which *quel(le),* 1
white *blanc(he),* 3
who *qui,* 0; **Who's calling?** *Qui est à l'appareil?* 9
whom *qui,* 6; **With whom?** *Avec qui?* 6
why *pourquoi,* 0; **Why don't you...?** *Pourquoi tu ne... pas?* 9; **Why not?** *Pourquoi pas?* 6
wife *la femme,* 7

win *gagner,* 9
window *la fenêtre,* 0; **to window-shop** *faire les vitrines,* 6
windsurfing *la planche à voile,* 11; **to go windsurfing** *faire de la planche à voile,* 11
winter *l'hiver* (m.), 4; **in the winter** *en hiver,* 4
with *avec,* 6; **with me** *avec moi,* 6; **With whom?** *Avec qui?* 6
withdraw *retirer,* 12; **withdraw money** *retirer de l'argent,* 12
without *sans,* 11; **You can't leave without...** *Tu ne peux pas partir sans...,* 11
work *travailler,* 9
worry: Don't worry! *Ne t'en fais pas!* 9
would like: I'd like to buy... *Je voudrais acheter...,* 3

year *l'an* (m.); **I am...years old.** *J'ai... ans.* 1
yellow *jaune,* 3
yes *oui,* 1; **Yes, please.** *Oui, s'il te/vous plaît.* 8
yesterday *hier,* 9
yet: not yet *ne... pas encore,* 9
yogurt *les yaourts* (m.), 8
you *tu, vous,* 0; **And you?** *Et toi?* 1
young *jeune,* 7
your *ton/ta/tes,* 7; *votre/vos,* 7

zoo *le zoo,* 6

Grammar Index

Grammar Index

Page numbers in boldface type refer to the **Grammaire** and **Note de grammaire** presentations. Other page numbers refer to grammar structures presented in the **Comment dit-on... ?, Tu te rappelles?, Vocabulaire,** and **A la française** sections. Page numbers beginning with **R** refer to the Grammar Summary in this Reference Section.

à: expressions with **jouer** 113; contractions with **le, la, l',** and **les 113,** 177, 360, R21; with cities and countries **330,** R21

adjectives: demonstrative adjectives **85,** R17; adjective agreement and placement 86, **87, 210,** R15–R18; possessive adjectives 203, **205,** R18; adjectives as nouns **301,** R18

à quelle heure: 58, 183, **185,** R20

adverbs: adverbs of frequency **122;** adverb placement with the **passé composé 272,** R18

agreement of adjectives: **87, 210,** R15–R18

aller: 151, 173, **174,** 328, 329, R26; **aller** in the **passé composé** 270, 338, R28

articles: definite articles **le, la, l',** and **les 28,** R19; definite articles with days of the week **173;** indefinite articles **un, une,** and **des** 79, **81,** R19; partitive articles **du, de la,** and **de l'** 235, **236,** 364, R19

avec qui: 183, **185,** R20

avoir: 55, R26; **avoir besoin de 238; avoir envie de** 329; with **passé composé** 269, **271,** 273, **277,** 303, 338, R28

ce, cet, cette, and **ces 85,** R17

c'est: versus **il/elle est** + adjective **310**

cognates: 6–7, 27, 84, 112

commands: 11, 148, 151, **152,** 240, 333, R28; commands with object pronouns 151, 240, **279,** 336, R22–R23

contractions: See **à** or **de.**

countries: prepositions with countries **330,** R21

de: expressions with **faire** 113; contractions **116, 369,** R21; indefinite articles (negative) **81;** indicating relationship or ownership **204;** partitive article **236,** R19; with expressions of quantity **242**

definite articles: **28,** R19

demonstrative adjectives: **85,** R17

devoir: 213, R27; **devrais** 279, 330

dire: 276, R27

direct object pronouns: **279, 309,** 336, R22

dormir: 334, R26

elle(s): See pronouns.

en: pronoun 242, 247, **248,** 333, R23; preposition before geographic names **330,** R21

-er verbs: 26, 31, 32, **33,** 119, R24; with **passé composé 271,** 273, 338, R28

est-ce que: 115, 185, R20

être: 61, 179, 183, 203, 209, 210, **211,** R26; with **passé composé** 270, 337, 338, R28

faire: with **de** + activity **113, 116;** weather 118, R22, R26

falloir: il me/te faut 82, 238, 301, 365, R22

future (near): **aller** + infinitive 84, 151, 173, 328, 329, R27; with the present tense 175, 334

il(s): See pronouns.

il est/ils sont: + adjective: 209; versus **c'est** + adjective **310**

imperatives: 11, 148, 151, **152,** 240, 333, R28

indefinite articles: 79, **81,** R19

indirect object pronouns: 276, **279,** 336, R23

interrogatives: 58, 183, **185,** 329, R20; **quel** 25; **quels** 55; **pourquoi** 179, 240, 279, 300, 330

-ir verbs: **303,** R24; with **passé composé 303,** R28

je: See pronouns.

lui: See pronouns.

leur: See pronouns.

mettre: 299, R27

ne... jamais: 122, R18
ne... ni... ni... : 208, 209
ne... pas: 26, 61; with indefinite articles 80, 81, 338, R19
ne... rien: 122, 146, 179, 329, 330; with the **passé composé 333**
negation: **26,** 61; indefinite articles (**ne... pas de**) 80, 81, 116, R19; with **rien** 122, 146, 179, 329, 330, 333; with the **passé composé** 338
negative statements or questions and **si:** 54, R20
nous: See pronouns.

object pronouns: See pronouns.
on: with suggestions 122, 145
où: 183, **185,** 329, R20

partir: 334, R26
partitive articles: 235, **236,** 364, R19
passé composé: with **avoir** 269, **271,** 273, 277, 338, R28; with **être** 270, 337, 338, R28
placement of adjectives: **87,** R17
placement of adverbs: **122, 272,** R18
possessive adjectives: **205,** R18
pourquoi: 179, 240, 279, 300, 330
pouvoir: 122, 146, 179, 213, 240, **241,** R27; **pourrais** 364
prendre: 148, **149,** R27
prepositions: **369,** R21; expressions with **faire** and **jouer 113;** prepositions **à** and **en 330,** R21; preposition **de 204, 242,** R21; preposition **chez** 183
pronouns: subject pronouns 24, 26, **33, 116,** R22; direct object pronouns **279, 309,** 336, R22; indirect object pronouns 276, **279,** 336, R23; pronouns and infinitives 279, 301; pronoun **en** 242, 247, **248,** 333, R23; pronoun **y** 151, 240, 327, 364, 366, **367,** R23

quand: 118, 183, **185,** R20
quantities: **242**
quel(s), quelle(s): See question words.
qu'est-ce que: 185, 329, 330, 337

question formation: **115,** R20
question words: 58, 183, **185,** 329, R20; **quel** 25; **quels** 55; **pourquoi** 179, 240, 279, 300, 330
qui: 183, **185,** R20
quoi: 55, **185,** 300

re-: prefix 241
-re verbs: **277,** R24; with **passé composé 277,** 338, R28
rien: See **ne... rien.**

si: 54, R20; indicating condition 213, 364
sortir: 334, R26
subject pronouns: 24, 26, **33, 116,** R22

time: 58, 183, **185**
tu: See pronouns.

un, une, des: 79, **81,** R19

venir: 179
verbs: commands 10, 148, 151, **152,** 240, 333, R28; **-er** 26, 31, 32, **33,** 119, R24; **-ir** verbs 303, R24; **passé composé** with **avoir** 269, **271,** 273, **277,** 303, 338, R28; **passé composé** with **être** 270, 337, 338, R28; **-re** verbs **277,** R24
vouloir: 179, **180,** R27
vous: See pronouns.

y: 151, 240, 327, 364, 366, **367,** R23

Credits

ACKNOWLEDGMENTS

For permission to reprint copyrighted material, grateful acknowledgment is made to the following sources:

Agence Vu: Two photographs from "Je passe ma vie au téléphone" by Anne Vaisman, photographs by Claudine Doury, from *Phosphore*, no. 190, February 1997. Copyright © 1997 by Agence Vu.

Air France: Front of Air France boarding pass, "Carte d'accès à bord."

Bayard Presse International: From "Allez, c'est à vous de choisir," text by Florence Farcouli, illustrations by Olivier Tossan, from *Okapi*, no. 568-9, September 1995. Copyright © 1995 by Bayard Presse International. From "Je passe ma vie au téléphone" by Anne Vaisman from *Phosphore*, no. 190, February 1997. Copyright © 1997 by Bayard Presse International.

C'Rock Radio, Vienne: Logo for C'Rock Radio, 89.5 MHz.

Cacharel: Four adapted photographs with captions of Cacharel products from *Rentrée très classe à prix petits : Nouvelles Galeries Lafayette.*

Canal B, Bruz: Logo for Canal B Radio, 94 MHz.

Cathédrale d'images: Advertisement, "Cathédrale d'images," from *Évasion Plus.*

Comité Français d'Education pour la Santé, 2, rue Auguste Comte-92170 Vanves: From "Les groupes d'aliments" from the brochure *Comment équilibrer votre alimentation*, published and edited by the Comité Français d'Education pour la Santé.

CSA, France: "Sondage: les lycéens ont-ils le moral?" Copyright © 1989 by CSA.

Editions S.A.E.P.: Recipe and photograph for "Croissants au coco et au sésame," recipe and photograph for "Mousseline africaine de petits légumes," "Signification des symboles accompagnant les recettes," and jacket cover from *La Cuisine Africaine* by Pierrette Chalendar. Copyright © 1993 by S.A.E.P.

EF Foundation: From "Le rêve américain devient réalité, en séjour Immersion avec EF: Vivre à l'américaine," photograph, and "Vacances de Printemps" from "Les U.S.A. en cours Principal: le séjour EF idéal" from *EF Voyages Linguistiques: Hiver, Printemps et Eté 1993.*

Femme Actuelle: Text from "En direct des refuges: Poupette, 3 ans" by Nicole Lauroy from *Femme Actuelle*, no. 414, August 31–September 6, 1992. Copyright © 1992 by Femme Actuelle. Text from "En direct des refuges: Jupiter, 7 mois" by Nicole Lauroy from *Femme Actuelle*, no. 436, February 1993. Copyright © 1993 by Femme Actuelle. Text from "En direct des refuges: Flora, 3 ans" by Nicole Lauroy from *Femme Actuelle*, no. 457, July 1993. Copyright © 1993 by Femme Actuelle. Text from "En direct des refuges: Dady, 2 ans" and from "Mayo a trouvé une famille" by Nicole Lauroy from *Femme Actuelle*, no. 466, August 30–September 5, 1993. Copyright © 1993 by Femme Actuelle. Text from "En direct des refuges: Camel, 5 ans" by Nicole Lauroy from *Femme Actuelle*, no. 472, October 11–17, 1993. Copyright © 1993 by Femme Actuelle.

France Miniature: Cover, illustration and adapted text from brochure, *Le Pays France Miniature.*

France Télécom: Front and back of the Télécarte.

Galeries Lafayette: Four adapted photographs with captions of Cacharel products and two photographs with captions of NAF NAF products from *Rentrée très classe à prix petits: Nouvelles Galeries Lafayette.*

Grands Bateaux de Provence: Advertisement, "Bateaux 'Mireio'," from *Evasion Plus.*

Grottes de Thouzon: Advertisement, "Grottes de Thouzon," photograph by M. Crotet, from *Evasion Plus*, Provence, Imprimerie Vincent, 1994.

Groupe Filipacchi: Advertisement, "Casablanca," from *7 à Paris*, no. 534, February 2–18, 1992, p. 43.

Hachette Livre: From "Où dormir?" and "Où manger?" from "Arles (13200)" from *Le Guide du Routard : Provence-Côte d'Azur, 2000/2001.* Copyright by Hachette Livre (Hachette Tourisme).

L'Harmattan: Excerpts from French text and six illustrations from *Cheval de bois/Chouval bwa* by Isabelle and Henri Cadoré, illustrated by Bernadette Coléno. Copyright © 1993 by L'Harmattan.

Loca Center: Advertisement, "Loca Center," from *Guide des Services: La Martinique à domicile.*

Ministère de la Culture: From "Les jeunes aiment sortir" (Retitled: "Les loisirs préférés") from *Francoscopie: Comment vivent les Français, 1997* by Gérard Mermet.

Le Monde: From "Baccalauréat 1996. Les hauts et les bas: Taux de réussite par série" from *Le Monde de l'Education*, no. 240, September 1996. Copyright © 1996 by Le Monde.

Musée de l'Empéri: Adapted advertisement, "Château-Musée de l'Empéri," from *Evasion Plus.*

NAF NAF: Two photographs with captions of NAF NAF products from *Rentrée très classe à prix petits : Nouvelles Galeries Lafayette.*

NRJ, Paris: Adaptation of logo for NRJ Radio, 100.3 MHz.

OUÏ FM, Paris: Logo for OUÏ FM Radio, 102.3 MHz.

Parc Astérix S.A.: Cover of brochure, *Parc Astérix,* 1992. Advertisement for Parc Astérix from *Paris Vision,* 1993, p. 29.

Parc Zoologique de Paris: Cover and map from brochure, *Parc Zoologique de Paris.*

RCV: La Radio Rock, Lille: Logo for RCV: La Radio Rock, 99 MHz.

Village des Sports: Advertisement, "Village des Sports: c'est l'fun, fun, fun!," from *Région de Québec.*

PHOTOGRAPHY CREDITS

Abbreviations used: (t) top, (b) bottom, (l) left, (r) right, (c) center.

Rencontre culturelle students, HRW Photo/John Langford Panorama fabric, Copyright © 1992 by Dover Publications, Inc.

All other fabric: HRW Photo.

All globes: Mountain High Maps® Copyright ©1997 Digital Wisdom, Inc.

TABLE OF CONTENTS: vii, HRW Photo/Sam Dudgeon; viii (both), HRW Photo/Marty Granger/Edge Productions; ix (t), © Owen Franken/Stock Boston; ix (b), HRW Photo/Marty Granger/Edge Productions; x, HRW Photo/Marty Granger/Edge Productions; xi (both), HRW Photo/Marty Granger/Edge Productions; xii (t), HRW Photo/Edge Productions; xii (b), © Hilary Wilkes/ International Stock Photography; xiii, © Owen Franken/ CORBIS; xiv, © Julio Donoso/Woodfin Camp & Associates; xv (both), HRW Photo/Edge Productions; xvi, © Owen Franken/CORBIS; xvii (both), HRW Photo/ Marty Granger/Edge Productions; xviii, © Benelux Press/Leo de Wys; xix, HRW Photo/Marty Granger/Edge Productions; xx, Corbis Images; xxi, HRW Photo/Marty Granger/Edge Productions; xxii, HRW Photo/Marty Granger/Edge Productions.

PRELIMINARY CHAPTER: xxvi (t, c), © Joe Viesti/Viesti Collection, Inc.; xxvi (b), © Robert Fried/Stock Boston; 1 (tl), D&P Valenti/H. Armstrong Roberts; 1 (tr), Stone/ Tim MacPherson; 1 (c), ©Michael Dwyer/Stock Boston; 1 (bl), © Owen Franken/Stock Boston; 1 (br), Viesti Collection, Inc.; 2 (t, c), Archive Photos; 2 (bl), Stephane Cardinale/People Avenue/CORBIS; 2 (br), AP/Wide World Photos; 3 (t), Vedat Acickalin/SIPA PRESS; 3 (c), Gastaud/SIPA Press; 3 (bl), George Lange/CORBIS OUTLINE; 3 (br), Shawn Botterill/Allsport; 4 (tl), Arianespace/SIPA Press; 4 (tc), Nabil Zorkot; 4 (tr), Boisière/SIPA Press; 4 (cl), © Robert Frerck/Odyssey/ Chicago; 4 (cr), K. Scholz/H. Armstrong Roberts; 4 (bl), HRW Photo/May Polycarpe; 4 (br), © Telegraph Colour Library/FPG International; 5 (l), Pictor Uniphoto; 5 (r), HRW Photo/John Langford; 6 (row 1, l), Digital imagery® © 2003 PhotoDisc, Inc.; 6 (row 1, cl), © Stockbyte; 6 (row 1, c), Digital imagery® © 2003 PhotoDisc, Inc.; 6 (row 1, cr), HRW Photo/Victoria Smith; 6 (row 1, r), Mountain High Maps® Copyright©1997 Digital Wisdom, Inc.; 6 (row 2, l), David Simson/Stock Boston; 6 (row 2, cl, c), Corbis Images; 6 (row 2, cr), CORBIS/Stuart Westmorland; 6 (row 2, r), Digital imagery® © 2003 PhotoDisc, Inc.; 6 (row 3, l, cl), Digital imagery® © 2003 PhotoDisc, Inc.; 6 (row 3, c), ©1998 Artville, LLC; 6 (row 3, cr), EyeWire, Inc.; 6 (row 3, r), © Stockbyte; 6 (row 4, l), CORBIS/Gunter Marx; 6 (row 4, cl), HRW Photo/ Victoria Smith; 6 (row 4, c, cr, r), Digital imagery® © 2003 PhotoDisc, Inc.; 6 (row 5, all), Digital imagery® © 2003 PhotoDisc, Inc.; 6 (row 6), Digital imagery® ©2003 PhotoDisc, Inc.; 7 (tl), Clay Myers/The Wildlife Collection; 7 (tc), Leonard Lee Rue/FPG International; 7 (tr), Tim Laman/The Wildlife Collection; 7 (bl), Jack Swenson/The Wildlife Collection; 7 (bc), Tim Laman/ The Wildlife Collection; 7 (br), Martin Harvey/The Wildlife Collection; 9 (tl, tc, tr), HRW Photo/Victoria Smith; 9 (c, cl, bl, bc), HRW Photo/Marty Granger/Edge Productions; 9 (cr), David Frazier Photolibrary; 9 (br), HRW Photo/Louis Boireau; 10, ©David Stover/Pictor; 11 (both), HRW Photo/Victoria Smith.

LOCATION: POITIERS: 12-13 (all), HRW Photo/Marty Granger/Edge Productions; 14 (both), Tom Craig/FPG International; 15 (t, c, bl), HRW Photo/Marty Granger/Edge Productions; 15 (br), HRW Photo.

CHAPTER 1 16-17, HRW Photo/Marty Granger/Edge Productions; 18 (tr inset), HRW Photo/Louis Boireau/ Edge Productions; 18 (remaining), HRW Photo/Marty Granger/Edge Productions; 19 (all), HRW Photo/ Marty Granger/Edge Productions; 20 (all), HRW Photo/Marty Granger/Edge Productions; 21 (tc), HRW Photo/Sam Dudgeon; 21 (br), HRW Photo/Alan Oddie; 21 (remaining), HRW Photo/Marty Granger/Edge Productions; 22 (cl), HBJ Photo/Mark Antman; 22 (c), HRW photo; 22 (cr), HRW photo/John Langford 22; (l), HRW Photo/Marty Granger/Edge Productions; 22 (r), IPA/The Image Works; 23 (all), HRW Photo/Marty Granger/Edge Productions; 24, HRW Photo/Marty Granger/Edge Productions; 25, Toussaint/Sipa Press; 30 (all), HRW Photo/Marty Granger/Edge Productions; 34 (tl), HRW Photo/Sam Dudgeon; 34 (tc), HRW Photo/Marty Granger/Edge Productions; 34 (tr), Robert Brenner/PhotoEdit; 34 (cl), HRW Photo/David Frazier; 34 (c), HBJ Photo/Pierre Capretz; 34 (cr), Marc Antman/ The Image Works; 34 (bl), Christine Galida/HRW Photo; 34 (bc), © Stephen Frisch/Stock Boston; 34 (br), © TRIP/ ASK Images; 36 (t), Frank Siteman/The Picture Cube; 36 (tc), Richard Hutchings/PhotoEdit; 36 (bc), David C. Bitters/The Picture Cube; 36 (b), R. Lucas/The Image Works; 37 (t), HRW Photo/Russell Dian; 37 (tc), HRW Photo/May Polycarpe; 37 (bc), R. Lucas/The Image Works; 37 (b), © Arthur Tilley/FPG International; 41 (l), HRW Photo/Sam Dudgeon; 41 (r), HRW Photo/David Frazier; 42 (tr), © Telegraph Colour Library/FPG International; 42 (tl, tc, br), HRW Photo/Marty Granger/Edge Productions; 42 (bl), David Young-Wolff/PhotoEdit.

CHAPTER 2 46-47, © Owen Franken/Stock Boston; 48 (all), HRW Photo/Marty Granger/Edge Productions; 49 (br inset), ©1997 Radlund & Associates for Artville; 49 (remaining), HRW Photo/Marty Granger/Edge Productions; 56 (l), HRW Photo/Louis Boireau/Edge

Productions; 56 (remaining), HRW Photo/Marty Granger/Edge Productions.

CHAPTER 3 74-75, HRW Photo/Marty Granger/ Edge Productions; 76 (all), HRW Photo/Edge Productions; 77 (all), HRW Photo/Edge Productions; 79 (all), HRW Photo/Sam Dudgeon; 80, HRW Photo/Sam Dudgeon; 81 (r), HRW Photo/Eric Beggs; 81 (remaining), HRW Photo/Sam Dudgeon; 83 (l,c), HRW Photo/Marty Granger/ Edge Productions; 83 (r), HRW photo/Louis Boireau/Edge Productions; 86 (all), HRW Photo/Sam Dudgeon; 88, © European Communities; 89 (both), © European Communities; 92 (t), Digital imagery® © 2003 PhotoDisc, Inc.; (92 t inset), Sam Dudgeon; 92 (ctr), HRW Photo; 92 (ctl), Digital imagery® © 2003 PhotoDisc, Inc.; 92 (cbr), Digital imagery® © 2003 PhotoDisc, Inc.; 92 (b), Artville, LLC; 92 (cbl), HRW Photo; 93 (bc), Digital imagery® © 2003 PhotoDisc, Inc.; 93 (remaining), HRW Photo; 95 (both), HRW Photo/Sam Dudgeon; 100 (all), HRW Photo/Sam Dudgeon.

LOCATION: QUEBEC 102-103, J. A. Kraulis/Masterfile; 104 (t, c, bl), HRW Photo/Marty Granger/Edge Productions; 104 (br), Wolfgang Kaehler; 105 (t), HRW Photo/ Marty Granger/Edge Productions; 105 (bl), HRW Photo/Marty Granger/Edge Productions; 105 (br), HRW Photo/Marty Granger/Edge Productions; 105 (cl), Hervey Smyth, Vue de la Prise de Québec, le 13 septembre 1759, Engraving, 35.9 x 47.8 cm, Musée du Québec, 78.375, Photo by Jean-Guy Kérouac.; 105 (cr), HRW Photo/Marty Granger/Edge Productions.

CHAPTER 4 106-107, HRW Photo/Marty Granger/ Edge Productions; 108 (c), HRW Photo/Marty Granger/ Edge Productions; 109 (all), HRW Photo/Marty Granger/Edge Productions; 111 (all), HRW Photo/Marty Granger/Edge Productions; 112 (tl), HRW Photo/ Marty Granger/Edge Productions; 112 (tc), David Young-Wolff/PhotoEdit; 112 (tr), HRW Photo/Sam Dudgeon; 112 (cl), Bill Bachmann/PhotoEdit; 112 (c, cr, bc, HRW Photo/Marty Granger/Edge Productions; 112 (bl), David Lissy/Leo de Wys; 112 (br), HRW Photo; 114 (tl, tc), HRW Photo/Victoria Smith; 114 (tr), © 2000 Robert Fried; 117 (l), Robert Fried Photography; 117 (cl, r), HRW Photo/ Sam Dudgeon; 117 (c), HBJ Photo/May Polycarpe; 117 (cr), HRW Photo/Marty Granger/Edge Productions; 120 (tl), © Telegraph Colour Library/FPG International; 120 (tc), Dean Abramson/Stock Boston; 120 (tr), Corbis Images; 120 (remaining), © Bill Stanton/International Stock Photography; 121 (l), HRW photo/Louis Boireau/ Edge Productions; 121 (c, r), HRW Photo/Marty Granger/ Edge Productions; 128, HRW Photo; 129, HRW Photo/ Marty Granger/Edge Productions; 131, HRW Photo/ Marty Granger/Edge Productions.

LOCATION: PARIS 136-137, Paul Steel/The Stock Market; 138 (all), HRW Photo/Marty Granger/Edge Productions;

139 (tr), Bob Handelman/ STONE; 139 (tl, br), HRW Photo/Marty Granger/Edge Productions; 139 (bl), Peter Menzel/Stock Boston.

CHAPTER 5 140-141, © Hilary Wilkes/International Stock Photography; 142 (all), HRW Photo/Edge Productions; 143 (all), HRW Photo/Edge Productions; 147 (drinks br), Digital imagery® ©2003 PhotoDisc, Inc.; 147 (remaining), HRW Photo/Victoria Smith; 150 (l, c), HRW Photo/Marty Granger/Edge Productions; 150 (r), HRW Photo/Louis Boireau/Edge Productions; 152 (both), HRW Photo/Sam Dudgeon; 154 (cr), HRW Photo/Michelle Bridwell; 154 (remaining), HRW Photo/Sam Dudgeon; 159 (t, b), Pomme de Pain; 159 (c), Steven Mark Needham/ Envision; 160, © Telegraph Colour Library/FPG International.

CHAPTER 6 168-169, © Owen Franken/CORBIS; 170 (cr), Sebastien Raymond/Sipa Press; 170 (remaining), HRW Photo/Marty Granger/Edge Productions; 171 (cr), Corbis Images; 171 (remaining), HRW Photo/Marty Granger/ Edge Productions; 172, Corbis Images; 172 (inset), HRW Photo/Marty Granger/Edge Productions; 175 (tl, tc, tr, br), HRW Photo/Marty Granger/Edge Productions; 175 (bc), David R. Frazier Photolibrary; 175 (bl), HRW Photo/Sam Dudgeon; 176 (tr), Tabuteau/The Image Works; 176 (cl), Maratea/International Stock Photography; 176 (ccl), Greg Meadors/Stock Boston; 176 (bl), Robert Fried/Stock Boston; 176 (bcl), Courtesy Marion Bermondy; 176 (bcr), HBJ Photo/Mark Antman; 176 (br), R. Lucas/The Image Works; 176 (remaining), HRW Photo/Marty Granger/ Edge Productions; 178 (l), HRW Photo/Louis Boireau/ Edge Productions; 178 (c, r), HRW Photo/Marty Granger/ Edge Productions; 182 (tl), Creasource/Series/PictureQuest; 182 (tr), HRW Photo/Marty Granger/Edge Productions; 182 (b), Ulrike Welsch/PhotoEdit; 185, HRW Photo/Marty Granger/Edge Productions; 191 (all), HRW Photo/Marty Granger/Edge Productions; 192, HRW Photo/Dianne Schrader; 194 (tl), HRW Photo/Pierre Capretz; 194 (tr), SuperStock; 194 (b), HRW Photo/Dianne Schrader.

CHAPTER 7 198-199, © Julio Donoso/Woodfin Camp & Associates; 200 (tl, tc, cl), HRW Photo/Marty Granger/ Edge Productions; 200 (tr), HRW Photo/Marty Granger/ Edge Productions; 200 (cr), HRW Photo/Russell Dian; 200 (b), HRW Photo; 200 (b inset), Digital imagery® ©2003 PhotoDisc, Inc.; 201 (tl, tr, c), HRW Photo; 201 (b), HRW Photo/Marty Granger/Edge Productions; 202 (l, cl), HRW Photo/Russell Dian; 202 (cr, r), HRW Photo; 203, HRW Photo/Russell Dian; 204 (Row 3 cl), HRW Photo/Marty Granger/Edge Productions; 204 (Row 4 cl), Courtesy Marion Bermondy; 204 (Row 4 cr), David Austen/Stock Boston; 204 (Row 4 r), John Lei/Stock Boston; 204 (remaining), HRW Photo; 205 (l), HRW Photo/Daniel Aubry; 205 (cl), David Young-Wolff/PhotoEdit; 205 (c), HRW Photo/May Polycarpe; 205 (cr), Tony Freeman/ PhotoEdit; 205 (r), HRW Photo/Sam Dudgeon; 209 (l), Firooz Zahedi/The Kobal Collection/Paramount Studios;

209 (r), TM © 20th Century Fox Film Corp., 1992; 212 (all), HRW Photo/Marty Granger/Edge Productions; 216 (t, b), Walter Chandoha; 216 (c), HRW Photo; 217 (t, c), Walter Chandoha; 217 (b), Gerard Lacz/Peter Arnold, Inc.; 220, ©1999 Image Farm Inc.; 220 (inset), HRW Photo/Russell Dian; 221, ©1999 Image Farm Inc.; 221 (inset), HRW Photo/Russell Dian.

LOCATION: ABIDJAN 226-227, Betty Press/Panos Pictures; 228 (t, br), Nabil Zorkot; 228 (b), John Elk III/Bruce Coleman, Inc.; 229 (t), Nabil Zorkot; 229 (bl), M. & E. Bernheim/Woodfin Camp & Associates; 229 (br), Nabil Zorkot.

CHAPTER 8 230-231, HRW Photo/Edge Productions; 232 (all), HRW Photo/Edge Productions; 233 (all), HRW Photo/Edge Productions; 234 (c), HRW Photo/Sam Dudgeon ; 234 (remaining), HRW Photo; 237, Charles & Josette Lenars/CORBIS; 239 (l, r), HRW Photo/Marty Granger/Edge Productions; 239 (c), HRW photo/Edge Productions; 244 (all), HRW Photo; 245 (tl), HRW Photo/Lance Shriner; 245 (tr), HRW Photo; 245 (bl), HRW Photo/Sam Dudgeon; 245 (br), HRW Photo/Eric Beggs;. 252, HRW Photo.

LOCATION: ARLES 260-261, HRW Photo/Marty Granger/Edge Productions; 262 (tl), HRW Photo; 262 (tr), Erich Lessing/Art Resource; 262 (b), © Ruggero Vanni/CORBIS; 263 (br), HRW Photo/Marty Granger/ Edge Productions; 263 (bl), G. Carde/SuperStock; 263 (t), W. Gontscharoff/SuperStock.

CHAPTER 9 264-265, © Owen Franken/CORBIS; 266 (all), HRW Photo/Marty Grange/Edge Productions; 267 (all), HRW Photo/Marty Granger/Edge Productions; 268 (r), Ermakoff/The Image Works; 268 (remaining), HRW Photo/Marty Granger/Edge Productions; 269 (r), © Digital Vision; 269 (l), HRW Photo/John Langford; 270 (l), HRW Photo/Michael Young; 270 (r), HRW Photo/ Victoria Smith; 275 (tl), © Telegraph Colour Library/FPG International; 275 (tcl), HRW Photo/John Langford; 275 (tcr), © Digital Vision; 275 (tr), ©Esbin-Anderson/The Image Works; 275 (bl), Robert Fried; 275 (br), Anthony Redpath/The Stock Market; 278 (all), HRW Photo/Marty Granger/ Edge Productions; 284, © Marcel Scholing/Zefa; 287, HRW Photo/Marty Granger/Edge Productions.

CHAPTER 10 292-293, HRW Photo/Marty Granger/Edge Productions; 294 (all), HRW Photo/Marty Granger/ Edge Productions; 295 (all), HRW Photo/Marty Granger/Edge Productions; 296 (all), HRW Photo/ Marty Granger/Edge Productions; 302, HRW Photo/Michelle Bridwell; 305 (all), HRW Photo/Marty Granger/Edge Productions; 312 (all), HRW Photo/Sam Dudgeon; 313 (all), HRW Photo/Sam Dudgeon; 316, HRW Photo/Marty Granger/Edge Productions; 318, HRW Photo; 320 (both), HRW Photo/Sam Dudgeon.

CHAPTER 11 322-323, © Benelux Press/Leo de Wys; 324 (cl inset), HRW Photo/May Polycarpe; 324 (cr inset), HRW photo/Edge Productions; 324 (bl inset), David Florenz/Option Photo; 324 (remaining), HRW Photo/ Marty Granger/Edge Productions; 325 (all), HRW Photo/Marty Granger/Edge Productions; 326 (all), HRW Photo/Marty Granger/Edge Productions; 329, © Telegraph Colour Library/FPG International; 331 (tl), © Robert Frerck/Woodfin Camp & Associates; 331 (tc), Digital imagery® © 2003 PhotoDisc, Inc.; 331 (tr), CORBIS Images; 331 (bl), © E. Bordis/Leo de Wys, Inc.; 331 (bc), © IFA Bilderteam/Leo de Wys, Inc.; 331 (br), Digital imagery® © 2003 PhotoDisc, Inc.; 332 (l), HRW Photo/Edge Productions; 332 (c, r), HRW Photo/Marty Granger/Edge Productions; 333, © European Communities; 335, Pierre Jaques/FOC photo; 337 (l), HRW Photo/May Polycarpe; 337 (r), HRW Photo/Sam Dudgeon; 337 (bkgd), Digital imagery® © 2003 PhotoDisc, Inc.; 338 (tl), HRW Photo/Marty Granger/ Edge Productions; 338 (tr), Robert Fried/Stock Boston; 338 (bl), Francis De Richem/The Image Works; 338 (bc), Joachim Messer/Leo de Wys; 338 (br), J. Messerschmidt/ Leo de Wys; 342, J. Messerschmidt/Leo de Wys; 345 (l), HRW Photo/Marty Granger/Edge Productions; 345 (r), Corbis Images.

LOCATION: FORT-DE-FRANCE 350-353 (all), HRW Photo/Marty Granger/Edge Productions.

CHAPTER 12 354-355, HRW Photo/Marty Granger/Edge Productions; 354 (l inset), HRW Photo/Victoria Smith; 356 (all), HRW Photo/Marty Granger/Edge Productions; 357 (all), HRW Photo/Marty Granger/ Edge Productions; 358 (all), HRW Photo/Marty Granger/Edge Productions; 359 (tl), HRW Photo; 359 (tc, tr, bl, br), HRW Photo/Marty Granger/ Edge Productions; 359 (cl), HBJ Photo/Patrick Courtault; 359 (c), HBJ Photo/Pierre Capretz; 359 (cr), IPA/The Image Works; 359 (bc), Robert Fried/Stock Boston; 362 (tl, bc), Chris Huxley/Leo de Wys; 362 (tc, tr, bl), HRW Photo/ Marty Granger/Edge Productions; 362 (br), HRW Photo; 365 (tl), HRW Photo/Helen Kolda; 365 (tc), © AFP/ CORBIS; 365 (tr), HRW Photo/Sam Dudgeon (by F. Johan and N. Vogel ©Casterman); 365 (bl, br), HRW Photo/Sam Dudgeon; 365 (bc),HRW Photo/Russell Dian; 366 (tl), Elizabeth Zuckerman/PhotoEdit; 366 (tc, cl, cr), HRW Photo/Marty Granger/Edge Productions; 366 (tr), Amy Etra/PhotoEdit; 366 (c), HRW Photo/Louis Boireau; 366 (bl), Robert Rathe/Stock Boston; 366 (bc), Dean Abramson/Stock Boston; 366 (br), Marc Antman/The Image Works; 368 (all), HRW Photo/Marty Granger/Edge Productions; 372 (l), HRW Photo/Marty Granger/Edge Productions; 372 (r), Chris Huxley/Leo de Wys; 376 (bl), David R. Frazier Photolibrary; 376 (remaining), HRW Photo/Marty Granger/Edge Productions; 380 (cr), Chris

Huxley/Leo de Wys; 380 (remaining), HRW Photo/Marty Granger/Edge Productions.

REVISIONS All photos HRW Photo/Marty Granger Edge Productions except: xx, HRW Photo/Sam Dudgeon; REVISIONS 3 (br), HRW Photo/Alan Oddie; REVISIONS 6 (tl), HRW Photo; (cr), ©Brooklyn Production/CORBIS Images/HRW; (bcr), HBJ Photo/May Polycarpe; (br), Robert Brenner/PhotoEdit; REVISIONS 8, HRW Photo/Sam Dudgeon; REVISIONS 9 (b), HRW Photo/Louis Boireau; REVISIONS 16, HRW Photo/Victoria Smith; REVISIONS 17 (b), Owen Franken/Stock Boston; REVISIONS 18 (all), HRW Photo/Victoria Smith; REVISIONS 21 (cl), Greg Meadors/Stock Boston; (cr), HBJ Photo/Mark Antman; (r), Tabuteau/The Image Works; REVISIONS 22 (tr), Tabuteau/The Image Works; (bcr), Robert Fried/Stock Boston; (br), Maratea/International Stock Photography; REVISIONS 24 (tl), HRW Photo/Columbia Photo; (tc), HRW Photo/Sam Dudgeon; (tr), HRW Photo; (bc, br), Digital Image copyright © 2004 PhotoDisc; REVISIONS 25 (tc, tr), Digital Image copyright © 2004 Artville; (br), HRW Photo/Victoria Smith; (bc), HRW Photo; REVISIONS 26 (all), HRW Photo/Sam Dudgeon; REVISIONS 27 (t), HRW Photo/Sam Dudgeon; (b,c), HRW Photo/Victoria Smith.

ADDITIONAL VOCABULARY R9 (tl, bl), HRW Photo/Sam Dudgeon; R9 (br, br inset), Digital imagery® ©2003 PhotoDisc, Inc.; R9 (tr 1 and 2), Digital imagery® © 2003 PhotoDisc, Inc.; R9 (tr 3 and 4), HRW Photo/Sam Dudgeon; R10 (cr), HRW Photo/Russell Dian; R10 (remaining), Digital imagery® © 2003 PhotoDisc, Inc.; R11 (tl, bl), Corbis Images; R11 (tr), HRW Photo/Michelle Bridwell; R11 (cl), HRW Photo/Sam Dudgeon; R11 (cr, bc, br), Digital imagery® © 2003 PhotoDisc, Inc.; R12 (t), Corbis Images; R12 (bl, br), Digital imagery® © 2003 PhotoDisc, Inc.; R13 (cr), © Digital Vision; R13 (remaining), Digital imagery® © 2003 PhotoDisc, Inc.; R14 (tl, bl, bc), Digital imagery® © 2003 PhotoDisc, Inc.; R14 (tr), Corbis Images; R14 (br), EyeWire, Inc. Image Club Graphics ©1997 Adobe Systems, Inc.

ILLUSTRATION AND CARTOGRAPHY CREDITS

Abbreviations used: (t) top, (b) bottom, (l) left, (r) right, (c) center.

All art, unless otherwise noted, by Holt, Rinehart & Winston.

PRELIMINARY CHAPTER: Page xxiii, GeoSystems; xxiv, GeoSystems; xxv, GeoSystems; 6, Bruce Roberts; 9, Ellen Beier; 11, Jocelyne Bouchard.

LOCATION: POITIERS
Chapter One: Page 12, MapQuest.com; 22, Vincent Rio; 23, Jocelyne Bouchard; 26, Jocelyne Bouchard; 27, Yves Larvor; 28, Camille Meyer; 29, Yves Larvor; 30, MapQuest.com; 31, Yves Larvor; 33, Vincent Rio; 49, Yves Larvor. **Chapter Two:** Page 51, Yves Larvor; 52 (t), Bruce Roberts; 52 (b), Brian Stevens; 54, Bruce Roberts; 56, Pascal Garnier; 58, Keith Petrus; 59, Guy Maestracci; 60, MapQuest.com; 62, Brian Stevens; 72, Bruce Roberts.
Chapter Three: Page 79, Yves Larvor; 80, Vincent Rio; 81, Michel Loppé; 82, Brian Stevens; 83, MapQuest.com; 84, Brian Stevens; 87, Vincent Rio; 89, Michel Loppé; 90, Jean-Pierre Foissy; 91, Michel Loppé; 94, Brian Stevens; 100, Bruce Roberts.

LOCATION: QUEBEC
Chapter Four: Page 102, MapQuest.com; 113, Michel Loppé; 115, Yves Larvor; 117, Jocelyne Bouchard; 118, Brian Stevens; 119, Jocelyne Bouchard; 120, MapQuest.com; 134, Jocelyne Bouchard.

LOCATION: PARIS
Chapter Five: Page 136, MapQuest.com; 145, Andrew Bylo; 146, Vincent Rio; 147, Jocelyne Bouchard; 148, Vincent Rio; 149, Camille Meyer; 150, MapQuest.com; 155, Guy Maestracci; 156, Jean-Pierre Foissy; 161, Vincent Rio; 166, Yves Larvor. **Chapter Six:** Page 174, Jocelyne Bouchard; 177 (t), Yves Larvor; 177 (c), Guy Maestracci; 178, MapQuest.com; 179, Jean-Pierre Foissy; 180, Brian Stevens; 181, Jean-Pierre Foissy; 183, Jean-Pierre Foissy; 184, Jocelyne Bouchard; 193, Guy Maestracci; 196 (t), Jocelyne Bouchard, 196 (b), Guy Maestracci. **Chapter Seven:** Page 203, Vincent Rio; 206 (cr), Guy Maestracci; 206 (b), Jocelyne Bouchard; 207, Vincent Rio; 208, Pascal Garnier; 209, Brian Stevens; 210, Jean-Pierre Foissy; 211, Vincent Rio; 212, MapQuest.com; 213 (tr), Pascal Garnier; 213 (br), Guy Maestracci; 214 (t), Vincent Rio; 214 (b), Pascal Garnier; 218, Jocelyn Bouchard; 223, Guy Maestracci; 224, Pascal Garnier.

LOCATION: ABIDJAN
Chapter Eight: Page 226, MapQuest.com; 235, Yves Larvor; 236, Camille Meyer; 237, George Kimani; 239, MapQuest.com; 240, Andrew Bylo; 242, Yves Larvor; 246 (t), Michel Loppé; 246 (b), Jocelyne Bouchard; 247, Michel Loppé; 248 (bl), George Kimani; 248 (tr), Jocelyne Bouchard; 254, George Kimani; 255, Yves Larvor; 258, Yves Larvor.

LOCATION: ARLES
Chapter Nine: Page 260, MapQuest.com; 269, Jean-Pierre Foissy; 271, Camille Meyer; 273, Guy Maestracci; 272, Jocelyne Bouchard; 278, MapQuest.com; 280, Brian Stevens; 285, Vincent Rio; 290, Jocelyne Bouchard.
Chapter Ten: Page 297, Jocelyne Bouchard; 298 (c), Michel Loppé; 298 (t), Yves Larvor; 299, Vincent Rio; 300, Jean-Pierre Foissy; 305, MapQuest.com; 306, Jean-Pierre Foissy; 268 (t), Brian Stevens; 268 (c), Jocelyne Bouchard; 270, Jean-Pierre Foissy; 307, Michel Loppé; 308, Guy Maestracci; 310, Jean-Pierre Foissy; 320, Yves Larvor.
Chapter Eleven: Page 327 (c), Brian Stevens; 327 (b), Russell Moore; 328, Guy Maestracci; 332, MapQuest.com; 333, Michel Loppé; 334, Yves Larvor; 336, Jean-Pierre Foissy; 343, Bruce Roberts; 344, Yves Larvor; 354, Yves Larvor.

LOCATION: FORT-DE-FRANCE
Chapter Twelve: Page 350, MapQuest.com; 361, Anne de Masson; 363, Anne de Masson; 364, Jean-Pierre Foissy; 366, Brian Stevens; 367, MapQuest.com; 369, Anne Stanley; 370, Anne de Masson; 371, Anne de Masson; 372, Anne Stanley; 377, Yves Larvor; 379, Anne Stanley; 380, Anne de Masson; 381, Anne de Masson; 382, Anne de Masson.

REVISIONS: REVISIONS 2, Ellen Beier; REVISIONS 3 (c), Yves Larvor; REVISIONS 3 (br), Guy Maestracci; REVISIONS 12, Yves Larvor; REVISIONS 14, Brian Stevens; REVISIONS 23, Jean-Pierre Foissy.